Early Praise for *The Definitive ANTLR 4 Reference*

Parr's clear writing and lighthearted style make it a pleasure to learn the practical details of building language processors.

➤ **Dan Bornstein**
Designer of the Dalvik VM for Android

ANTLR is an exceptionally powerful and flexible tool for parsing formal languages. At Twitter, we use it exclusively for query parsing in our search engine. Our grammars are clean and concise, and the generated code is efficient and stable. This book is our go-to reference for ANTLR v4—engaging writing, clear descriptions, and practical examples all in one place.

➤ **Samuel Luckenbill**
Senior manager of search infrastructure, Twitter, Inc.

ANTLR v4 really makes parsing easy, and this book makes it even easier. It explains every step of the process, from designing the grammar to making use of the output.

➤ **Niko Matsakis**
Core contributor to the Rust language and researcher at Mozilla Research

I sure wish I had ANTLR 4 and this book four years ago when I started to work on a C++ grammar in the NetBeans IDE and the Sun Studio IDE. Excellent content and very readable.

➤ **Nikolay Krasilnikov**
Senior software engineer, Oracle Corp.

This book is an absolute requirement for getting the most out of ANTLR. I refer to it constantly whenever I'm editing a grammar.

➤ **Rich Unger**
Principal member of technical staff, Apex Code team, Salesforce.com

I have been using ANTLR to create languages for six years now, and the new v4 is absolutely wonderful. The best news is that Terence has written this fantastic book to accompany the software. It will please newbies and experts alike. If you process data or implement languages, do yourself a favor and buy this book!

➤ **Rahul Gidwani**
Senior software engineer, Xoom Corp.

Never have the complexities surrounding parsing been so simply explained. This book provides brilliant insight into the ANTLR v4 software, with clear explanations from installation to advanced usage. An array of real-life examples, such as JSON and R, make this book a must-have for any ANTLR user.

➤ **David Morgan**
Student, computer and electronic systems, University of Strathclyde

The Definitive ANTLR 4 Reference

Terence Parr

The Pragmatic Bookshelf
Dallas, Texas • Raleigh, North Carolina

Many of the designations used by manufacturers and sellers to distinguish their products are claimed as trademarks. Where those designations appear in this book, and The Pragmatic Programmers, LLC was aware of a trademark claim, the designations have been printed in initial capital letters or in all capitals. The Pragmatic Starter Kit, The Pragmatic Programmer, Pragmatic Programming, Pragmatic Bookshelf, PragProg and the linking *g* device are trademarks of The Pragmatic Programmers, LLC.

Every precaution was taken in the preparation of this book. However, the publisher assumes no responsibility for errors or omissions, or for damages that may result from the use of information (including program listings) contained herein.

Our Pragmatic courses, workshops, and other products can help you and your team create better software and have more fun. For more information, as well as the latest Pragmatic titles, please visit us at *http://pragprog.com*.

Cover image by BabelStone (Own work) [CC-BY-SA-3.0 (http://creativecommons.org/licenses/by-sa/3.0)], via Wikimedia Commons:
http://commons.wikimedia.org/wiki/File%3AShang_dynasty_inscribed_scapula.jpg

The team that produced this book includes:

Susannah Pfalzer (editor)
Potomac Indexing, LLC (indexer)
Kim Wimpsett (copyeditor)
David J Kelly (typesetter)
Janet Furlow (producer)
Juliet Benda (rights)
Ellie Callahan (support)

Printed in the United States of America.
ISBN-13: 978-1-93435-699-9
Printed on acid-free paper.
Book version: P2.0—September 2014

Contents

Part II — Developing Language Applications with ANTLR Grammars

Part III — Advanced Topics

Acknowledgments

It's been roughly 25 years since I started working on ANTLR. In that time, many people have helped shape the tool syntax and functionality, for which I'm most grateful. Most importantly for ANTLR version 4, Sam Harwell[1] was my coauthor. He helped write the software but also made critical contributions to the Adaptive *LL(*)* grammar analysis algorithm. Sam is also building the ANTLRWorks2 grammar IDE.

The following people provided technical reviews: Oliver Ziegermann, Sam Rose, Kyle Ferrio, Maik Schmidt, Colin Yates, Ian Dees, Tim Ottinger, Kevin Gisi, Charley Stran, Jerry Kuch, Aaron Kalair, Michael Bevilacqua-Linn, Javier Collado, Stephen Wolff, and Bernard Kaiflin. I also appreciate those people who reported errors in beta versions of the book and v4 software. Kim Shrier and Graham Wideman deserve special attention because they provided such detailed reviews. Graham's technical reviews were so elaborate, voluminous, and extensive that I wasn't sure whether to shake his hand vigorously or go buy a handgun.

Finally, I'd like to thank Pragmatic Bookshelf editor Susannah Davidson Pfalzer, who has stuck with me through three books! Her suggestions and careful editing really improved this book.

1. http://tunnelvisionlabs.com

Welcome Aboard!

ANTLR v4 is a powerful parser generator that you can use to read, process, execute, or translate structured text or binary files. It's widely used in academia and industry to build all sorts of languages, tools, and frameworks. Twitter search uses ANTLR for query parsing, with more than 2 billion queries a day. The languages for Hive and Pig and the data warehouse and analysis systems for Hadoop all use ANTLR. Lex Machina[1] uses ANTLR for information extraction from legal texts. Oracle uses ANTLR within the SQL Developer IDE and its migration tools. The NetBeans IDE parses C++ with ANTLR. The HQL language in the Hibernate object-relational mapping framework is built with ANTLR.

Aside from these big-name, high-profile projects, you can build all sorts of useful tools such as configuration file readers, legacy code converters, wiki markup renderers, and JSON parsers. I've built little tools for creating object-relational database mappings, describing 3D visualizations, and injecting profiling code into Java source code, and I've even done a simple DNA pattern matching example for a lecture.

From a formal language description called a *grammar*, ANTLR generates a parser for that language that can automatically build parse trees, which are data structures representing how a grammar matches the input. ANTLR also automatically generates tree walkers that you can use to visit the nodes of those trees to execute application-specific code.

This book is both a reference for ANTLR v4 and a guide to using it to solve language recognition problems. You're going to learn how to do the following:

- Identify grammar patterns in language samples and reference manuals in order to build your own grammars.

1. http://lexmachina.com

- Build grammars for simple languages like JSON all the way up to complex programming languages like R. You'll also solve some tricky recognition problems from Python and XML.
- Implement language applications based upon those grammars by walking the automatically generated parse trees.
- Customize recognition error handling and error reporting for specific application domains.
- Take absolute control over parsing by embedding Java actions into a grammar.

Unlike a textbook, the discussions are example-driven in order to make things more concrete and to provide starter kits for building your own language applications.

Who Is This Book For?

This book is specifically targeted at any programmer interested in learning how to build data readers, language interpreters, and translators. This book is about how to build things with ANTLR specifically, of course, but you'll learn a lot about lexers and parsers in general. Beginners and experts alike will need this book to use ANTLR v4 effectively. To get your head around the advanced topics in Part III, you'll need some experience with ANTLR by working through the earlier chapters. Readers should know Java to get the most out of the book.

The Honey Badger Release

ANTLR v4 is named the "Honey Badger" release after the fearless hero of the YouTube sensation *The Crazy Nastyass Honey Badger*.[a] It takes whatever grammar you give it; it doesn't give a damn!

a. http://www.youtube.com/watch?v=4r7wHMg5Yjg

What's So Cool About ANTLR V4?

The v4 release of ANTLR has some important new capabilities that reduce the learning curve and make developing grammars and language applications much easier. The most important new feature is that ANTLR v4 gladly accepts every grammar you give it (with one exception regarding indirect left recursion, described shortly). There are no grammar conflict or ambiguity warnings as ANTLR translates your grammar to executable, human-readable parsing code.

If you give your ANTLR-generated parser valid input, the parser will always recognize the input properly, no matter how complicated the grammar. Of course, it's up to you to make sure the grammar accurately describes the language in question.

ANTLR parsers use a new parsing technology called *Adaptive LL(*)* or *ALL(*)* ("all star") that I developed with Sam Harwell.[2] *ALL(*)* is an extension to v3's *LL(*)* that performs grammar analysis dynamically at runtime rather than statically, before the generated parser executes. Because *ALL(*)* parsers have access to actual input sequences, they can always figure out how to recognize the sequences by appropriately weaving through the grammar. Static analysis, on the other hand, has to consider all possible (infinitely long) input sequences.

In practice, having *ALL(*)* means you don't have to contort your grammars to fit the underlying parsing strategy as you would with most other parser generator tools, including ANTLR v3. If you've ever pulled your hair out because of an ambiguity warning in ANTLR v3 or a reduce/reduce conflict in yacc, ANTLR v4 is for you!

The next awesome new feature is that ANTLR v4 dramatically simplifies the grammar rules used to match syntactic structures like programming language arithmetic expressions. Expressions have always been a hassle to specify with ANTLR grammars (and to recognize by hand with recursive-descent parsers). The most natural grammar to recognize expressions is invalid for traditional top-down parser generators like ANTLR v3. Now, with v4, you can match expressions with rules that look like this:

```
expr : expr '*' expr  // match subexpressions joined with '*' operator
     | expr '+' expr  // match subexpressions joined with '+' operator
     | INT            // matches simple integer atom
     ;
```

Self-referential rules like expr are recursive and, in particular, *left recursive* because at least one of its alternatives immediately refers to itself.

ANTLR v4 automatically rewrites left-recursive rules such as expr into non-left-recursive equivalents. The only constraint is that the left recursion must be direct, where rules immediately reference themselves. Rules cannot reference another rule on the left side of an alternative that eventually comes back to reference the original rule without matching a token. See Section 5.4, *Dealing with Precedence, Left Recursion, and Associativity*, on page 71 for more details.

2. http://tunnelvisionlabs.com

In addition to those two grammar-related improvements, ANTLR v4 makes it much easier to build language applications. ANTLR-generated parsers automatically build convenient representations of the input called *parse trees* that an application can walk to trigger code snippets as it encounters constructs of interest. Previously, v3 users had to augment the grammar with tree construction operations. In addition to building trees automatically, ANTLR v4 also automatically generates parse-tree walkers in the form of *listener* and *visitor pattern* implementations. Listeners are analogous to XML document handler objects that respond to SAX events triggered by XML parsers.

ANTLR v4 is much easier to learn because of those awesome new features but also because of what it does not carry forward from v3.

- The biggest change is that v4 deemphasizes embedding actions (code) in the grammar, favoring listeners and visitors instead. The new mechanisms decouple grammars from application code, nicely encapsulating an application instead of fracturing it and dispersing the pieces across a grammar. Without embedded actions, you can also reuse the same grammar in different applications without even recompiling the generated parser. ANTLR still allows embedded actions, but doing so is considered advanced in v4. Such actions give the highest level of control but at the cost of losing grammar reuse.

- Because ANTLR automatically generates parse trees and tree walkers, there's no need for you to build tree grammars in v4. You get to use familiar design patterns like the visitor instead. This means that once you've learned ANTLR grammar syntax, you get to move back into the comfortable and familiar realm of the Java programming language to implement the actual language application.

- ANTLR v3's *LL(*)* parsing strategy is weaker than v4's *ALL(*)*, so v3 sometimes relied on backtracking to properly parse input phrases. Backtracking makes it hard to debug a grammar by stepping through the generated parser because the parser might parse the same input multiple times (recursively). Backtracking can also make it harder for the parser to give a good error message upon invalid input.

ANTLR v4 is the result of a minor detour (twenty-five years) I took in graduate school. I guess I'm going to have to change my motto slightly.

> Why program by hand in five days what you can spend *twenty-five* years of your life automating?

ANTLR v4 is exactly what I want in a parser generator, so I can finally get back to the problem I was originally trying to solve in the 1980s. Now, if I could just remember what that was.

What's in This Book?

This book is the best, most complete source of information on ANTLR v4 that you'll find anywhere. The free, online documentation provides enough to learn the basic grammar syntax and semantics but doesn't explain ANTLR concepts in detail. Only this book explains how to identify grammar patterns in languages and how to express them as ANTLR grammars. The examples woven throughout the text give you the leg up you need to start building your own language applications. This book helps you get the most out of ANTLR and is required reading to become an advanced user.

This book is organized into four parts.

- Part I introduces ANTLR, provides some background knowledge about languages, and gives you a tour of ANTLR's capabilities. You'll get a taste of the syntax and what you can do with it.

- Part II is all about designing grammars and building language applications using those grammars in combination with tree walkers.

- Part III starts out by showing you how to customize the error handling of ANTLR-generated parsers. Next, you'll learn how to embed actions in the grammar because sometimes it's simpler or more efficient to do so than building a tree and walking it. Related to actions, you'll also learn how to use *semantic predicates* to alter the behavior of the parser to handle some challenging recognition problems.

  The final chapter solves some challenging language recognition problems, such as recognizing XML and context-sensitive newlines in Python.

- Part IV is the reference section and lays out all of the rules for using the ANTLR grammar meta-language and its runtime library.

Readers who are totally new to grammars and language tools should definitely start by reading Chapter 1, *Meet ANTLR*, on page 3 and Chapter 2, *The Big Picture*, on page 9. Experienced ANTLR v3 users can jump directly to Chapter 4, *A Quick Tour*, on page 33 to learn more about v4's new capabilities.

The source code for all examples in this book is available online. For those of you reading this electronically, you can click the box above the source code, and it will display the code in a browser window. If you're reading the paper version of this book or would simply like a complete bundle of the code, you can grab it at the book website.[3] To focus on the key elements being discussed, most of the code snippets shown in the book itself are partial. The downloads show the full source.

Also be aware that all files have a copyright notice as a comment at the top, which kind of messes up the sample input files. Please remove the copyright notice from files, such as t.properties in the listeners code subdirectory, before using them as input to the parsers described in this book. Readers of the electronic version can also cut and paste from the book, which does not display the copyright notice, as shown here:

listeners/t.properties
```
user="parrt"
machine="maniac"
```

Learning More About ANTLR Online

At the http://www.antlr.org website, you'll find the ANTLR download, the ANTLRWorks2 graphical user interface (GUI) development environment, documentation, prebuilt grammars, examples, articles, and a file-sharing area. The tech support mailing list[4] is a newbie-friendly public Google group.

Terence Parr
University of San Francisco, November 2012

3. http://pragprog.com/titles/tpantlr2/source_code
4. https://groups.google.com/d/forum/antlr-discussion

Part I

Introducing ANTLR and Computer Languages

In Part I, we'll get ANTLR installed, try it on a simple "hello world" grammar, and look at the big picture of language application development. With those basics down, we'll build a grammar to recognize and translate lists of integers in curly braces like {1, 2, 3}. Finally, we'll take a whirlwind tour of ANTLR features by racing through a number of simple grammars and applications.

CHAPTER 1

Meet ANTLR

Our goals in this first part of the book are to get a general overview of ANTLR's capabilities and to explore language application architecture. Once we have the big picture, we'll learn ANTLR slowly and systematically in Part II using lots of real-world examples. To get started, let's install ANTLR and then try it on a simple "hello world" grammar.

1.1 Installing ANTLR

ANTLR is written in Java, so you need to have Java installed before you begin.[1] This is true even if you're going to use ANTLR to generate parsers in another language such as C# or C++. (I expect to have other targets in the near future.) ANTLR requires Java version 1.6 or newer.

Why This Book Uses the Command-Line Shell

Throughout this book, we'll be using the command line (shell) to run ANTLR and build our applications. Since programmers use a variety of development environments and operating systems, the operating system shell is the only "interface" we have in common. Using the shell also makes each step in the language application development and build process explicit. I'll be using the Mac OS X shell throughout for consistency, but the commands should work in any Unix shell and, with trivial variations, on Windows.

Installing ANTLR itself is a matter of downloading the latest jar, such as antlr-4.0-complete.jar,[2] and storing it somewhere appropriate. The jar contains all dependencies necessary to run the ANTLR tool and the runtime library

1. http://www.java.com/en/download/help/download_options.xml
2. See http://www.antlr.org/download.html, but you can also build ANTLR from the source by pulling from https://github.com/antlr/antlr4.

needed to compile and execute recognizers generated by ANTLR. In a nutshell, the ANTLR tool converts grammars into programs that recognize sentences in the language described by the grammar. For example, given a grammar for JSON, the ANTLR tool generates a program that recognizes JSON input using some support classes from the ANTLR runtime library.

The jar also contains two support libraries: a sophisticated tree layout library[3] and StringTemplate,[4] a template engine useful for generating code and other structured text (see the sidebar *The StringTemplate Engine*, on page 4). At version 4.0, ANTLR is still written in ANTLR v3, so the complete jar contains the previous version of ANTLR as well.

The StringTemplate Engine

StringTemplate is a Java template engine (with ports for C#, Python, Ruby, and Scala) for generating source code, web pages, emails, or any other formatted text output. StringTemplate is particularly good at multitargeted code generators, multiple site skins, and internationalization/localization. It evolved over years of effort developing jGuru.com. StringTemplate also generates that website and powers the ANTLR v3 and v4 code generators. See the About[a] page on the website for more information.

a. http://www.stringtemplate.org/about.html

You can manually download ANTLR from the ANTLR website using a web browser, or you can use the command-line tool curl to grab it.

```
$ cd /usr/local/lib
$ curl -O http://www.antlr.org/download/antlr-4.0-complete.jar
```

On Unix, /usr/local/lib is a good directory to store jars like ANTLR's. On Windows, there doesn't seem to be a standard directory, so you can simply store it in your project directory. Most development environments want you to drop the jar into the dependency list of your language application project. There is no configuration script or configuration file to alter—you just need to make sure that Java knows how to find the jar.

Because this book uses the command line throughout, you need to go through the typical onerous process of setting the CLASSPATH[5] environment variable. With CLASSPATH set, Java can find both the ANTLR tool and the runtime library. On Unix systems, you can execute the following from the shell or add it to the shell start-up script (.bash_profile for bash shell):

3. http://code.google.com/p/treelayout
4. http://www.stringtemplate.org
5. http://docs.oracle.com/javase/tutorial/essential/environment/paths.html

```
$ export CLASSPATH=".:/usr/local/lib/antlr-4.0-complete.jar:$CLASSPATH"
```

It's critical to have the dot, the current directory identifier, somewhere in the CLASSPATH. Without that, the Java compiler and Java virtual machine won't see classes in the current directory. You'll be compiling and testing things from the current directory all the time in this book.

You can check to see that ANTLR is installed correctly now by running the ANTLR tool without arguments. You can either reference the jar directly with the java -jar option or directly invoke the org.antlr.v4.Tool class.

```
$ java -jar /usr/local/lib/antlr-4.0-complete.jar  # launch org.antlr.v4.Tool
ANTLR Parser Generator  Version 4.0
 -o ___              specify output directory where all output is generated
 -lib ___            specify location of .tokens files
...
$ java org.antlr.v4.Tool    # launch org.antlr.v4.Tool
ANTLR Parser Generator  Version 4.0
-o ___               specify output directory where all output is generated
-lib ___             specify location of .tokens files
...
```

Typing either of those java commands to run ANTLR all the time would be painful, so it's best to make an alias or shell script. Throughout the book, I'll use alias antlr4, which you can define as follows on Unix:

```
$ alias antlr4='java -jar /usr/local/lib/antlr-4.0-complete.jar'
```

Or, you could put the following script into /usr/local/bin (readers of the ebook can click the install/antlr4 title bar to get the file):

install/antlr4

```
#!/bin/sh
java -cp "/usr/local/lib/antlr4-complete.jar:$CLASSPATH" org.antlr.v4.Tool $*
```

On Windows you can do something like this (assuming you put the jar in C:\libraries):

install/antlr4.bat

```
java -cp C:\libraries\antlr-4.0-complete.jar;%CLASSPATH% org.antlr.v4.Tool %*
```

Either way, you get to say just antlr4.

```
$ antlr4
ANTLR Parser Generator  Version 4.0
-o ___               specify output directory where all output is generated
-lib ___             specify location of .tokens files
...
```

If you see the help message, then you're ready to give ANTLR a quick test-drive!

1.2 Executing ANTLR and Testing Recognizers

Here's a simple grammar that recognizes phrases like hello parrt and hello world:

install/Hello.g4

```
grammar Hello;              // Define a grammar called Hello
r  : 'hello' ID ;           // match keyword hello followed by an identifier
ID : [a-z]+ ;               // match lower-case identifiers
WS : [ \t\r\n]+ -> skip ; // skip spaces, tabs, newlines, \r (Windows)
```

To keep things tidy, let's put grammar file Hello.g4 in its own directory, such as /tmp/test. Then we can run ANTLR on it and compile the results.

```
$ cd /tmp/test
$ # copy-n-paste Hello.g4 or download the file into /tmp/test
$ antlr4 Hello.g4  # Generate parser and lexer using antlr4 alias from before
$ ls
Hello.g4                  HelloLexer.java     HelloParser.java
Hello.tokens              HelloLexer.tokens
HelloBaseListener.java  HelloListener.java
$ javac *.java     # Compile ANTLR-generated code
```

Running the ANTLR tool on Hello.g4 generates an executable recognizer embodied by HelloParser.java and HelloLexer.java, but we don't have a main program to trigger language recognition. (We'll learn what parsers and lexers are in the next chapter.) That's the typical case at the start of a project. You'll play around with a few different grammars before building the actual application. It'd be nice to avoid having to create a main program to test every new grammar.

ANTLR provides a flexible testing tool in the runtime library called TestRig. It can display lots of information about how a recognizer matches input from a file or standard input. TestRig uses Java reflection to invoke compiled recognizers. Like before, it's a good idea to create a convenient alias or batch file. I'm going to call it grun throughout the book (but you can call it whatever you want).

```
$ alias grun='java org.antlr.v4.runtime.misc.TestRig'
```

The test rig takes a grammar name, a starting rule name kind of like a main() method, and various options that dictate the output we want. Let's say we'd like to print the tokens created during recognition. Tokens are vocabulary symbols like keyword hello and identifier parrt. To test the grammar, start up grun as follows:

```
⇒ $ grun Hello r -tokens     # start the TestRig on grammar Hello at rule r
⇒ hello parrt                # input for the recognizer that you type
⇒ EOF                        # type ctrl-D on Unix or Ctrl+Z on Windows
```

```
[@0,0:4='hello',<1>,1:0]    # these three lines are output from grun
[@1,6:10='parrt',<2>,1:6]
[@2,12:11='<EOF>',<-1>,2:0]
```

After you hit a newline on the grun command, the computer will patiently wait for you to type in hello parrt followed by a newline. At that point, you must type the end-of-file character to terminate reading from standard input; otherwise, the program will stare at you for eternity. Once the recognizer has read all of the input, TestRig prints out the list of tokens per the use of option -tokens on grun.

Each line of the output represents a single token and shows everything we know about the token. For example, [@1,6:10='parrt',<2>,1:6] indicates that the token is the second token (indexed from 0), goes from character position 6 to 10 (inclusive starting from 0), has text parrt, has token type 2 (ID), is on line 1 (from 1), and is at character position 6 (starting from zero and counting tabs as a single character).

We can print the parse tree in LISP-style text form (*root children*) just as easily.

```
$ grun Hello r -tree
hello parrt
EOF
(r hello parrt)
```

The easiest way to see how a grammar recognizes the input, though, is by looking at the parse tree visually. Running TestRig with the grun -gui option, grun Hello r -gui, produces the following dialog box:

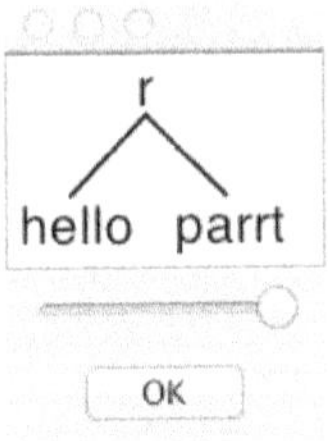

Running TestRig without any command-line options prints a small help message.

```
$ grun
java org.antlr.v4.runtime.misc.TestRig GrammarName startRuleName
  [-tokens] [-tree] [-gui] [-ps file.ps] [-encoding encodingname]
  [-trace] [-diagnostics] [-SLL]
  [input-filename(s)]
Use startRuleName='tokens' if GrammarName is a lexer grammar.
Omitting input-filename makes rig read from stdin.
```

As we go along in the book, we'll use many of those options; here's briefly what they do:

-tokens prints out the token stream.

-tree prints out the parse tree in LISP form.

-gui displays the parse tree visually in a dialog box.

-ps file.ps generates a visual representation of the parse tree in PostScript and stores it in file.ps. The parse tree figures in this chapter were generated with -ps.

-encoding encodingname specifies the test rig input file encoding if the current locale would not read the input properly. For example, we need this option to parse a Japanese-encoded XML file in Section 12.4, *Parsing and Lexing XML*, on page 226.

-trace prints the rule name and current token upon rule entry and exit.

-diagnostics turns on diagnostic messages during parsing. This generates messages only for unusual situations such as ambiguous input phrases.

-SLL uses a faster but slightly weaker parsing strategy.

Now that we have ANTLR installed and have tried it on a simple grammar, let's take a step back to look at the big picture and learn some important terminology in the next chapter. After that, we'll try a simple starter project that recognizes and translates lists of integers such as {1, 2, 3}. Then, we'll walk through a number of interesting examples in Chapter 4, *A Quick Tour*, on page 33 that demonstrate ANTLR's capabilities and that illustrate a few of the domains where ANTLR applies.

CHAPTER 2

The Big Picture

Now that we have ANTLR installed and some idea of how to build and run a small example, we're going to look at the big picture. In this chapter, we'll learn about the important processes, terminology, and data structures associated with language applications. As we go along, we'll identify the key ANTLR objects and learn a little bit about what ANTLR does for us behind the scenes.

2.1 Let's Get Meta!

To implement a language, we have to build an application that reads sentences and reacts appropriately to the phrases and input symbols it discovers. (A language is a set of valid sentences, a sentence is made up of phrases, and a phrase is made up of subphrases and vocabulary symbols.) Broadly speaking, if an application computes or "executes" sentences, we call that application an *interpreter*. Examples include calculators, configuration file readers, and Python interpreters. If we're converting sentences from one language to another, we call that application a *translator*. Examples include Java to C# converters and compilers.

To react appropriately, the interpreter or translator has to recognize all of the valid sentences, phrases, and subphrases of a particular language. Recognizing a phrase means we can identify the various components and can differentiate it from other phrases. For example, we recognize input `sp = 100;` as a programming language assignment statement. That means we know that `sp` is the assignment target and `100` is the value to store. Similarly, if we were recognizing English sentences, we'd identify the parts of speech, such as the subject, predicate, and object. Recognizing assignment `sp = 100;` also means that the language application sees it as clearly distinct from, say, an import statement. After recognition, the application would then perform a suitable operation such as `performAssignment("sp", 100)` or `translateAssignment("sp", 100)`.

Programs that recognize languages are called *parsers* or *syntax analyzers*. *Syntax* refers to the rules governing language membership, and in this book we're going to build ANTLR *grammars* to specify language syntax. A grammar is just a set of rules, each one expressing the structure of a phrase. The ANTLR tool translates grammars to parsers that look remarkably similar to what an experienced programmer might build by hand. (ANTLR is a program that writes other programs.) Grammars themselves follow the syntax of a language optimized for specifying other languages: ANTLR's *meta-language*.

Parsing is much easier if we break it down into two similar but distinct tasks or stages. The separate stages mirror how our brains read English text. We don't read a sentence character by character. Instead, we perceive a sentence as a stream of words. The human brain subconsciously groups character sequences into words and looks them up in a dictionary before recognizing grammatical structure. This process is more obvious if we're reading Morse code because we have to convert the dots and dashes to characters before reading a message. It's also obvious when reading long words such as *Humuhumunukunukuapua'a*, the Hawaiian state fish.

The process of grouping characters into words or symbols (*tokens*) is called *lexical analysis* or simply *tokenizing*. We call a program that tokenizes the input a *lexer*. The lexer can group related tokens into token classes, or *token types*, such as `INT` (integers), `ID` (identifiers), `FLOAT` (floating-point numbers), and so on. The lexer groups vocabulary symbols into types when the parser cares only about the type, not the individual symbols. Tokens consist of at least two pieces of information: the token type (identifying the lexical structure) and the text matched for that token by the lexer.

The second stage is the actual parser and feeds off of these tokens to recognize the sentence structure, in this case an assignment statement. By default, ANTLR-generated parsers build a data structure called a *parse tree* or *syntax tree* that records how the parser recognized the structure of the input sentence and its component phrases. The following diagram illustrates the basic data flow of a language recognizer:

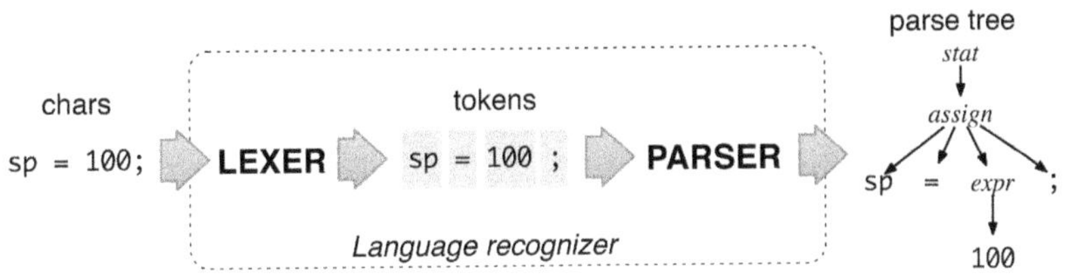

The interior nodes of the parse tree are phrase names that group and identify their children. The root node is the most abstract phrase name, in this case *stat* (short for "statement"). The leaves of a parse tree are always the input tokens. Sentences, linear sequences of symbols, are really just serializations of parse trees we humans grok natively in hardware. To get an idea across to someone, we have to conjure up the same parse tree in their heads using a word stream.

By producing a parse tree, a parser delivers a handy data structure to the rest of the application that contains complete information about how the parser grouped the symbols into phrases. Trees are easy to process in subsequent steps and are well understood by programmers. Better yet, the parser can generate parse trees automatically.

By operating off parse trees, multiple applications that need to recognize the same language can reuse a single parser. The other choice is to embed application-specific code snippets directly into the grammar, which is what parser generators have done traditionally. ANTLR v4 still allows this (see Chapter 10, *Attributes and Actions*, on page 177), but parse trees make for a much tidier and more decoupled design.

Parse trees are also useful for translations that require multiple passes (tree walks) because of computation dependencies where one stage needs information from a previous stage. In other cases, an application is just a heck of a lot easier to code and test in multiple stages because it's so complex. Rather than reparse the input characters for each stage, we can just walk the parse tree multiple times, which is much more efficient.

Because we specify phrase structure with a set of rules, parse-tree subtree roots correspond to grammar rule names. As a preview of things to come, here's the grammar rule that corresponds to the first level of the *assign* subtree from the diagram:

```
assign : ID '=' expr ';' ; // match an assignment statement like "sp = 100;"
```

Understanding how ANTLR translates such rules into human-readable parsing code is fundamental to using and debugging grammars, so let's dig deeper into how parsing works.

2.2 Implementing Parsers

The ANTLR tool generates *recursive-descent parsers* from grammar rules such as assign that we just saw. Recursive-descent parsers are really just a collection of recursive methods, one per rule. The *descent* term refers to the fact that parsing begins at the root of a parse tree and proceeds toward the leaves (tokens). The rule we invoke first, the *start symbol*, becomes the root of the parse tree. That would mean calling method stat() for the parse tree in the previous section. A more general term for this kind of parsing is *top-down parsing*; recursive-descent parsers are just one kind of top-down parser implementation.

To get an idea of what recursive-descent parsers look like, here's the (slightly cleaned up) method that ANTLR generates for rule assign:

```
// assign : ID '=' expr ';' ;
void assign() {     // method generated from rule assign
    match(ID);      // compare ID to current input symbol then consume
    match('=');
    expr();         // match an expression by calling expr()
    match(';');
}
```

The cool part about recursive-descent parsers is that the call graph traced out by invoking methods stat(), assign(), and expr() mirrors the interior parse tree nodes. (Take a quick peek back at the parse tree figure.) The calls to match() correspond to the parse tree leaves. To build a parse tree manually in a handbuilt parser, we'd insert "add new subtree root" operations at the start of each rule method and an "add new leaf node" operation to match().

Method assign() just checks to make sure all necessary tokens are present and in the right order. When the parser enters assign(), it doesn't have to choose between more than one *alternative*. An alternative is one of the choices on the right side of a rule definition. For example, the stat rule that invokes assign likely has a list of other kinds of statements.

```
/** Match any kind of statement starting at the current input position */
stat: assign          // First alternative ('|' is alternative separator)
    | ifstat          // Second alternative
    | whilestat
   ...
    ;
```

A parsing rule for stat looks like a switch.

```
void stat() {
    switch ( «current input token» ) {
        CASE ID    : assign(); break;
        CASE IF    : ifstat(); break; // IF is token type for keyword 'if'
        CASE WHILE : whilestat(); break;
        ...
        default    : «raise no viable alternative exception»
    }
}
```

Method stat() has to make a *parsing decision* or *prediction* by examining the next input token. Parsing decisions predict which alternative will be successful. In this case, seeing a WHILE keyword predicts the third alternative of rule stat. Rule method stat() therefore calls whilestat(). You might've heard the term *lookahead token* before; that's just the next input token. A lookahead token is any token that the parser sniffs before matching and consuming it.

Sometimes, the parser needs lots of lookahead tokens to predict which alternative will succeed. It might even have to consider all tokens from the current position until the end of file! ANTLR silently handles all of this for you, but it's helpful to have a basic understanding of decision making so debugging generated parsers is easier.

To visualize parsing decisions, imagine a maze with a single entrance and a single exit that has words written on the floor. Every sequence of words along a path from entrance to exit represents a sentence. The structure of the maze is analogous to the rules in a grammar that define a language. To test a sentence for membership in a language, we compare the sentence's words with the words along the floor as we traverse the maze. If we can get to the exit by following the sentence's words, that sentence is valid.

To navigate the maze, we must choose a valid path at each fork, just as we must choose alternatives in a parser. We have to decide which path to take by comparing the next word or words in our sentence with the words visible down each path emanating from the fork. The words we can see from the fork are analogous to lookahead tokens. The decision is pretty easy when each path starts with a unique word. In rule stat, each alternative begins with a unique token, so stat() can distinguish the alternatives by looking at the first lookahead token.

When the words starting each path from a fork overlap, a parser needs to look further ahead, scanning for words that distinguish the alternatives. ANTLR automatically throttles the amount of lookahead up-and-down as necessary for each decision. If the lookahead is the same down multiple paths to the exit (end of file), there are multiple interpretations of the current input phrase. Resolving such ambiguities is our next topic. After that, we'll figure out how to use parse trees to build language applications.

2.3 You Can't Put Too Much Water into a Nuclear Reactor

An ambiguous phrase or sentence is one that has more than one interpretation. In other words, the words fit more than one grammatical structure. The section title "You Can't Put Too Much Water into a Nuclear Reactor" is an ambiguous sentence from a *Saturday Night Live* sketch I saw years ago. The characters weren't sure if they should be careful *not* to put too much water into the reactor or if they should put lots of water into the reactor.

For Whom No Thanks Is Too Much

One of my favorite ambiguous sentences is on the dedication page of my friend Kevin's Ph.D. thesis: "To my Ph.D. supervisor, for whom no thanks is too much." It's unclear whether he was grateful or ungrateful. Kevin claimed it was the latter, so I asked why he had taken a postdoc job working for the same guy. His reply: "Revenge."

Ambiguity can be funny in natural language but causes problems for computer-based language applications. To interpret or translate a phrase, a program has to uniquely identify the meaning. That means we have to provide unambiguous grammars so that the generated parser can match each input phrase in exactly one way.

We haven't studied grammars in detail yet, but let's include a few ambiguous grammars here to make the notion of ambiguity more concrete. You can refer to this section if you run into ambiguities later when building a grammar.

Some ambiguous grammars are obvious.

```
stat: ID '=' expr ';'  // match an assignment; can match "f();"
    | ID '=' expr ';'  // oops! an exact duplicate of previous alternative
    ;
expr: INT ;
```

Most of the time, though, the ambiguity will be more subtle, as in the following grammar that can match a function call via both alternatives of rule stat:

```
stat: expr ';'         // expression statement
    | ID '(' ')' ';'   // function call statement
    ;
expr: ID '(' ')'
    | INT
```

```
    ;
```

Here are the two interpretations of input f(); starting in rule stat:

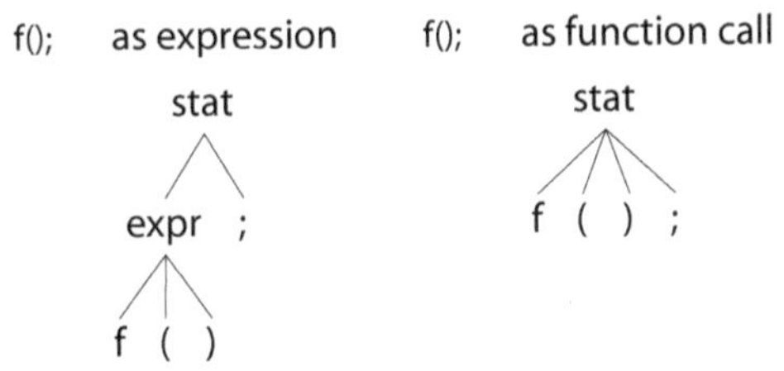

The parse tree on the left shows the case where f() matches to rule expr. The tree on the right shows f() matching to the start of rule stat's second alternative.

Since most language inventors design their syntax to be unambiguous, an ambiguous grammar is analogous to a programming bug. We need to reorganize the grammar to present a single choice to the parser for each input phrase. If the parser detects an ambiguous phrase, it has to pick one of the viable alternatives. ANTLR resolves the ambiguity by choosing the first alternative involved in the decision. In this case, the parser would choose the interpretation of f(); associated with the parse tree on the left.

Ambiguities can occur in the lexer as well as the parser, but ANTLR resolves them so the rules behave naturally. ANTLR resolves lexical ambiguities by matching the input string to the rule specified first in the grammar. To see how this works, let's look at an ambiguity that's common to most programming languages: the ambiguity between keywords and identifier rules. Keyword begin (followed by a nonletter) is also an identifier, at least lexically, so the lexer can match b-e-g-i-n to either rule.

```
BEGIN : 'begin' ;  // match b-e-g-i-n sequence; ambiguity resolves to BEGIN
ID    : [a-z]+ ;   // match one or more of any lowercase letter
```

For more on this lexical ambiguity, see *Matching Identifiers*, on page 76.

Note that lexers try to match the longest string possible for each token, meaning that input beginner would match only to rule ID. The lexer would not match beginner as BEGIN followed by an ID matching input ner.

Sometimes the syntax for a language is just plain ambiguous and no amount of grammar reorganization will change that fact. For example, the natural grammar for arithmetic expressions can interpret input such as 1+2*3 in two ways, either by performing the operations left to right (as Smalltalk does) or in precedence order like most languages. We'll learn how to implicitly specify the operator precedence order for expressions in Section 5.4, *Dealing with Precedence, Left Recursion, and Associativity*, on page 71.

The venerable C language exhibits another kind of ambiguity, which we can resolve using context information such as how an identifier is defined. Consider the code snippet `i*j;`. Syntactically, it looks like an expression, but its meaning, or semantics, depends on whether `i` is a type name or variable. If `i` is a type name, then the snippet isn't an expression. It's a declaration of variable `j` as a pointer to type `i`. We'll see how to resolve these ambiguities in Chapter 11, *Altering the Parse with Semantic Predicates*, on page 191.

Parsers by themselves test input sentences only for language membership and build a parse tree. That's crucial stuff, but it's time to see how language applications use parse trees to interpret or translate the input.

2.4 Building Language Applications Using Parse Trees

To make a language application, we have to execute some appropriate code for each input phrase or subphrase. The easiest way to do that is to operate on the parse tree created automatically by the parser. The nice thing about operating on the tree is that we're back in familiar Java territory. There's no further ANTLR syntax to learn in order to build an application.

Let's start by looking more closely at the data structures and class names ANTLR uses for recognition and for parse trees. A passing familiarity with the data structures will make future discussions more concrete.

Earlier we learned that lexers process characters and pass tokens to the parser, which in turn checks syntax and creates a parse tree. The corresponding ANTLR classes are `CharStream`, `Lexer`, `Token`, `Parser`, and `ParseTree`. The "pipe" connecting the lexer and parser is called a `TokenStream`. The diagram below illustrates how objects of these types connect to each other in memory.

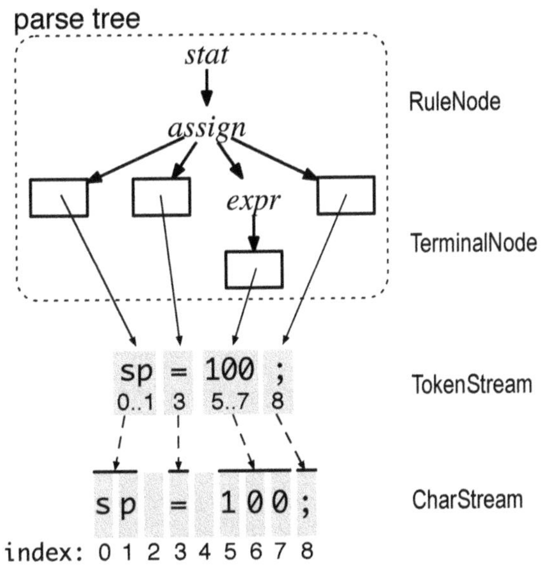

These ANTLR data structures share as much data as possible to reduce memory requirements. The diagram shows that leaf (token) nodes in the parse tree are containers that point at tokens in the token stream. The tokens record start and stop character indexes into the CharStream, rather than making copies of substrings. There are no tokens associated with whitespace characters (indexes 2 and 4) since we can assume our lexer tosses out whitespace.

The figure also shows ParseTree subclasses RuleNode and TerminalNode that correspond to subtree roots and leaf nodes. RuleNode has familiar methods such as getChild() and getParent(), but RuleNode isn't specific to a particular grammar. To better support access to the elements within specific nodes, ANTLR generates a RuleNode subclass for each rule. The following figure shows the specific classes of the subtree roots for our assignment statement example, which are StatContext, AssignContext, and ExprContext:

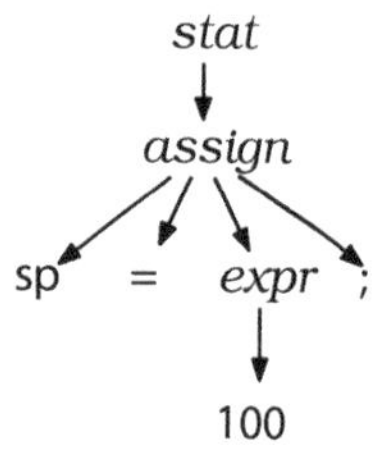

Parse tree

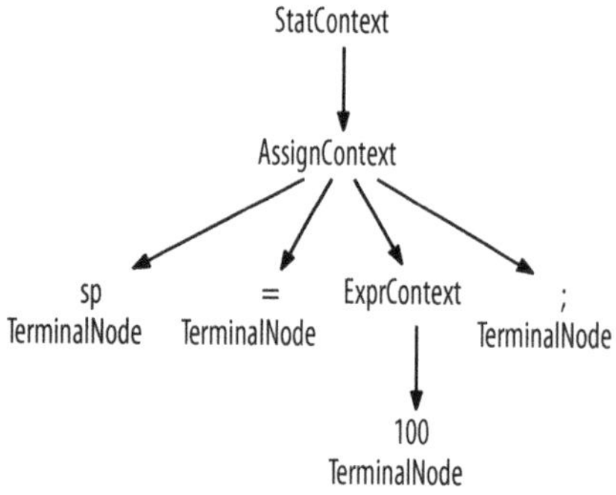

Parse tree node class names

These are called *context* objects because they record everything we know about the recognition of a phrase by a rule. Each context object knows the start and stop tokens for the recognized phrase and provides access to all of the elements of that phrase. For example, AssignContext provides methods ID() and expr() to access the identifier node and expression subtree.

Given this description of the concrete types, we could write code by hand to perform a depth-first walk of the tree. We could perform whatever actions we wanted as we discovered and finished nodes. Typical operations are things such as computing results, updating data structures, or generating output. Rather than writing the same tree-walking boilerplate code over again for each application, though, we can use the tree-walking mechanisms that ANTLR generates automatically.

2.5 Parse-Tree Listeners and Visitors

ANTLR provides support for two tree-walking mechanisms in its runtime library. By default, ANTLR generates a parse-tree *listener* interface that responds to events triggered by the built-in tree walker. The listeners themselves are exactly like SAX document handler objects for XML parsers. SAX listeners receive notification of events like startDocument() and endDocument(). The methods in a listener are just callbacks, such as we'd use to respond to a checkbox click in a GUI application. Once we look at listeners, we'll see how ANTLR can also generate tree walkers that follow the visitor design pattern.[1]

Parse-Tree Listeners

To walk a tree and trigger calls into a listener, ANTLR's runtime provides class ParseTreeWalker. To make a language application, we build a ParseTreeListener im-

1. http://en.wikipedia.org/wiki/Visitor_pattern

plementation containing application-specific code that typically calls into a larger surrounding application.

ANTLR generates a ParseTreeListener subclass specific to each grammar with enter and exit methods for each rule. As the walker encounters the node for rule assign, for example, it triggers enterAssign() and passes it the AssignContext parse-tree node. After the walker visits all children of the assign node, it triggers exitAssign(). The tree diagram shown below shows ParseTreeWalker performing a depth-first walk, represented by the thick dashed line.

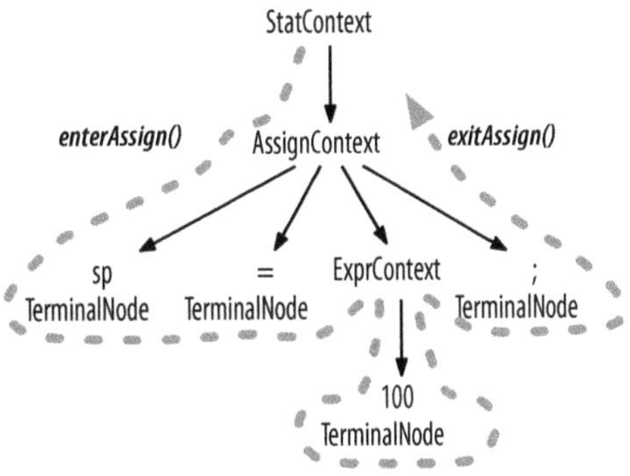

It also identifies where in the walk ParseTreeWalker calls the enter and exit methods for rule assign. (The other listener calls aren't shown.)

And the diagram in Figure 1, *ParseTreeWalker call sequence*, on page 20 shows the complete sequence of calls made to the listener by ParseTreeWalker for our statement tree.

The beauty of the listener mechanism is that it's all automatic. We don't have to write a parse-tree walker, and our listener methods don't have to explicitly visit their children.

Parse-Tree Visitors

There are situations, however, where we want to control the walk itself, explicitly calling methods to visit children. Option -visitor asks ANTLR to generate a visitor interface from a grammar with a visit method per rule. Here's the familiar visitor pattern operating on our parse tree:

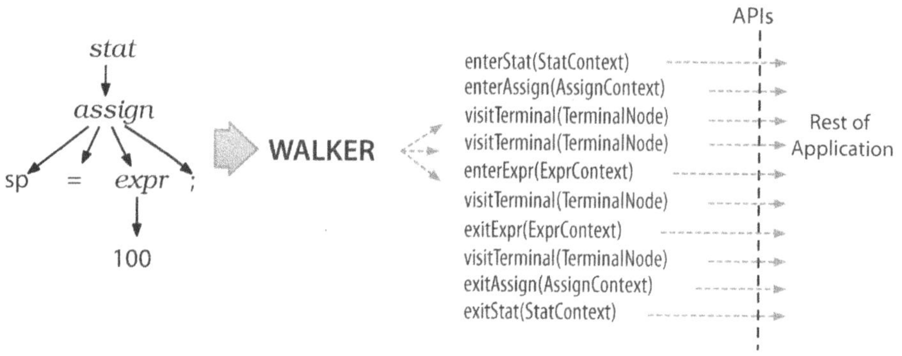

Figure 1—ParseTreeWalker call sequence

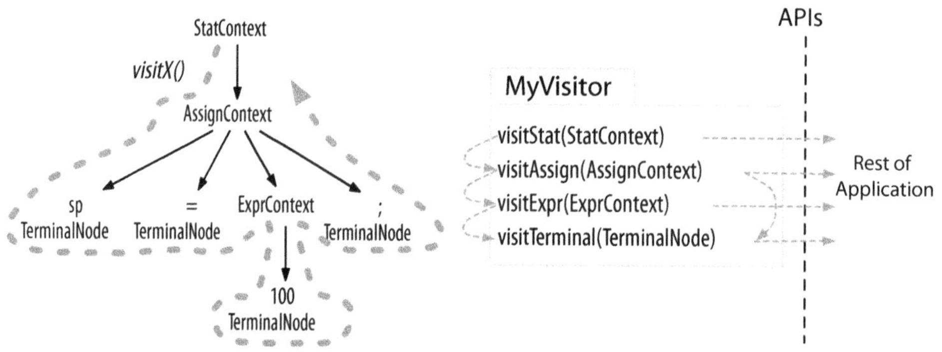

The thick dashed line shows a depth-first walk of the parse tree. The thin dashed lines indicate the method call sequence among the visitor methods. To initiate a walk of the tree, our application-specific code would create a visitor implementation and call visit().

```
ParseTree tree = ... ; // tree is result of parsing
MyVisitor v = new MyVisitor();
v.visit(tree);
```

ANTLR's visitor support code would then call visitStat() upon seeing the root node. From there, the visitStat() implementation would call visit() with the children as arguments to continue the walk. Or, visitMethod() could explicitly call visitAssign(), and so on.

ANTLR gives us a leg up over writing everything ourselves by generating the visitor interface and providing a class with default implementations for the visitor methods. This way, we avoid having to override every method in the interface, letting us focus on just the methods of interest. We'll learn all about visitors and listeners in Chapter 7, *Decoupling Grammars from Application-Specific Code*, on page 111.

Parsing Terms

This chapter introduced a number of important language recognition terms.

Language A language is a set of valid sentences; sentences are composed of phrases, which are composed of subphrases, and so on.

Grammar A grammar formally defines the syntax rules of a language. Each rule in a grammar expresses the structure of a subphrase.

Syntax tree or parse tree This represents the structure of the sentence where each subtree root gives an abstract name to the elements beneath it. The subtree roots correspond to grammar rule names. The leaves of the tree are symbols or tokens of the sentence.

Token A token is a vocabulary symbol in a language; these can represent a category of symbols such as "identifier" or can represent a single operator or keyword.

Lexer or tokenizer This breaks up an input character stream into tokens. A lexer performs lexical analysis.

Parser A parser checks sentences for membership in a specific language by checking the sentence's structure against the rules of a grammar. The best analogy for parsing is traversing a maze, comparing words of a sentence to words written along the floor to go from entrance to exit. ANTLR generates top-down parsers called *ALL(*)* that can use all remaining input symbols to make decisions. Top-down parsers are goal-oriented and start matching at the rule associated with the coarsest construct, such as `program` or `inputFile`.

Recursive-descent parser This is a specific kind of top-down parser implemented with a function for each rule in the grammar.

Lookahead Parsers use lookahead to make decisions by comparing the symbols that begin each alternative.

So, now we have the big picture. We looked at the overall data flow from character stream to parse tree and identified the key class names in the ANTLR runtime. And we just saw a summary of the listener and visitor mechanisms used to connect parsers with application-specific code. Let's make this all more concrete by working through a real example in the next chapter.

CHAPTER 3

A Starter ANTLR Project

For our first project, let's build a grammar for a tiny subset of C or one of its derivatives like Java. In particular, let's recognize integers in, possibly nested, curly braces like {1, 2, 3} and {1, {2, 3}, 4}. These constructs could be int array or struct initializers. A grammar for this syntax would come in handy in a variety of situations. For one, we could use it to build a source code refactoring tool for C that converted integer arrays to byte arrays if all of the initialized values fit within a byte. We could also use this grammar to convert initialized Java short arrays to strings. For example, we could transform the following:

```
static short[] data = {1,2,3};
```

into the following equivalent string with Unicode constants:

```
static String data = "\u0001\u0002\u0003"; // Java char are unsigned short
```

where Unicode character specifiers, such as \u0001, use four hexadecimal digits representing a 16-bit character value, that is, a short.

The reason we might want to do this translation is to overcome a limitation in the Java .class file format. A Java class file stores array initializers as a sequence of explicit array-element initializers, equivalent to data[0]=1; data[1]=2; data[2]=3;, instead of a compact block of packed bytes.[1] Because Java limits the size of initialization methods, it limits the size of the arrays we can initialize. In contrast, a Java class file stores a string as a contiguous sequence of shorts. Converting array initializers to strings results in a more compact class file and avoids Java's initialization method size limit.

By working through this starter example, you'll learn a bit of ANTLR grammar syntax, what ANTLR generates from a grammar, how to incorporate the

1. To learn more about this topic, check out the slides from my JVM Language Summit presentation: http://parrt.cs.usfca.edu/doc/impl-parsers-in-java.pdf.

generated parser into a Java application, and how to build a translator with a parse-tree listener.

3.1 The ANTLR Tool, Runtime, and Generated Code

To get started, let's peek inside ANTLR's jar. There are two key ANTLR components: the ANTLR tool itself and the ANTLR runtime (parse-time) API. When we say "run ANTLR on a grammar," we're talking about running the ANTLR tool, class org.antlr.v4.Tool. Running ANTLR generates code (a parser and a lexer) that recognizes sentences in the language described by the grammar. A lexer breaks up an input stream of characters into tokens and passes them to a parser that checks the syntax. The runtime is a library of classes and methods needed by that generated code such as Parser, Lexer, and Token. First we run ANTLR on a grammar and then compile the generated code against the runtime classes in the jar. Ultimately, the compiled application runs in conjunction with the runtime classes.

The first step to building a language application is to create a grammar that describes a language's syntactic rules (the set of valid sentences). We'll learn how to write grammars in Chapter 5, *Designing Grammars*, on page 59, but for the moment, here's a grammar that'll do what we want:

starter/ArrayInit.g4

```
/** Grammars always start with a grammar header. This grammar is called
 *  ArrayInit and must match the filename: ArrayInit.g4
 */
grammar ArrayInit;

/** A rule called init that matches comma-separated values between {...}. */
init  : '{' value (',' value)* '}' ;  // must match at least one value

/** A value can be either a nested array/struct or a simple integer (INT) */
value : init
      | INT
      ;

// parser rules start with lowercase letters, lexer rules with uppercase
INT :   [0-9]+ ;             // Define token INT as one or more digits
WS  :   [ \t\r\n]+ -> skip ; // Define whitespace rule, toss it out
```

Let's put grammar file ArrayInit.g4 in its own directory, such as /tmp/array (by cutting and pasting or downloading the source code from the book website). Then, we can run ANTLR (the tool) on the grammar file.

```
$ cd /tmp/array
$ antlr4 ArrayInit.g4  # Generate parser and lexer using antlr4 alias
```

From grammar ArrayInit.g4, ANTLR generates lots of files that we'd normally have to write by hand.

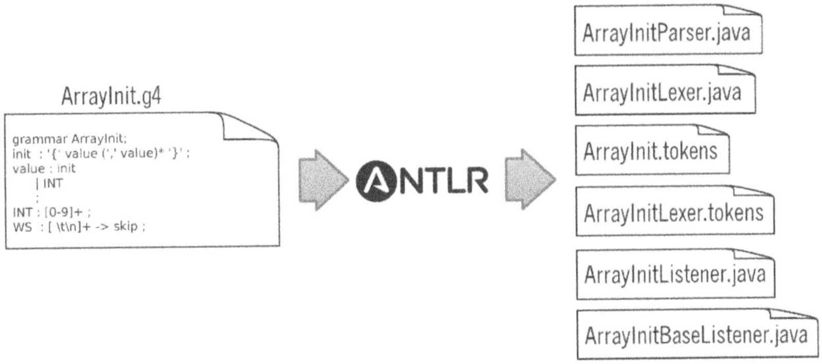

At this point, we're just trying to get the gist of the development process, so here's a quick description of the generated files:

ArrayInitParser.java This file contains the parser class definition specific to grammar ArrayInit that recognizes our array language syntax.

```
public class ArrayInitParser extends Parser { ... }
```

It contains a method for each rule in the grammar as well as some support code.

ArrayInitLexer.java ANTLR automatically extracts a separate parser and lexer specification from our grammar. This file contains the lexer class definition, which ANTLR generated by analyzing the lexical rules INT and WS as well as the grammar literals '{', ',', and '}'. Recall that the lexer tokenizes the input, breaking it up into vocabulary symbols. Here's the class outline:

```
public class ArrayInitLexer extends Lexer { ... }
```

ArrayInit.tokens ANTLR assigns a token type number to each token we define and stores these values in this file. It's needed when we split a large grammar into multiple smaller grammars so that ANTLR can synchronize all the token type numbers. See *Importing Grammars*, on page 38.

ArrayInitListener.java, ArrayInitBaseListener.java By default, ANTLR parsers build a tree from the input. By walking that tree, a tree walker can fire "events" (callbacks) to a listener object that we provide. ArrayInitListener is the interface that describes the callbacks we can implement. ArrayInitBaseListener is a set of empty default implementations. This class makes it easy for us to override just the callbacks we're interested in. (See Section 7.2, *Implementing Applications with Parse-Tree Listeners*, on page 114.) ANTLR can also generate tree visitors for us with the -visitor command-line option. (See *Traversing Parse Trees with Visitors*, on page 121.)

We'll use the listener classes to translate short array initializers to String objects shortly (sorry about the pun), but first let's verify that our parser correctly matches some sample input.

ANTLR Grammars Are Stronger Than Regular Expressions

Those of you familiar with regular expressions[a] might be wondering if ANTLR is overkill for such a simple recognition problem. It turns out that we can't use regular expressions to recognize initializations because of nested initializers. Regular expressions have no memory in the sense that they can't remember what they matched earlier in the input. Because of that, they don't know how to match up left and right curlies. We'll get to this in more detail in *Pattern: Nested Phrase*, on page 67.

a. http://en.wikipedia.org/wiki/Regular_expression

3.2 Testing the Generated Parser

Once we've run ANTLR on our grammar, we need to compile the generated Java source code. We can do that by simply compiling everything in our /tmp/array directory.

```
$ cd /tmp/array
$ javac *.java     # Compile ANTLR-generated code
```

If you get a ClassNotFoundException error from the compiler, that means you probably haven't set the Java CLASSPATH correctly. On UNIX systems, you'll need to execute the following command (and likely add to your start-up script such as .bash_profile):

```
$ export CLASSPATH=".:/usr/local/lib/antlr-4.0-complete.jar:$CLASSPATH"
```

To test our grammar, we use the TestRig via alias grun that we saw in the previous chapter. Here's how to print out the tokens created by the lexer:

```
$ grun ArrayInit init -tokens
{99, 3, 451}
EOF
[@0,0:0='{',<1>,1:0]
[@1,1:2='99',<4>,1:1]
[@2,3:3=',',<2>,1:3]
[@3,5:5='3',<4>,1:5]
[@4,6:6=',',<2>,1:6]
[@5,8:10='451',<4>,1:8]
[@6,11:11='}',<3>,1:11]
[@7,13:12='<EOF>',<-1>,2:0]
```

After typing in array initializer {99, 3, 451}, we have to hit EOF[2] on a line by itself. By default, ANTLR loads the entire input before processing. (That's the most common case and the most efficient.)

Each line of the output represents a single token and shows everything we know about the token. For example, [@5,8:10='451',<4>,1:8] indicates that it's the token at index 5 (indexed from 0), goes from character position 8 to 10 (inclusive starting from 0), has text 451, has token type 4 (INT), is on line 1 (from 1), and is at character position 8 (starting from zero and counting tabs as a single character). Notice that there are no tokens for the space and newline characters. Rule WS in our grammar tosses them out because of the -> skip directive.

To learn more about how the parser recognized the input, we can ask for the parse tree with the -tree option.

```
⇒ $ grun ArrayInit init -tree
⇒ {99, 3, 451}
⇒ EOF
❮ (init { (value 99) , (value 3) , (value 451) })
```

Option -tree prints out the parse tree in LISP-like text form (*root children*). Or, we can use the -gui option to visualize the tree in a dialog box. Try it with a nested group of integers as input: {1,{2,3},4}.

```
⇒ $ grun ArrayInit init -gui
⇒ {1,{2,3},4}
⇒ EOF
```

Here's the parse tree dialog box that pops up:

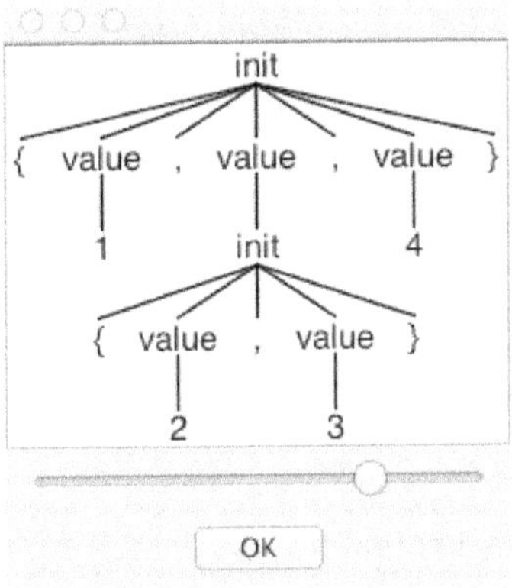

2. The end-of-file character is Ctrl+D on Unix and Ctrl+Z on Windows.

In English, the parse tree says, "The input is an initializer with three values surrounded by curly braces. The first and third values are the integers 1 and 4. The second value is itself an initializer with two values surrounded by curly braces. Those values are integers 2 and 3."

Those interior nodes, init and value, are really handy because they identify all of the various input elements by name. It's kind of like identifying the verb and subject in an English sentence. The best part is that ANTLR creates that tree automatically for us based upon the rule names in our grammar. We'll build a translator based on this grammar at the end of this chapter using a built-in tree walker to trigger callbacks like enterInit() and enterValue().

Now that we can run ANTLR on a grammar and test it, it's time to think about how to call this parser from a Java application.

3.3 Integrating a Generated Parser into a Java Program

Once we have a good start on a grammar, we can integrate the ANTLR-generated code into a larger application. In this section, we'll look at a simple Java main() that invokes our initializer parser and prints out the parse tree like TestRig's -tree option. Here's a boilerplate Test.java file that embodies the overall recognizer data flow we saw in Section 2.1, *Let's Get Meta!*, on page 9:

starter/Test.java

```
// import ANTLR's runtime libraries
import org.antlr.v4.runtime.*;
import org.antlr.v4.runtime.tree.*;

public class Test {
    public static void main(String[] args) throws Exception {
        // create a CharStream that reads from standard input
        ANTLRInputStream input = new ANTLRInputStream(System.in);

        // create a lexer that feeds off of input CharStream
        ArrayInitLexer lexer = new ArrayInitLexer(input);

        // create a buffer of tokens pulled from the lexer
        CommonTokenStream tokens = new CommonTokenStream(lexer);

        // create a parser that feeds off the tokens buffer
        ArrayInitParser parser = new ArrayInitParser(tokens);

        ParseTree tree = parser.init(); // begin parsing at init rule
        System.out.println(tree.toStringTree(parser)); // print LISP-style tree
    }
}
```

The program uses a number of classes like CommonTokenStream and ParseTree from ANTLR's runtime library that we'll learn more about starting in Section 4.1, *Matching an Arithmetic Expression Language*, on page 34.

Here's how to compile everything and run Test:

```
⇒ $ javac ArrayInit*.java Test.java
⇒ $ java Test
⇒ {1,{2,3},4}
⇒ EOF
❮ (init { (value 1) , (value (init { (value 2) , (value 3) })) , (value 4) })
```

ANTLR parsers also automatically report and recover from syntax errors. For example, here's what happens if we enter an initializer that's missing the final curly brace:

```
⇒ $ java Test
⇒ {1,2
⇒ EOF
❮ line 2:0 missing '}' at '<EOF>'
  (init { (value 1) , (value 2) <missing '}'>)
```

At this point, we've seen how to run ANTLR on a grammar and integrate the generated parser into a trivial Java application. An application that merely checks syntax is not that impressive, though, so let's finish up by building a translator that converts short array initializers to String objects.

3.4 Building a Language Application

Continuing with our array initializer example, our next goal is to translate not just recognize initializers. For example, let's translate Java short arrays like {99 , 3 , 451 } to "\u0063\u0003\u01c3" where 63 is the hexadecimal representation of the 99 decimal.

To move beyond recognition, an application has to extract data from the parse tree. The easiest way to do that is to have ANTLR's built-in parse-tree walker trigger a bunch of callbacks as it performs a depth-first walk. As we saw earlier, ANTLR automatically generates a listener infrastructure for us. These listeners are like the callbacks on GUI widgets (for example, a button would notify us upon a button press) or like SAX events in an XML parser.

To write a program that reacts to the input, all we have to do is implement a few methods in a subclass of ArrayInitBaseListener. The basic strategy is to have each listener method print out a translated piece of the input when called to do so by the tree walker.

The beauty of the listener mechanism is that we don't have to do any tree walking ourselves. In fact, we don't even have to know that the runtime is walking a tree to call our methods. All we know is that our listener gets notified at the beginning and end of phrases associated with rules in the grammar. As we'll see in Section 7.2, *Implementing Applications with Parse-Tree Listeners*, on page 114, this approach reduces how much we have to learn about ANTLR —we're back in familiar programming language territory for anything but phrase recognition.

Starting a translation project means figuring out how to convert each input token or phrase to an output string. To do that, it's a good idea to manually translate a few representative samples in order to pick out the general phrase-to-phrase conversions. In this case, the translation is pretty straightforward.

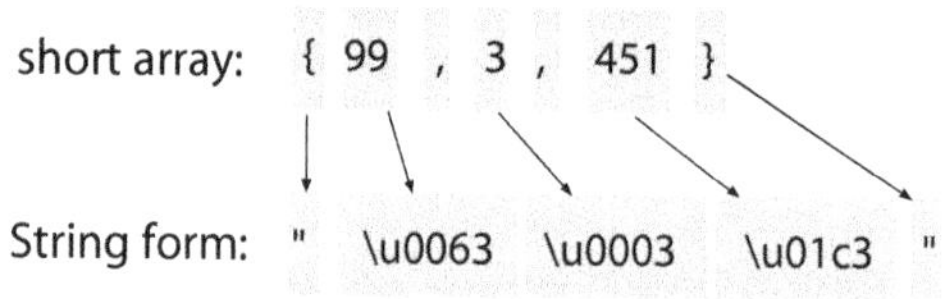

In English, the translation is a series of "*X goes to Y*" rules.

1. Translate { to ".
2. Translate } to ".
3. Translate integers to four-digit hexadecimal strings prefixed with \u.

To code the translator, we need to write methods that print out the converted strings upon seeing the appropriate input token or phrase. The built-in tree walker triggers callbacks in a listener upon seeing the beginning and end of the various phrases. Here's a listener implementation for our translation rules:

starter/ShortToUnicodeString.java

```
/** Convert short array inits like {1,2,3} to "\u0001\u0002\u0003" */
public class ShortToUnicodeString extends ArrayInitBaseListener {
    /** Translate { to " */
    @Override
    public void enterInit(ArrayInitParser.InitContext ctx) {
        System.out.print('"');
    }

    /** Translate } to " */
    @Override
    public void exitInit(ArrayInitParser.InitContext ctx) {
        System.out.print('"');
    }
```

```
    /** Translate integers to 4-digit hexadecimal strings prefixed with \\u */
    @Override
    public void enterValue(ArrayInitParser.ValueContext ctx) {
        // Assumes no nested array initializers
        int value = Integer.valueOf(ctx.INT().getText());
        System.out.printf("\\u%04x", value);
    }
}
```

We don't need to override every enter/exit method; we do just the ones we care about. The only unfamiliar expression is ctx.INT(), which asks the context object for the integer INT token matched by that invocation of rule value. Context objects record everything that happens during the recognition of a rule.

The only thing left to do is to create a translator application derived from the Test boilerplate code shown earlier.

starter/Translate.java

```
// import ANTLR's runtime libraries
import org.antlr.v4.runtime.*;
import org.antlr.v4.runtime.tree.*;

public class Translate {
    public static void main(String[] args) throws Exception {
        // create a CharStream that reads from standard input
        ANTLRInputStream input = new ANTLRInputStream(System.in);
        // create a lexer that feeds off of input CharStream
        ArrayInitLexer lexer = new ArrayInitLexer(input);
        // create a buffer of tokens pulled from the lexer
        CommonTokenStream tokens = new CommonTokenStream(lexer);
        // create a parser that feeds off the tokens buffer
        ArrayInitParser parser = new ArrayInitParser(tokens);
        ParseTree tree = parser.init(); // begin parsing at init rule

➤       // Create a generic parse tree walker that can trigger callbacks
➤       ParseTreeWalker walker = new ParseTreeWalker();
➤       // Walk the tree created during the parse, trigger callbacks
➤       walker.walk(new ShortToUnicodeString(), tree);
➤       System.out.println(); // print a \n after translation
    }
}
```

The only difference from the boilerplate code is the highlighted section that creates a tree walker and asks it to walk the tree returned from the parser. As the tree walker traverses, it triggers calls into our ShortToUnicodeString listener.

Please note: To focus our attention and to reduce bloat, the remainder of the book will typically show just the important or novel bits of code rather than entire files. If you're reading the electronic version of this book, you can always click the code snippet titles; the title bars are links to the full source code on the Web. You can also grab the full source code bundle on the book's website.[3]

Let's build the translator and try it on our sample input.

```
⇒ $ javac ArrayInit*.java Translate.java
⇒ $ java Translate
⇒ {99, 3, 451}
⇒ EOF
❮ "\u0063\u0003\u01c3"
```

It works! We've just built our first translator, without even touching the grammar. All we had to do was implement a few methods that printed the appropriate phrase translations. Moreover, we can generate completely different output simply by passing in a different listener. Listeners effectively isolate the language application from the grammar, making the grammar reusable for other applications.

In the next chapter, we'll take a whirlwind tour of ANTLR grammar notation and the key features that make ANTLR powerful and easy to use.

3. http://pragprog.com/titles/tpantlr2/source_code

CHAPTER 4

A Quick Tour

So far, we have learned how to install ANTLR and have looked at the key processes, terminology, and building blocks needed to build a language application. In this chapter, we're going to take a whirlwind tour of ANTLR by racing through a number of examples that illustrate its capabilities. We'll be glossing over a lot of details in the interest of brevity, so don't worry if things aren't crystal clear. The goal is just to get a feel for what you can do with ANTLR. We'll look underneath the hood starting in Chapter 5, *Designing Grammars*, on page 59. For those with experience using previous versions of ANTLR, this chapter is a great way to retool.

This chapter is broken down into four broad topics that nicely illustrate the feature set. It's a good idea to download the code[1] for this book (or follow the links in the ebook version) and work through the examples as we go along. That way, you'll get used to working with grammar files and building ANTLR applications. Keep in mind that many of the code snippets you see interspersed in the text aren't complete files so that we can focus on the interesting bits.

First, we're going to work with a grammar for a simple arithmetic expression language. We'll test it initially using ANTLR's built-in test rig and then learn more about the boilerplate main program that launches parsers shown in Section 3.3, *Integrating a Generated Parser into a Java Program*, on page 28. Then, we'll look at a nontrivial parse tree for the expression grammar. (Recall that a parse tree records how a parser matches an input phrase.) For dealing with very large grammars, we'll see how to split a grammar into manageable chunks using grammar imports. Next, we'll check out how ANTLR-generated parsers respond to invalid input.

1. http://pragprog.com/titles/tpantlr2/source_code

Second, after looking at the parser for arithmetic expressions, we'll use a visitor pattern to build a calculator that walks expression grammar parse trees. ANTLR parsers automatically generate visitor interfaces and blank method implementations so we can get started painlessly.

Third, we'll build a translator that reads in a Java class definition and spits out a Java interface derived from the methods in that class. Our implementation will use the tree listener mechanism that ANTLR also generates automatically.

Fourth, we'll learn how to embed *actions* (arbitrary code) directly in the grammar. Most of the time, we can build language applications with visitors or listeners, but for the ultimate flexibility, ANTLR allows us to inject our own application-specific code into the generated parser. These actions execute during the parse and can collect information or generate output like any other arbitrary code snippets. In conjunction with *semantic predicates* (Boolean expressions), we can even make parts of our grammar disappear at runtime! For example, we might want to turn the `enum` keyword on and off in a Java grammar to parse different versions of the language. Without semantic predicates, we'd need two different versions of the grammar.

Finally, we'll zoom in on a few ANTLR features at the lexical (token) level. We'll see how ANTLR deals with input files that contain more than one language. Then we'll look at the awesome `TokenStreamRewriter` class that lets us tweak, mangle, or otherwise manipulate token streams, all without disturbing the original input stream. Finally, we'll revisit our interface generator example to learn how ANTLR can ignore whitespace and comments during Java parsing but retain them for later processing.

Let's begin our tour by getting acquainted with ANTLR grammar notation. Make sure you have the `antlr4` and `grun` aliases or scripts defined, as explained in Section 1.2, *Executing ANTLR and Testing Recognizers*, on page 6.

4.1 Matching an Arithmetic Expression Language

For our first grammar, we're going to build a simple calculator. Doing something with expressions makes sense because they're so common. To keep things simple, we'll allow only the basic arithmetic operators (add, subtract, multiply, and divide), parenthesized expressions, integer numbers, and variables. We'll also restrict ourselves to integers instead of allowing floating-point numbers.

Here's some sample input that illustrates all language features:

tour/t.expr

```
193
a = 5
b = 6
a+b*2
(1+2)*3
```

In English, a *program* in our expression language is a sequence of statements terminated by newlines. A statement is either an expression, an assignment, or a blank line. Here's an ANTLR grammar that'll parse those statements and expressions for us:

tour/Expr.g4

```
grammar Expr;

/** The start rule; begin parsing here. */
prog:   stat+ ;

stat:   expr NEWLINE
    |   ID '=' expr NEWLINE
    |   NEWLINE
    ;

expr:   expr ('*'|'/') expr
    |   expr ('+'|'-') expr
    |   INT
    |   ID
    |   '(' expr ')'
    ;

ID  :   [a-zA-Z]+ ;      // match identifiers
INT :   [0-9]+ ;         // match integers
NEWLINE:'\r'? '\n' ;     // return newlines to parser (is end-statement signal)
WS  :   [ \t]+ -> skip ; // toss out whitespace
```

Without going into too much detail, let's look at some of the key elements of ANTLR's grammar notation.

- Grammars consist of a set of rules that describe language syntax. There are rules for syntactic structure like stat and expr as well as rules for vocabulary symbols (tokens) such as identifiers and integers.
- Rules starting with a lowercase letter comprise the parser rules.
- Rules starting with an uppercase letter comprise the lexical (token) rules.
- We separate the alternatives of a rule with the | operator, and we can group symbols with parentheses into *subrules*. For example, subrule ('*'|'/') matches either a multiplication symbol or a division symbol.

We'll tackle all of this stuff in detail when we get to Chapter 5, *Designing Grammars*, on page 59.

One of ANTLR v4's most significant new features is its ability to handle (most kinds of) left-recursive rules. A left-recursive rule is one that invokes itself at the start of an alternative. For example, in this grammar, rule expr has alternatives on lines 11 and 12 that recursively invoke expr on the left edge. Specifying arithmetic expression notation this way is dramatically easier than what we'd need for the typical top-down parser strategy. In that strategy, we'd need multiple rules, one for each operator precedence level. For more on this feature, see Section 5.4, *Dealing with Precedence, Left Recursion, and Associativity*, on page 71.

The notation for the token definitions should be familiar to those with regular expression experience. We'll look at lots of lexical (token) rules in Chapter 6, *Exploring Some Real Grammars*, on page 85. The only unusual syntax is the -> skip operation on the WS whitespace rule. It's a directive that tells the lexer to match but throw out whitespace. (Every possible input character must be matched by at least one lexical rule.) We avoid tying the grammar to a specific target language by using formal ANTLR notation instead of an arbitrary code snippet in the grammar that tells the lexer to skip.

OK, let's take grammar Expr out for a joy ride. Download it either by clicking the tour/Expr.g4 link on the previous code listing, if you're viewing the ebook version, or by cutting and pasting the grammar into a file called Expr.g4.

The easiest way to test grammars is with the built-in TestRig, which we can access using alias grun. For example, here is the build and test sequence on a Unix box to parse input file t.expr:

```
$ antlr4 Expr.g4
$ ls Expr*.java
ExprBaseListener.java   ExprListener.java
ExprLexer.java          ExprParser.java
$ javac Expr*.java
$ grun Expr prog -gui t.expr # launches org.antlr.v4.runtime.misc.TestRig
```

Because of the -gui option, the test rig pops up a window showing the parse tree, as shown in Figure 2, *Window showing the parse tree*, on page 37.

The parse tree is analogous to the function call tree our parser would trace as it recognizes input. (ANTLR generates a function for each rule.)

It's OK to develop and test grammars using the test rig, but ultimately we'll need to integrate our ANTLR-generated parser into an application. The main

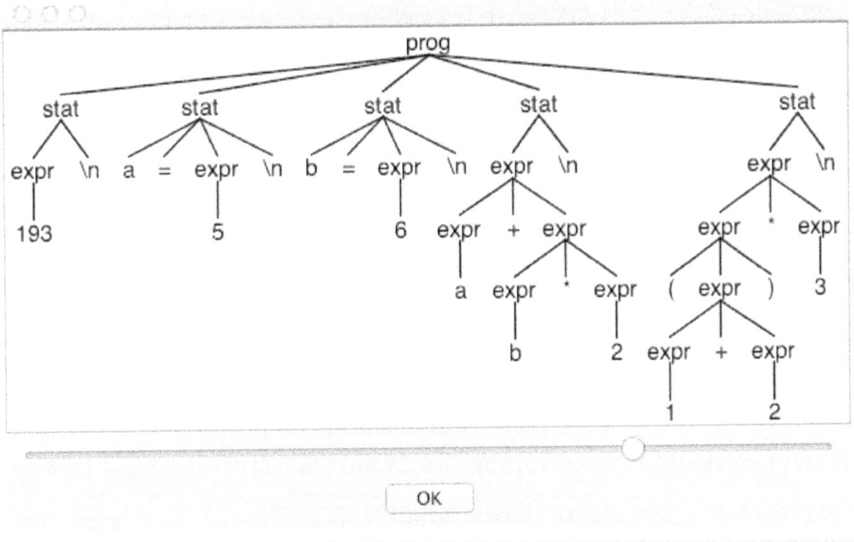

Figure 2—Window showing the parse tree

program given below shows the code necessary to create all necessary objects and launch our expression language parser starting at rule `prog`:

tour/ExprJoyRide.java

```
1  import org.antlr.v4.runtime.*;
2  import org.antlr.v4.runtime.tree.*;
3  import java.io.FileInputStream;
4  import java.io.InputStream;
5  public class ExprJoyRide {
6      public static void main(String[] args) throws Exception {
7          String inputFile = null;
8          if ( args.length>0 ) inputFile = args[0];
9          InputStream is = System.in;
10         if ( inputFile!=null ) is = new FileInputStream(inputFile);
11         ANTLRInputStream input = new ANTLRInputStream(is);
12         ExprLexer lexer = new ExprLexer(input);
13         CommonTokenStream tokens = new CommonTokenStream(lexer);
14         ExprParser parser = new ExprParser(tokens);
15         ParseTree tree = parser.prog(); // parse; start at prog
16         System.out.println(tree.toStringTree(parser)); // print tree as text
17     }
18 }
```

Lines 7..11 create an input stream of characters for the lexer. Lines 12..14 create the lexer and parser objects and a token stream "pipe" between them. Line 15 actually launches the parser. (Calling a rule method is like invoking that rule; we can call any parser rule method we want.) Finally, line 16 prints out the parse tree returned from the rule method prog() in text form.

Here is how to build the test program and run it on input file t.expr:

```
$ javac ExprJoyRide.java Expr*.java
$ java ExprJoyRide t.expr
(prog
  (stat (expr 193) \n)
  (stat a = (expr 5) \n)
  (stat b = (expr 6) \n)
  (stat (expr (expr a) + (expr (expr b) * (expr 2))) \n)
  (stat (expr (expr ( (expr (expr 1) + (expr 2)) )) * (expr 3)) \n)
)
```

The (slightly cleaned up) text representation of the parse tree is not as easy to read as the visual representation, but it's useful for functional testing.

This expression grammar is pretty small, but grammars can run into the thousands of lines. In the next section, we'll learn how to keep such large grammars manageable.

Importing Grammars

It's a good idea to break up very large grammars into logical chunks, just like we do with software. One way to do that is to split a grammar into parser and lexer grammars. That's not a bad idea because there's a surprising amount of overlap between different languages lexically. For example, identifiers and numbers are usually the same across languages. Factoring out lexical rules into a "module" means we can use it for different parser grammars. Here's a lexer grammar containing all of the lexical rules:

tour/CommonLexerRules.g4

```
lexer grammar CommonLexerRules; // note "lexer grammar"

ID  :   [a-zA-Z]+ ;       // match identifiers
INT :   [0-9]+ ;          // match integers
NEWLINE:'\r'? '\n' ;      // return newlines to parser (end-statement signal)
WS  :   [ \t]+ -> skip ;  // toss out whitespace
```

Now we can replace the lexical rules from the original grammar with an import statement.

tour/LibExpr.g4

```
grammar LibExpr;         // Rename to distinguish from original
import CommonLexerRules; // includes all rules from CommonLexerRules.g4
/** The start rule; begin parsing here. */
prog:   stat+ ;
```

```
stat:   expr NEWLINE
    |   ID '=' expr NEWLINE
    |   NEWLINE
    ;

expr:   expr ('*'|'/') expr
    |   expr ('+'|'-') expr
    |   INT
    |   ID
    |   '(' expr ')'
    ;
```

The build and test sequence is the same as it was without the import. We do not run ANTLR on the imported grammar itself.

```
⇒ $ antlr4 LibExpr.g4 # automatically pulls in CommonLexerRules.g4
⇒ $ ls Lib*.java
❮ LibExprBaseListener.java        LibExprListener.java
  LibExprLexer.java               LibExprParser.java
⇒ $ javac LibExpr*.java
⇒ $ grun LibExpr prog -tree
⇒ 3+4
⇒ EOF
❮ (prog (stat (expr (expr 3) + (expr 4)) \n))
```

So far, we've assumed valid input, but error handling is an important part of almost all language applications. Let's see what ANTLR does with erroneous input.

Handling Erroneous Input

ANTLR parsers automatically report and recover from syntax errors. For example, if we forget a closing parenthesis in an expression, the parser automatically emits an error message.

```
⇒ $ java ExprJoyRide
⇒ (1+2
⇒ 3
⇒ EOF
❮ line 1:4 mismatched input '\n' expecting {')', '+', '*', '-', '/'}
  (prog
    (stat (expr ( (expr (expr 1) + (expr 2)) <missing ')'>) \n)
    (stat (expr 3) \n)
  )
```

Equally important is that the parser recovers to correctly match the second expression (the 3).

When using the -gui option on grun, the parse-tree dialog automatically highlights error nodes in red.

```
⇒ $ grun LibExpr prog -gui
⇒ (1+2
⇒ 34*69
⇒ EOF
```

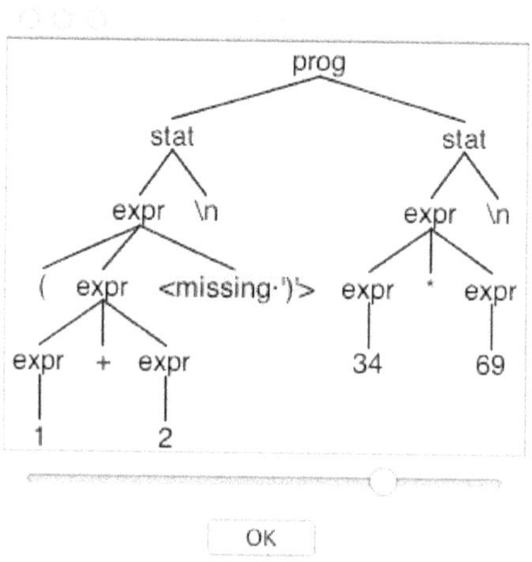

Notice that ANTLR successively recovered from the error in the first expression again to properly match the second.

ANTLR's error mechanism has lots of flexibility. We can alter the error messages, catch recognition exceptions, and even alter the fundamental error handling strategy. We'll cover this in Chapter 9, *Error Reporting and Recovery*, on page 151.

That completes our quick tour of grammars and parsing. We've looked at a simple expression grammar and how to launch it using the built-in test rig and a sample main program. We also saw how to get text and visual representations of parse trees that show how our grammar recognizes input phrases. The `import` statement lets us break up grammars into *modules*. Now, let's move beyond language recognition to interpreting expressions (computing their values).

4.2 Building a Calculator Using a Visitor

To get the previous arithmetic expression parser to compute values, we need to write some Java code. ANTLR v4 encourages us to keep grammars clean and use parse-tree visitors and other walkers to implement language applications. In this section, we'll use the well-known visitor pattern to implement our little calculator. To make things easier for us, ANTLR automatically generates a visitor interface and blank visitor implementation object.

Before we get to the visitor, we need to make a few modifications to the grammar. First, we need to label the alternatives of the rules. (The labels can be any identifier that doesn't collide with a rule name.) Without labels on the alternatives, ANTLR generates only one visitor method per rule. (Chapter 7, *Decoupling Grammars from Application-Specific Code*, on page 111 uses a similar grammar to explain the visitor mechanism in more detail.) In our case, we'd like a different visitor method for each alternative so that we can get different "events" for each kind of input phrase. Labels appear on the right edge of alternatives and start with the # symbol in our new grammar, LabeledExpr.

tour/LabeledExpr.g4

```
stat:   expr NEWLINE                # printExpr
    |   ID '=' expr NEWLINE         # assign
    |   NEWLINE                     # blank
    ;

expr:   expr op=('*'|'/') expr      # MulDiv
    |   expr op=('+'|'-') expr      # AddSub
    |   INT                         # int
    |   ID                          # id
    |   '(' expr ')'                # parens
    ;
```

Next, let's define some token names for the operator literals so that, later, we can reference token names as Java constants in the visitor.

tour/LabeledExpr.g4

```
MUL :   '*' ; // assigns token name to '*' used above in grammar
DIV :   '/' ;
ADD :   '+' ;
SUB :   '-' ;
```

Now that we have a properly enhanced grammar, let's start coding our calculator and see what the main program looks like. Our main program in file Calc.java is nearly identical to the main() in ExprJoyRide.java from earlier. The first difference is that we create lexer and parser objects derived from grammar LabeledExpr, not Expr.

tour/Calc.java

```
LabeledExprLexer lexer = new LabeledExprLexer(input);
CommonTokenStream tokens = new CommonTokenStream(lexer);
LabeledExprParser parser = new LabeledExprParser(tokens);
ParseTree tree = parser.prog(); // parse
```

We also can remove the print statement that displays the tree as text. The other difference is that we create an instance of our visitor class, EvalVisitor, which we'll get to in just a second. To start walking the parse tree returned from method prog(), we call visit().

tour/Calc.java
```
EvalVisitor eval = new EvalVisitor();
eval.visit(tree);
```

All of our supporting machinery is now in place. The only thing left to do is implement a visitor that computes and returns values by walking the parse tree. To get started, let's see what ANTLR generates for us when we type.

```
$ antlr4 -no-listener -visitor LabeledExpr.g4
```

First, ANTLR generates a visitor interface with a method for each labeled alternative name.

```
public interface LabeledExprVisitor<T> {
    T visitId(LabeledExprParser.IdContext ctx);             # from label id
    T visitAssign(LabeledExprParser.AssignContext ctx);     # from label assign
    T visitMulDiv(LabeledExprParser.MulDivContext ctx);     # from label MulDiv
    ...
}
```

The interface definition uses Java generics with a parameterized type for the return values of the visit methods. This allows us to derive implementation classes with our choice of return value type to suit the computations we want to implement.

Next, ANTLR generates a default visitor implementation called LabeledExprBaseVisitor that we can subclass. In this case, our expression results are integers and so our EvalVisitor should extend LabeledExprBaseVisitor<Integer>. To implement the calculator, we override the methods associated with statement and expression alternatives. Here it is in its full glory. You can either cut and paste or save the tour/EvalVisitor link (ebook version).

tour/EvalVisitor.java
```
import java.util.HashMap;
import java.util.Map;

public class EvalVisitor extends LabeledExprBaseVisitor<Integer> {
    /** "memory" for our calculator; variable/value pairs go here */
    Map<String, Integer> memory = new HashMap<String, Integer>();

    /** ID '=' expr NEWLINE */
    @Override
    public Integer visitAssign(LabeledExprParser.AssignContext ctx) {
        String id = ctx.ID().getText();  // id is left-hand side of '='
        int value = visit(ctx.expr());   // compute value of expression on right
        memory.put(id, value);           // store it in our memory
        return value;
    }
```

```
    /** expr NEWLINE */
    @Override
    public Integer visitPrintExpr(LabeledExprParser.PrintExprContext ctx) {
        Integer value = visit(ctx.expr()); // evaluate the expr child
        System.out.println(value);         // print the result
        return 0;                          // return dummy value
    }

    /** INT */
    @Override
    public Integer visitInt(LabeledExprParser.IntContext ctx) {
        return Integer.valueOf(ctx.INT().getText());
    }

    /** ID */
    @Override
    public Integer visitId(LabeledExprParser.IdContext ctx) {
        String id = ctx.ID().getText();
        if ( memory.containsKey(id) ) return memory.get(id);
        return 0;
    }

    /** expr op=('*'|'/') expr */
    @Override
    public Integer visitMulDiv(LabeledExprParser.MulDivContext ctx) {
        int left = visit(ctx.expr(0));  // get value of left subexpression
        int right = visit(ctx.expr(1)); // get value of right subexpression
        if ( ctx.op.getType() == LabeledExprParser.MUL ) return left * right;
        return left / right; // must be DIV
    }

    /** expr op=('+'|'-') expr */
    @Override
    public Integer visitAddSub(LabeledExprParser.AddSubContext ctx) {
        int left = visit(ctx.expr(0));  // get value of left subexpression
        int right = visit(ctx.expr(1)); // get value of right subexpression
        if ( ctx.op.getType() == LabeledExprParser.ADD ) return left + right;
        return left - right; // must be SUB
    }

    /** '(' expr ')' */
    @Override
    public Integer visitParens(LabeledExprParser.ParensContext ctx) {
        return visit(ctx.expr()); // return child expr's value
    }
}
```

And here is the build and test sequence that evaluates expressions in t.expr:

```
⇒ $ antlr4 -no-listener -visitor LabeledExpr.g4   # -visitor is required!!!
⇒ $ ls LabeledExpr*.java
❮ LabeledExprBaseVisitor.java     LabeledExprParser.java
  LabeledExprLexer.java           LabeledExprVisitor.java
⇒ $ javac Calc.java LabeledExpr*.java
⇒ $ cat t.expr
❮ 193
  a = 5
  b = 6
  a+b*2
  (1+2)*3
⇒ $ java Calc t.expr
❮ 193
  17
  9
```

The takeaway is that we built a calculator without having to insert raw Java actions into the grammar, as we would need to do in ANTLR v3. The grammar is kept application independent and programming language neutral. The visitor mechanism also keeps everything beyond the recognition-related stuff in familiar Java territory. There's no extra ANTLR notation to learn in order to build a language application on top of a generated parser.

Before moving on, you might take a moment to try to extend this expression language by adding a clear statement. It's a great way to get your feet wet and do something real without having to know all of the details. The clear command should clear out the memory map, and you'll need a new alternative in rule stat to recognize it. Label the alternative with # clear and then run ANTLR on the grammar to get the augmented visitor interface. Then, to make something happen upon clear, implement visitor method visitClear(). Compile and run Calc following the earlier sequence.

Let's switch gears now and think about translation rather than evaluating or interpreting input. In the next section, we're going to use a variation of the visitor called a *listener* to build a translator for Java source code.

4.3 Building a Translator with a Listener

Imagine your boss assigns you to build a tool that generates a Java interface file from the methods in a Java class definition. Panic ensues if you're a junior programmer. As an experienced Java developer, you might suggest using the Java reflection API or the javap tool to extract method signatures. If your Java tool building kung fu is very strong, you might even try using a bytecode library such as ASM.[2] Then your boss says, "Oh, yeah. Preserve whitespace

2. http://asm.ow2.org

and comments within the bounds of the method signature." There's no way around it now. We have to parse Java source code. For example, we'd like to read in Java code like this:

tour/Demo.java
```
import java.util.List;
import java.util.Map;
public class Demo {
	void f(int x, String y) { }
	int[ ] g(/*no args*/) { return null; }
	List<Map<String, Integer>>[] h() { return null; }
}
```

and generate an interface with the method signatures, preserving the whitespace and comments.

tour/IDemo.java
```
interface IDemo {
	void f(int x, String y);
	int[ ] g(/*no args*/);
	List<Map<String, Integer>>[] h();
}
```

Believe it or not, we're going to solve the core of this problem in about fifteen lines of code by listening to "events" fired from a Java parse-tree walker. The Java parse tree will come from a parser generated from an existing Java grammar included in the source code for this book. We'll derive the name of the generated interface from the class name and grab method signatures (return type, method name, and argument list) from method definitions. For a similar but more thoroughly explained example, see Section 8.3, *Generating a Call Graph*, on page 136.

The key "interface" between the grammar and our listener object is called JavaListener, and ANTLR automatically generates it for us. It defines all of the methods that class ParseTreeWalker from ANTLR's runtime can trigger as it traverses the parse tree. In our case, we need to respond to three events by overriding three methods: when the walker enters and exits a class definition and when it encounters a method definition. Here are the relevant methods from the generated listener interface:

```
public interface JavaListener extends ParseTreeListener {
    void enterClassDeclaration(JavaParser.ClassDeclarationContext ctx);
    void exitClassDeclaration(JavaParser.ClassDeclarationContext ctx);
    void enterMethodDeclaration(JavaParser.MethodDeclarationContext ctx);
    ...
}
```

The biggest difference between the listener and visitor mechanisms is that listener methods are called by the ANTLR-provided walker object, whereas visitor methods must walk their children with explicit visit calls. Forgetting to invoke visit() on a node's children means those subtrees don't get visited.

To build our listener implementation, we need to know what rules classDeclaration and methodDeclaration look like because listener methods have to grab phrase elements matched by the rules. File Java.g4 is a complete grammar for Java, but here are the two methods we need to look at for this problem:

tour/Java.g4
```
classDeclaration
    :   'class' Identifier typeParameters? ('extends' type)?
        ('implements' typeList)?
        classBody
    ;
```

tour/Java.g4
```
methodDeclaration
    :   type Identifier formalParameters ('[' ']')* methodDeclarationRest
    |   'void' Identifier formalParameters methodDeclarationRest
    ;
```

So that we don't have to implement all 200 or so interface methods, ANTLR generates a default implementation called JavaBaseListener. Our interface extractor can then subclass JavaBaseListener and override the methods of interest.

Our basic strategy will be to print out the interface header when we see the start of a class definition. Then, we'll print a terminating } at the end of the class definition. Upon each method definition, we'll spit out its signature. Here's the complete implementation:

tour/ExtractInterfaceListener.java
```
import org.antlr.v4.runtime.TokenStream;
import org.antlr.v4.runtime.misc.Interval;

public class ExtractInterfaceListener extends JavaBaseListener {
    JavaParser parser;
    public ExtractInterfaceListener(JavaParser parser) {this.parser = parser;}
    /** Listen to matches of classDeclaration */
    @Override
    public void enterClassDeclaration(JavaParser.ClassDeclarationContext ctx){
        System.out.println("interface I"+ctx.Identifier()+" {");
    }
    @Override
    public void exitClassDeclaration(JavaParser.ClassDeclarationContext ctx) {
        System.out.println("}");
    }
```

```
    /** Listen to matches of methodDeclaration */
    @Override
    public void enterMethodDeclaration(
        JavaParser.MethodDeclarationContext ctx
    )
    {
        // need parser to get tokens
        TokenStream tokens = parser.getTokenStream();
        String type = "void";
        if ( ctx.type()!=null ) {
            type = tokens.getText(ctx.type());
        }
        String args = tokens.getText(ctx.formalParameters());
        System.out.println("\t"+type+" "+ctx.Identifier()+args+";");
    }
}
```

To fire this up, we need a main program, which looks almost the same as the others in this chapter. Our application code starts after we've launched the parser.

tour/ExtractInterfaceTool.java

```
JavaLexer lexer = new JavaLexer(input);
CommonTokenStream tokens = new CommonTokenStream(lexer);
JavaParser parser = new JavaParser(tokens);
ParseTree tree = parser.compilationUnit(); // parse

ParseTreeWalker walker = new ParseTreeWalker(); // create standard walker
ExtractInterfaceListener extractor = new ExtractInterfaceListener(parser);
walker.walk(extractor, tree); // initiate walk of tree with listener
```

We also need to add `import org.antlr.v4.runtime.tree.*;` at the top of the file.

Given grammar Java.g4 and our `main()` in `ExtractInterfaceTool`, here's the complete build and test sequence:

```
⇒ $ antlr4 Java.g4
⇒ $ ls Java*.java ExtractInterface*.java
❮ ExtractInterfaceListener.java  JavaBaseListener.java   JavaListener.java
  ExtractInterfaceTool.java      JavaLexer.java          JavaParser.java
⇒ $ javac Java*.java Extract*.java
⇒ $ java ExtractInterfaceTool Demo.java
❮ interface IDemo {
          void f(int x, String y);
          int[ ] g(/*no args*/);
          List<Map<String, Integer>>[] h();
  }
```

This implementation isn't quite complete because it doesn't include in the interface file the import statements for the types referenced by the interface methods such as List. As an exercise, try handling the imports. It should convince you that it's easy to build these kinds of extractors or translators using a listener. We don't even need to know what the importDeclaration rule looks like because enterImportDeclaration() should simply print the text matched by the entire rule: parser.getTokenStream().getText(ctx).

The visitor and listener mechanisms work very well and promote the separation of concerns between parsing and parser application. Sometimes, though, we need extra control and flexibility.

4.4 Making Things Happen During the Parse

Listeners and visitors are great because they keep application-specific code out of grammars, making grammars easier to read and preventing them from getting entangled with a particular application. For the ultimate flexibility and control, however, we can directly embed code snippets (actions) within grammars. These actions are copied into the recursive-descent parser code ANTLR generates. In this section, we'll implement a simple program that reads in rows of data and prints out the values found in a specific column. After that, we'll see how to make special actions, called *semantic predicates*, dynamically turn parts of a grammar on and off.

Embedding Arbitrary Actions in a Grammar

We can compute values or print things out on-the-fly during parsing if we don't want the overhead of building a parse tree. On the other hand, it means embedding arbitrary code within the expression grammar, which is harder; we have to understand the effect of the actions on the parser and where to position those actions.

To demonstrate actions embedded in a grammar, let's build a program that prints out a specific column from rows of data. This comes up all the time for me because people send me text files from which I need to grab, say, the name or email column. For our purposes, let's use the following data:

tour/t.rows
```
parrt	Terence Parr	101
tombu	Tom Burns	020
bke	Kevin Edgar	008
```

The columns are tab-delimited, and each row ends with a newline character. Matching this kind of input is pretty simple grammatically.

```
file : (row NL)+ ; // NL is newline token: '\r'? '\n'
row  : STUFF+ ;
```

It gets mucked up, though, when we add actions. We need to create a constructor so that we can pass in the column number we want (counting from 1), and we need an action inside the (...)+ loop in rule row.

tour/Rows.g4
```
grammar Rows;

@parser::members { // add members to generated RowsParser
    int col;
    public RowsParser(TokenStream input, int col) { // custom constructor
        this(input);
        this.col = col;
    }
}

file: (row NL)+ ;

row
locals [int i=0]
    : (   STUFF
          {
          $i++;
          if ( $i == col ) System.out.println($STUFF.text);
          }
      )+
    ;

TAB  :  '\t' -> skip ;   // match but don't pass to the parser
NL   :  '\r'? '\n' ;     // match and pass to the parser
STUFF:  ~[\t\r\n]+ ;     // match any chars except tab, newline
```

The STUFF lexical rule matches anything that's not a tab or newline, which means we can have space characters in a column.

A suitable main program should be looking pretty familiar by now. The only thing different here is that we're passing in a column number to the parser using a custom constructor and telling the parser not to build a tree.

tour/Col.java
```
RowsLexer lexer = new RowsLexer(input);
CommonTokenStream tokens = new CommonTokenStream(lexer);
int col = Integer.valueOf(args[0]);
RowsParser parser = new RowsParser(tokens, col); // pass column number!
parser.setBuildParseTree(false); // don't waste time bulding a tree
parser.file(); // parse
```

There are a lot of details in there that we'll explore in Chapter 10, *Attributes and Actions*, on page 177. For now, actions are code snippets surrounded by curly braces. The members action injects that code into the member area of the generated parser class. The action within rule row accesses $i, the local variable defined with the locals clause. It also uses $STUFF.text to get the text for the most recently matched STUFF token.

Here's the build and test sequence, one test per column:

```
⇒ $ antlr4 -no-listener Rows.g4  # don't need the listener
⇒ $ javac Rows*.java Col.java
⇒ $ java Col 1 < t.rows         # print out column 1, reading from file t.rows
❮ parrt
  tombu
  bke
⇒ $ java Col 2 < t.rows
❮ Terence Parr
  Tom Burns
  Kevin Edgar
⇒ $ java Col 3 < t.rows
❮ 101
  020
  008
```

These actions extract and print values matched by the parser, but they don't alter the parse itself. Actions can also finesse how the parser recognizes input phrases. In the next section, we'll take the concept of embedded actions one step further.

Altering the Parse with Semantic Predicates

Until we get to Chapter 11, *Altering the Parse with Semantic Predicates*, on page 191, we can demonstrate the power of semantic predicates with a simple example. Let's look at a grammar that reads in sequences of integers. The trick is that part of the input specifies how many integers to group together. We don't know until runtime how many integers to match. Here's a sample input file:

tour/t.data

```
2 9 10 3 1 2 3
```

The first number says to match the two subsequent numbers, 9 and 10. The 3 following the 10 says to match three more as a sequence. Our goal is a grammar called Data that groups 9 and 10 together and then 1, 2, and 3 like this:

```
⇒ $ antlr4 -no-listener Data.g4
⇒ $ javac Data*.java
⇒ $ grun Data file -tree t.data
❮ (file (group 2 (sequence 9 10)) (group 3 (sequence 1 2 3)))
```

The parse tree clearly identifies the groups.

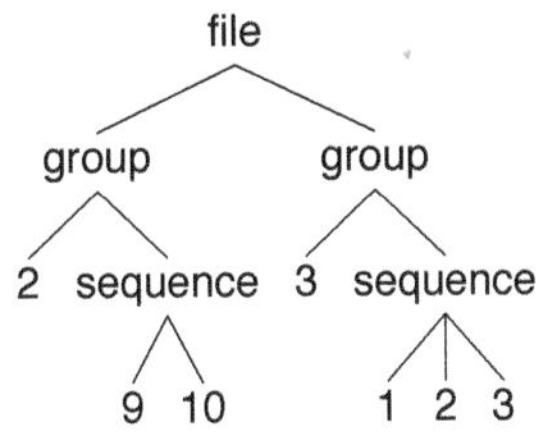

The key in the following Data grammar is a special Boolean-valued action called a *semantic predicate*: {$i<=$n}?. That predicate evaluates to true until we surpass the number of integers requested by the sequence rule parameter n. False predicates make the associated alternative "disappear" from the grammar and, hence, from the generated parser. In this case, a false predicate makes the (...)* loop terminate and return from rule sequence.

tour/Data.g4
```
grammar Data;

file : group+ ;

group: INT sequence[$INT.int] ;

sequence[int n]
locals [int i = 1;]
     : ( {$i<=$n}? INT {$i++;} )* // match n integers
     ;

INT :    [0-9]+ ;              // match integers
WS  :    [ \t\n\r]+ -> skip ; // toss out all whitespace
```

Visually, the internal grammar representation of rule sequence used by the parser looks something like this:

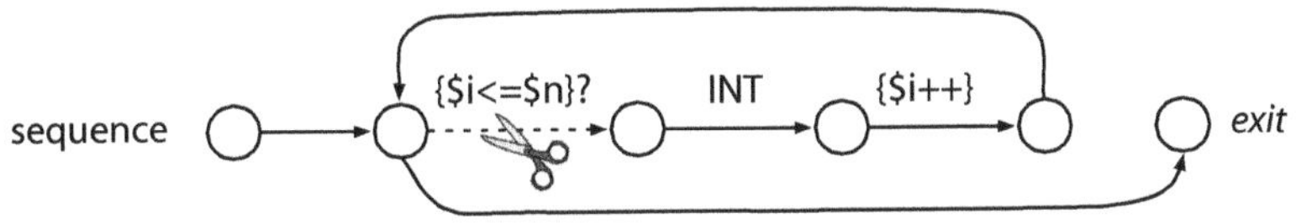

The scissors and dashed line indicate that the predicate can snip that path, leaving the parser with only one choice: the path to the exit.

Most of the time we won't need such micromanagement, but it's nice to know we have a weapon for handling pathological parsing problems.

During our tour so far, we've focused on parsing features, but there is a lot of interesting stuff going on at the lexical level. Let's take a look.

4.5 Cool Lexical Features

ANTLR has three great token-related features that are worth demonstrating in our tour. First, we'll see how to deal with formats like XML that have different lexical structures (inside and outside tags) in the same file. Next, we'll learn how to insert a field into a Java class by tweaking the input stream. It'll show how to generate output that is very similar to the input with minimal effort. And, lastly, we'll see how ANTLR parsers can ignore whitespace and comments without having to throw them out.

Island Grammars: Dealing with Different Formats in the Same File

All the sample input files we've seen so far contain a single language, but there are common file formats that contain multiple languages. For example, the `@author` tags and so on inside Java document comments follow a mini language; everything outside the comment is Java code. Template engines such as StringTemplate[3] and Django[4] have a similar problem. They have to treat all of the text surrounding the template expressions differently. These are often called *island grammars*.

ANTLR provides a well-known lexer feature called *lexical modes* that lets us deal easily with files containing mixed formats. The basic idea is to have the lexer switch back and forth between modes when it sees special sentinel character sequences.

XML is a good example. An XML parser treats everything other than tags and entity references (such as `£`) as text chunks. When the lexer sees <, it switches to "inside" mode and switches back to the default mode when it sees > or />. The following grammar demonstrates how this works. We'll explore this in more detail in Chapter 12, *Wielding Lexical Black Magic*, on page 205.

tour/XMLLexer.g4
```
lexer grammar XMLLexer;

// Default "mode": Everything OUTSIDE of a tag
OPEN        :   '<'                   -> pushMode(INSIDE) ;
COMMENT     :   '<!--' .*? '-->'      -> skip ;
EntityRef   :   '&' [a-z]+ ';' ;
TEXT        :   ~('<'|'&')+ ;            // match any 16 bit char minus < and &

// ---------------- Everything INSIDE of a tag --------------------
mode INSIDE;
```

3. http://www.stringtemplate.org
4. https://www.djangoproject.com

```
CLOSE       :   '>'                     -> popMode ; // back to default mode
SLASH_CLOSE :   '/>'                    -> popMode ;
EQUALS      :   '=' ;
STRING      :   '"' .*? '"' ;
SlashName   :   '/' Name ;
Name        :   ALPHA (ALPHA|DIGIT)* ;
S           :   [ \t\r\n]               -> skip ;

fragment
ALPHA       :   [a-zA-Z] ;

fragment
DIGIT       :   [0-9] ;
```

Let's use the following XML file as a sample input to that grammar:

tour/t.xml

```
<tools>
        <tool name="ANTLR">A parser generator</tool>
</tools>
```

Here's how to do a build and launch the test rig:

```
⇒ $ antlr4 XMLLexer.g4
⇒ $ javac XML*.java
⇒ $ grun XML tokens -tokens t.xml
❮ [@0,0:0='<',<1>,1:0]
  [@1,1:5='tools',<10>,1:1]
  [@2,6:6='>',<5>,1:6]
  [@3,7:8='\n\t',<4>,1:7]
  [@4,9:9='<',<1>,2:1]
  [@5,10:13='tool',<10>,2:2]
  [@6,15:18='name',<10>,2:7]
  [@7,19:19='=',<7>,2:11]
  [@8,20:26='"ANTLR"',<8>,2:12]
  [@9,27:27='>',<5>,2:19]
  [@10,28:45='A parser generator',<4>,2:20]
  [@11,46:46='<',<1>,2:38]
  [@12,47:51='/tool',<9>,2:39]
  [@13,52:52='>',<5>,2:44]
  [@14,53:53='\n',<4>,2:45]
  [@15,54:54='<',<1>,3:0]
  [@16,55:60='/tools',<9>,3:1]
  [@17,61:61='>',<5>,3:7]
  [@18,62:62='\n',<4>,3:8]
  [@19,63:62='<EOF>',<-1>,4:9]
```

Each line of that output represents a token and contains the token index, the start and stop character, the token text, the token type, and finally the line and character position within the line. This tells us how the lexer tokenized the input.

On the test rig command line, the XML tokens sequence is normally a grammar name followed by the start rule. In this case, we use the grammar name followed by special rule name tokens to tell the test rig it should run the lexer but not the parser. Then, we use test rig option -tokens to print out the list of matched tokens.

Knowledge of the token stream flowing from the lexer to the parser can be pretty useful. For example, some translation problems are really just tweaks of the input. We can sometimes get away with altering the original token stream rather than generating completely new output.

Rewriting the Input Stream

Let's build a tool that processes Java source code to insert serialization identifiers, serialVersionUID, for use with java.io.Serializable (like Eclipse does automatically). We want to avoid implementing every listener method in a JavaListener interface, generated from a Java grammar by ANTLR, just to capture the text and print it back out. It's easier to insert the appropriate constant field into the original token stream and then print out the altered input stream. No fuss, no muss.

Our main program looks exactly the same as the one in ExtractInterfaceTool.java from Section 4.3, *Building a Translator with a Listener*, on page 44 except that we print the token stream out when the listener has finished (highlighted with an arrow).

tour/InsertSerialID.java

```
ParseTreeWalker walker = new ParseTreeWalker(); // create standard walker
InsertSerialIDListener extractor = new InsertSerialIDListener(tokens);
walker.walk(extractor, tree); // initiate walk of tree with listener

// print back ALTERED stream
System.out.println(extractor.rewriter.getText());
```

To implement the listener, we need to trigger an insertion when we see the start of a class.

tour/InsertSerialIDListener.java

```
import org.antlr.v4.runtime.TokenStream;
import org.antlr.v4.runtime.TokenStreamRewriter;

public class InsertSerialIDListener extends JavaBaseListener {
    TokenStreamRewriter rewriter;
    public InsertSerialIDListener(TokenStream tokens) {
        rewriter = new TokenStreamRewriter(tokens);
    }
```

```
    @Override
    public void enterClassBody(JavaParser.ClassBodyContext ctx) {
        String field = "\n\tpublic static final long serialVersionUID = 1L;";
        rewriter.insertAfter(ctx.start, field);
    }
}
```

The key is the TokenStreamRewriter object that knows how to give altered views of a token stream without actually modifying the stream. It treats all of the manipulation methods as "instructions" and queues them up for lazy execution when traversing the token stream to render it back as text. The rewriter executes those instructions every time we call getText().

Let's build and test the listener on the Demo.java test file we used before.

```
⇒ $ antlr4 Java.g4
⇒ $ javac InsertSerialID*.java Java*.java
⇒ $ java InsertSerialID Demo.java
❮ import java.util.List;
  import java.util.Map;
  public class Demo {
          public static final long serialVersionUID = 1L;
          void f(int x, String y) { }
          int[ ] g(/*no args*/) { return null; }
          List<Map<String, Integer>>[] h() { return null; }
  }
```

With only a few lines of code, we were able to tweak a Java class definition without disturbing anything outside of our insertion point. This strategy is very effective for the general problem of source code instrumentation or refactoring. The TokenStreamRewriter is a powerful and extremely efficient means of manipulating a token stream.

One more lexical goodie before finishing our tour involves a mundane issue but one that is a beast to solve without a general scheme like ANTLR's token channels.

Sending Tokens on Different Channels

The Java interface extractor we looked at earlier magically preserves whitespace and comments in method signatures such as the following:

```
int[ ] g(/*no args*/) { return null; }
```

Traditionally, this has been a nasty requirement to fulfill. For most grammars, comments and whitespace are things the parser can ignore. If we don't want to explicitly allow whitespace and comments all over the place in a grammar, we need the lexer to throw them out. Unfortunately, that means the whitespace and comments are inaccessible to application code and any subsequent processing steps. The secret to preserving but ignoring comments and whitespace is to send those tokens to the parser on a "hidden channel." The parser tunes to only a single channel and so we can pass anything we want on the other channels. Here's how the Java grammar does it:

tour/Java.g4
```
COMMENT
    :   '/*' .*? '*/'     -> channel(HIDDEN) // match anything between /* and */
    ;
WS  :   [ \r\t\u000C\n]+ -> channel(HIDDEN)
    ;
```

The -> channel(HIDDEN) is a lexer command like the -> skip we discussed before. In this case, it sets the channel number of these tokens so that it's ignored by the parser. The token stream still maintains the original sequence of tokens but skips over the off-channel tokens when feeding the parser.

With these lexical features out of the way, we can wrap up our ANTLR tour. This chapter covered all of the major elements that make ANTLR easy to use and flexible. We didn't cover any of the details, but we saw ANTLR in action solving some small but real problems. We got a feel for grammar notation. We implemented visitors and listeners that let us calculate and translate without embedding actions in the grammar. We also saw that, sometimes, embedded actions are exactly what we want in order to satisfy our inner control freak. And, finally, we looked at some cool things we can do with ANTLR lexers and token streams.

It's time to slow down our pace and revisit all of the concepts explored in this chapter with the goal of learning all of the details. Each chapter in the next part of the book will take us another step toward becoming language implementers. We'll start by learning ANTLR notation and figuring out how to derive grammars from examples and language reference manuals. Once we have those fundamentals, we'll build some grammars for real-world languages and then learn the details of the tree listeners and visitors we just raced through. After that, we'll move on to some virtuoso topics in Part III.

Part II

Developing Language Applications with ANTLR Grammars

In Part II, we'll learn how to derive grammars from language specifications and sample inputs. We'll build grammars for comma-separated values, JSON, the DOT graphics format, a simple programming language, and R. Once we know how to design grammars, we'll dig into the details of building language applications by walking parse trees.

CHAPTER 5

Designing Grammars

In Part I, we got acquainted with ANTLR and saw a high-level view of grammars and language applications. Now we're going to slow down and learn the details needed to perform useful tasks such as building internal data structures, extracting information, and generating a translation of the input. The first step on our journey, though, is to learn how to build grammars. In this chapter, we'll look at the most commonly used lexical and syntactic language structures and figure out how to express them in ANTLR notation. Armed with these ANTLR building blocks, we'll combine them to build some real grammars in the next chapter.

To learn how to build grammars, we can't just wade through the various ANTLR constructs. First, we need to study the common language patterns and learn to identify them in computer language sentences. That is how we get a picture of the overall language structure. (A language pattern is a recurring grammatical structure, such as a sequence like subject–verb–object in English or subject–object–verb in Japanese.) Ultimately, we need the ability to divine a language's structure from a set of representative input files. Once we identify a language's structure, we can express it formally with an ANTLR grammar.

The good news is that there are relatively few fundamental language patterns to deal with, despite the vast number of languages invented over the past fifty years. This makes sense because people tend to design languages that follow the constraints our brains place on natural language. We expect token order to matter and expect dependencies between tokens. For example, `{(})` is ungrammatical because of the token order, and `(1+2` drives us crazy looking for the matching `)`. Languages also tend to be similar because designers follow common notation from mathematics. Even at the lexical level, languages tend to reuse the same structures, such as identifiers, integers, strings, and so on.

The constraints of word order and dependency, derived from natural language, blossom into four abstract computer language patterns.

- *Sequence*: This is a sequence of elements such as the values in an array initializer.
- *Choice*: This is a choice between multiple, alternative phrases such as the different kinds of statements in a programming language.
- *Token dependence*: The presence of one token requires the presence of its counterpart elsewhere in a phrase such as matching left and right parentheses.
- *Nested phrase*: This is a self-similar language construct such as nested arithmetic expressions or nested statement blocks in a programming language.

To implement these patterns, we really only need grammar rules comprised of alternatives, token references, and rule references (*Backus-Naur-Format* [BNF]). For convenience, though, we'll also group those elements into *subrules*. Subrules are just in-lined rules wrapped in parentheses. We can mark subrules as optional (?) and as zero-or-more (*) or one-or-more (+) loops to recognize the enclosed grammar fragments multiple times (*Extended Backus-Naur-Format* [EBNF]).

No doubt most readers will have seen some form of grammar or at least regular expressions during their career, but let's start at the very beginning so we're all on the same page.

5.1 Deriving Grammars from Language Samples

Writing a grammar is a lot like writing software except that we work with rules instead of functions or procedures. (Remember that ANTLR generates a function for each rule in your grammar.) But, before focusing on the rule innards, it's worth discussing the overall anatomy of a grammar and how to form an initial grammar skeleton. That's what we'll do in this section because it's an important first step in any language project. If you're itching to build and execute your first parser, you can revisit Chapter 4, *A Quick Tour*, on page 33 or jump to the first example in the next chapter: Section 6.1, *Parsing Comma-Separated Values*, on page 86. Feel free to pop back and forth to the examples in the next chapter as we learn the fundamentals here.

Grammars consist of a header that names the grammar and a set of rules that can invoke each other.

```
grammar MyG;
rule1 : «stuff» ;
rule2 : «more stuff» ;
...
```

Just like writing software, we have to figure out which rules we need, what *«stuff»* is, and which rule is the *start rule* (analogous to a main() method).

To figure all this out for a given language, we either have to know that language really well or have a set of representative input samples. Naturally, it helps to have a grammar for the language from a reference manual or even in the format of another parser generator. But for now, let's assume we don't have an existing grammar as a guide.

Proper grammar design mirrors functional decomposition or top-down design in the programming world. That means we work from the coarsest to the finest level, identifying language structures and encoding them as grammatical rules. So, the first task is to find a name for the coarsest language structure, which becomes our start rule. In English, we could use sentence. For an XML file, we could use document. For a Java file, we could use compilationUnit.

Designing the contents of the start rule is a matter of describing the overall format of the input in English pseudocode, kind of like we do when writing software. For example, "a comma-separated-value (CSV) file is a sequence of rows terminated by newlines." The essential word *file* to the left of *is a* is the rule name, and everything to the right of *is a* becomes the *«stuff»* on the right side of a rule definition.

```
file : «sequence of rows that are terminated by newlines» ;
```

Then we step down a level in granularity by describing the elements identified on the right side of the start rule. The nouns on the right side are typically references to either tokens or yet-to-be-defined rules. The tokens are elements that our brain normally latches onto as words, punctuation, or operators. Just as words are the atomic elements in an English sentence, tokens are the atoms in a parser grammar. The rule references, however, refer to other language structures that need to be broken down into more detail like *row*.

Stepping down another level of detail, we could say that a row is a sequence of *fields* separated by commas. Then, a *field* is a number or string. Our pseudocode looks like this:

```
file  : «sequence of rows that are terminated by newlines» ;
row   : «sequence of fields separated by commas» ;
field : «number or string» ;
```

When we run out of rules to define, we have a rough draft of our grammar.

Let's see how this technique works for describing some of the key structures in a Java file. (We can make the rule names stand out by italicizing them.) At the coarsest level, a Java *compilation unit* is an optional *package specifier*, followed by one or more *class definitions*. Stepping down a level, a class definition is keyword class, followed by an identifier, followed optionally by a *superclass specifier*, followed optionally by an *implements clause*, followed by a *class body*. A *class body* is a series of *members* enclosed in curly braces. A *member* is a nested class definition, a *field*, or a *method*. From here, we would describe *fields* and *methods* and then the *statements* within *methods*. You get the idea. Start at the highest possible level and work your way down, treating even large subphrases like Java class definitions as rules to define later. In grammar pseudocode, we'd start out like this:

```
compilationUnit  : «optional packageSpec then classDefinitions» ;
packageSpec      : 'package' identifier ';' ;
classDefinition  :
    'class' «optional superclassSpec optional implementsClause classBody» ;
superclassSpec   : 'extends' identifier ;
implementsClause :
    'implements' «one or more identifiers separated by comma» ;
classBody        : '{' «zero-or-more members» '}' ;
member           : «nested classDefinition or field or method» ;
...
```

Designing a grammar for a large language like Java is a lot easier if we have access to a grammar that we can use as a reference, but be careful. Blindly following an existing grammar can lead you astray, as we'll discuss next.

5.2 Using Existing Grammars as a Guide

Having access to existing grammar in non-ANTLR format is a great way to figure out how somebody else decided to break down the phrases in a language. At the very least, an existing grammar gives us a nice list of rule names to use as a guide. A word of caution, though. I recommend against cutting and pasting a grammar from a reference manual into ANTLR and massaging it until it works. Treat it as a guide rather than a piece of code.

Reference manuals are often pretty loose for grammar clarity reasons, meaning that the grammar recognizes lots of sentences not in the language. Or, the grammar might be ambiguous, able to match the same input sequence in more than one way. For example, a grammar might say that an expression can invoke a constructor or call a function. The problem is that input like T(i) could match both. Ideally, there would be no such ambiguities in our grammar.

We really need a single interpretation of each input sentence to translate it or perform some other task.

At the opposite extreme, grammars in reference manuals sometimes over-specify the rules. There are some constraints that we should enforce after parsing the input, rather than trying to enforce the constraints with grammatical structure. For example, when working on Section 12.4, *Parsing and Lexing XML*, on page 226, I scanned through the W3C XML language definition and got lost in all the details. As a trivial example, the XML grammar explicitly specifies where we must have whitespace in a tag and where it's optional. That's good to know, but we can simply have a lexer strip out whitespace inside of tags before sending it to the parser. Our grammar need not have tests for whitespace everywhere.

The specification also says that the `<?xml ...>` tag can have two special attributes: `encoding` and `standalone`. We need to know that constraint, but it's easier to allow any attribute name and then, after parsing, inspect the parse tree to ensure all such constraints are satisfied. In the end, XML is just a bunch of tags embedded in text, so its grammatical structure is fairly straightforward. The only challenge is treating what's inside and outside the tags differently. We'll look at this more in Section 12.3, *Islands in the Stream*, on page 221.

Identifying the grammar rules and expressing their right sides in pseudocode is challenging at first but gets easier and easier as you build grammars for more languages. You'll get lots of practice as you go through the examples in this book.

Once we have pseudocode, we need to translate it to ANTLR notation to get a working grammar. In the next section, we'll define four language patterns found in just about any language and see how they map to ANTLR constructs. After that, we'll figure out how to define the tokens referenced in our grammars, such as integer and identifier. Remember that we're looking at grammar development fundamentals in this chapter. It will give us the solid footing we need in order to tackle the real-world examples in the next chapter.

5.3 Recognizing Common Language Patterns with ANTLR Grammars

Now that we have a general top-down strategy for roughing out a grammar, we need to focus on the common language patterns: sequence, choice, token dependence, and nested phrase. We saw a few examples of these patterns in the previous section, but now we're going to see many more examples from a variety of languages. As we go along, we'll learn basic ANTLR notation by expressing the specific patterns as formal grammar rules. Let's start with the most common language pattern.

Pattern: Sequence

The structure you'll see most often in computer languages is a sequence of elements, such as the sequence of methods in a class definition. Even simple languages like the HTTP, POP, and SMTP network protocols exhibit the sequence pattern. Protocols expect a sequence of commands. For example, here's the sequence to log into a POP server and get the first message:

```
USER parrt
PASS secret
RETR 1
```

Even the commands themselves are sequences. Most commands are a keyword (reserved identifier), such as `USER` and `RETR`, followed by an operand and then newline. For example, in a grammar we'd say that the retrieve command is a keyword followed by an integer followed by a newline token. To specify such a sequence in a grammar, we simply list the elements in order. In ANTLR notation, the retrieve command is just sequence `'RETR' INT '\n'`, where `INT` represents the integer token type.

```
retr  : 'RETR' INT '\n' ; // match keyword integer newline sequence
```

Notice that we can include any simple sequence of letters, such as keywords or punctuation, directly as string literals like `'RETR'` in the grammar. (We'll explore lexical structures such as `INT` in Section 5.5, *Recognizing Common Lexical Structures*, on page 74.)

We use grammar rules to label language structures just like we label statement lists as functions in a programming language. In this case, we're labeling the `RETR` sequence as the `retr` rule. Elsewhere in the grammar, we can refer to the `RETR` sequence with the rule name as a shorthand.

Let's look at an arbitrarily long sequence such as the simple list of integers in a Matlab vector like `[1 2 3]`. As with a finite sequence, we want one element to follow the next, but we can't list all possible integer lists with rule fragments like `INT INT INT INT INT INT INT INT INT...`.

To encode a sequence of one or more elements, we use the + subrule operator. For example, `(INT)+` describes an arbitrarily long sequence of integers. As a shorthand, `INT+` is OK too. To specify that a list can be empty, we use the zero-or-more * operator: `INT*`. This operator is analogous to a loop in a programming language, which of course is how ANTLR-generated parsers implement them.

Variations on this pattern include the *sequence with terminator* and *sequence with separator*. CSV files demonstrate both nicely. Here's how we can express the pseudocode grammar from the previous section in ANTLR notation:

```
file : (row '\n')* ;        // sequence with a '\n' terminator
row  : field (',' field)* ; // sequence with a ',' separator
field: INT ;                // assume fields are just integers
```

Rule file uses the list with terminator pattern to match zero or more row '\n' sequences. The '\n' token terminates each element of the sequence. Rule row uses the list with separator pattern by matching a field followed by zero or more ',' field sequences. The ',' separates the fields. row matches sequences like 1 and 1,2 and 1,2,3, and so on.

We see the same constructs in programming languages. For example, here's how to recognize statement sequences in a programming language like Java where each statement is terminated by a semicolon:

```
stats : (stat ';')* ; // match zero or more ';'-terminated statements
```

And here is how to specify a comma-separated list of expressions such as we'd find in a function call argument list:

```
exprList : expr (',' expr)* ;
```

Even ANTLR's metalanguage uses sequence patterns. Here's partially how ANTLR expresses rule definition syntax in its own syntax:

```
// match 'rule-name :' followed by at least one alternative followed
// by zero or more alternatives separated by '|' symbols followed by ';'
rule : ID ':' alternative ('|' alternative )* ';' ;
```

Finally, there is a special kind of zero-or-one sequence, specified with the ?, that we use to express optional constructs. In a Java grammar, for example, we might find a sequence like ('extends' identifier)? that matches the optional superclass specification. Similarly, to match an optional initializer on a variable definition, we could say ('=' expr)?. The optional operator is kind of like a choice between something and nothing. As a preview to the next section, ('=' expr)? is the same as ('=' expr |).

Pattern: Choice (Alternatives)

A language with only one sentence would be pretty boring. Even the simplest languages, such as network protocols, have multiple valid sentences such as the USER and RETR commands of POP. This brings us to the choice pattern. We've already seen a choice in the Java grammar pseudocode *«nested classDefinition or field or method»* for rule member.

To express the notion of choice in a language, we use | as the "or" operator in ANTLR rules to separate grammatical choices called *alternatives* or *productions*. Grammars are full of choices.

Returning to our CSV grammar, we can make a more flexible field rule by allowing the choice of integers or strings.

```
field : INT | STRING ;
```

Looking through the grammars in the next chapter, we'll find lots of choice pattern examples, such as the list of type names in rule type from Section 6.4, *Parsing Cymbol*, on page 100.

```
type:   'float' | 'int' | 'void' ; // user-defined types
```

In Section 6.3, *Parsing DOT*, on page 95, we'll see the list of possible statements in a graph description.

```
stmt:   node_stmt
    |   edge_stmt
    |   attr_stmt
    |   id '=' id
    |   subgraph
    ;
```

Any time you find yourself saying "language structure *x* can be either this or that," then you've identified a choice pattern. Use | in rule *x*.

Grammar sequences and choices let us encode lots of language constructs, but there are two key remaining patterns to look at: token dependency and phrase nesting. They're typically used together in grammars, but let's start with token dependencies in isolation for simplicity.

Pattern: Token Dependency

Previously, we used INT+ to express the nonempty sequence of integers in a Matlab vector, [1 2 3]. To specify a vector with the surrounding square brackets, we need a way to express dependencies between tokens. If we see one symbol in a sentence, we must find its matching counterpart elsewhere in the sentence. To express this with a grammar, we use a sequence that specifies both symbols, usually enclosing or grouping other elements. In this case, we completely specify vectors like this:

```
vector : '[' INT+ ']' ; // [1], [1 2], [1 2 3], ...
```

Glance at any nontrivial program in your favorite language, and you'll see all sorts of grouping symbols that must occur in pairs: (...), {...}, and [...]. From

Section 6.4, *Parsing Cymbol*, on page 100, we find token dependencies between the parentheses of a method call and the square brackets of an array index.

```
expr:   ID '(' exprList? ')'     // func call like f(), f(x), f(1,2)
    |   expr '[' expr ']'        // array index like a[i], a[i][j]
   ...
    ;
```

We also see token dependencies between left and right parentheses in method declarations.

examples/Cymbol.g4

```
functionDecl
    :   type ID '(' formalParameters? ')' block // "void f(int x) {...}"
    ;
formalParameters
    :   formalParameter (',' formalParameter)*
    ;
formalParameter
    :   type ID
    ;
```

The grammar from Section 6.2, *Parsing JSON*, on page 88 matches up curly braces around object definitions such as `{ "name":"parrt", "passwd":"secret" }`.

examples/JSON.g4

```
object
    :   '{' pair (',' pair)* '}'
    |   '{' '}' // empty object
    ;
pair:   STRING ':' value ;
```

See Section 6.5, *Parsing R*, on page 104 for more examples of matching tokens.

Keep in mind that dependent symbols don't necessarily have to match. C-derived languages also have the `a?b:c` ternary operator where the `?` sets up a requirement to see `:` later in the phrase.

Also, just because we have matching tokens doesn't necessarily imply a nested phrase. For example, a vector might not allow nested vectors. In general, though, subphrases enclosed in matching symbols typically nest. We get constructs like `a[(i)]` and `{while (b) {i=1;}}`. This brings us to the final language pattern we're likely to need.

Pattern: Nested Phrase

A nested phrase has a self-similar language structure, one whose subphrases conform to that same structure. Expressions are the quintessential self-similar language structure and are made up of nested subexpressions separated by operators. Similarly, a while's code block is a code block nested within an outer code block. We express self-similar language structures using recursive rules in grammars. So, if the pseudocode for a rule references itself, we are going to need a recursive (self-referencing) rule.

Let's see how nesting works for code blocks. A while statement is the keyword while followed by a condition expression in parentheses followed by a statement. We can also treat multiple statements as a single block statement by wrapping them in curly braces. Expressing that grammatically looks like this:

```
stat: 'while' '(' expr ')' stat  // match WHILE statement
    | '{' stat* '}'              // match block of statements in curlies
   ...                           // and other kinds of statements
    ;
```

The looping statement, stat, of the while can be a single statement or a group of statements if we enclose them in {...}. Rule stat is *directly recursive* because it refers to itself in the first (and second) alternatives. If we moved the second alternative to its own rule, rules stat and block would be mutually *indirectly recursive*.

```
stat: 'while' '(' expr ')' stat  // match WHILE statement
    | block                      // match a block of statements
   ...                           // and other kinds of statements
    ;
block: '{' stat* '}' ;           // match block of statements in curlies
```

Most nontrivial languages have multiple self-similar constructs, leading to lots of recursive rules. Let's look at an expression rule for a simple language that has just three kinds of expressions: indexed array references, parenthesized expressions, and integers. Here's how we would express that in ANTLR notation:

```
expr: ID '[' expr ']'  // a[1], a[b[1]], a[(b[1])]
    | '(' expr ')'     // (1), (a[1]), (((1))), (a[1])
    | INT              // 1, 94117
    ;
```

Notice how the recursion happens naturally. The index component of an array index expression is itself an expression, so we just reference expr in that alternative. The fact that the array index alternative is itself an expression shouldn't bother us. The nature of the language construct dictates the use of a rule reference that just happens to be recursive.

Here are the parse trees for two sample inputs:

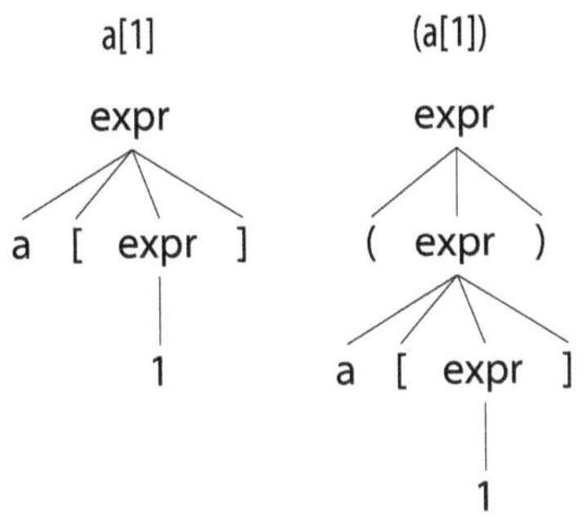

As we saw in Section 2.1, *Let's Get Meta!*, on page 9, the internal tree nodes are rule references, and the leaves are token references. A path from the root of the tree to any node represents the rule invocation stack for that element (or call stack for an ANTLR-generated recursive-descent parser). Paths representing recursive, nested subtrees have multiple references to the same rule. I like to think of the rule nodes as labeling the subtrees underneath. The root is `expr`, so the entire tree is an expression. The subtree with `expr` before `1` labels that integer as an expression.

Not all languages have expressions, such as data formats, but most languages you'll run into have fairly complex expressions (see Section 6.5, *Parsing R*, on page 104). Moreover, expression grammar specifications are not always obvious, so it's worth spending some time digging into the details of recognizing expressions. We'll do that next.

For future reference, here's a table summarizing ANTLR's core grammar notation:

Syntax	Description
x	Match token, rule reference, or subrule *x*.
x y ... *z*	Match a sequence of rule elements.
(... | ... | ...)	Subrule with multiple alternatives.
x?	Match *x* or skip it.
*x**	Match *x* zero or more times.
x+	Match *x* one or more times.
r : ... ;	Define rule r.
r : ... | ... | ... ;	Define rule r with multiple alternatives.

Table 1—ANTLR Core Notation

And here is a table summarizing what we've learned so far about common computer language patterns:

Pattern Name	Description

Sequence

This is a finite or arbitrarily long sequence of tokens or subphrases. Examples include variable declarations (type followed by identifier) and lists of integers. Here are some sample implementations:

```
x y ... z            // x followed by y, ..., z
'[' INT+ ']'         // Matlab vector of integers
```

Sequence with terminator

This is an arbitrarily long, potentially empty sequence of tokens or subphrases separated by a token, usually a semicolon or newline. Examples include statement lists from C-like languages and rows of data terminated with newlines. Here are some sample implementations:

```
(statement ';')*     // Java statement list
(row '\n')*          // Lines of data
```

Sequence with separator

This is a nonempty arbitrarily long sequence of tokens or subphrases separated by a token, usually a comma, semicolon, or period. Examples include function argument definition lists, function call argument lists, languages where statements are separated but not terminated, and directory names. Here are some sample implementations:

```
expr (',' expr)*         // function call arguments
( expr (',' expr)* )?    // optional function call arguments
'/'? name ('/' name)*    // simplified directory name
stat ('.' stat)*         // SmallTalk statement list
```

Choice

This is a set of alternative phrases. Examples include the different kinds of types, statements, expressions, or XML tags. Here are some sample implementations:

```
type : 'int' | 'float' ;
stat : ifstat | whilestat | 'return' expr ';' ;
expr : '(' expr ')' | INT | ID ;
tag  : '<' Name attribute* '>' | '<' '/' Name '>' ;
```

Token dependency

The presence of one token requires the presence of one or more subsequent tokens. Examples include matching parentheses, curly braces, square bracket, and angle brackets. Here are some sample implementations:

```
'(' expr ')'            // nested expression
ID '[' expr ']'         // array index
'{' stat* '}'           // statements grouped in curlies
'<' ID (',' ID)* '>'    // generic type specifier
```

Pattern Name	Description
Nested phrase	This is a self-similar language structure. Examples include expressions, nested Java classes, nested code blocks, and nested Python function definitions. Here are some sample implementations:

```
expr : '(' expr ')' | ID ;
classDef : 'class' ID '{' (classDef|method|field) '}' ;
```

5.4 Dealing with Precedence, Left Recursion, and Associativity

Expressions have always been a hassle to specify with top-down grammars and to recognize by hand with recursive-descent parsers, first because the most natural grammar is ambiguous and second because the most natural specification uses a special kind of recursion called *left recursion*. We'll discuss the latter in detail later, but for now, keep in mind that top-down grammars and parsers cannot deal with left recursion in their classic form.

To illustrate the problem, imagine a simple arithmetic expression language that has multiply and addition operators and integer "atoms." Expressions are self-similar, so it's natural for us to say that a multiplicative expression is two subexpressions joined by the * operator. Similarly, an additive expression is two subexpressions joined by a +. We can also have simple integers as expressions. Literally encoding this as a grammar leads to the following reasonable-looking rule:

```
expr : expr '*' expr  // match subexpressions joined with '*' operator
     | expr '+' expr  // match subexpressions joined with '+' operator
     | INT            // matches simple integer atom
     ;
```

The problem is that this rule is ambiguous for some input phrases. In other words, this rule can match a single input stream in more than one way, which you might recall from Section 2.3, *You Can't Put Too Much Water into a Nuclear Reactor*, on page 14. It's fine for simple integers and for single-operator expressions such as 1+2 and 1*2 because there is only one way to match them. For example, the rule can match 1+2 only using the second alternative, as shown by the left parse tree in the diagram in Figure 3, *Parse tree interpretations*, on page 72

The problem is that the rule as specified can interpret input such as 1+2*3 in the two ways depicted by the middle and right parse trees. They're different because the middle tree says to add 1 to the result of multiplying 2 and 3, whereas the tree on the right multiplies 3 by the result of adding 1 and 2.

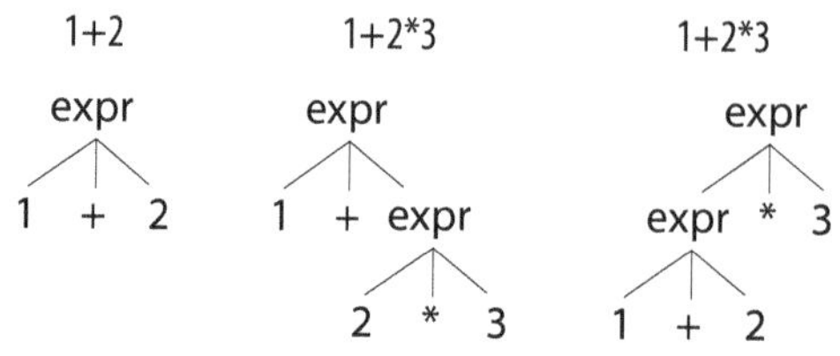

Figure 3—Parse tree interpretations

This is a question of operator precedence, and conventional grammars simply have no way to specify precedence. Most grammar tools, such as Bison,[1] use extra notation to specify the operator precedence.

Instead, ANTLR resolves ambiguities in favor of the alternative given first, implicitly allowing us to specify operator precedence. Rule `expr` has the multiplication alternative before the addition alternative, so ANTLR resolves the operator ambiguity for `1+2*3` in favor of the multiplication.

By default, ANTLR associates operators left to right as we'd expect for `*` and `+`. Some operators like exponentiation group right to left, though, so we have to manually specify the associativity on the operator token using option `assoc`. Here's an expression rule that properly interprets input like `2^3^4` as `2^(3^4)`:

```
expr : expr '^'<assoc=right> expr // ^ operator is right associative
     | INT
     ;
```

The following parse trees illustrates the difference between left and right associative versions of `^`. The parse tree on the right is the usual interpretation, but language designers are free to use either associativity.

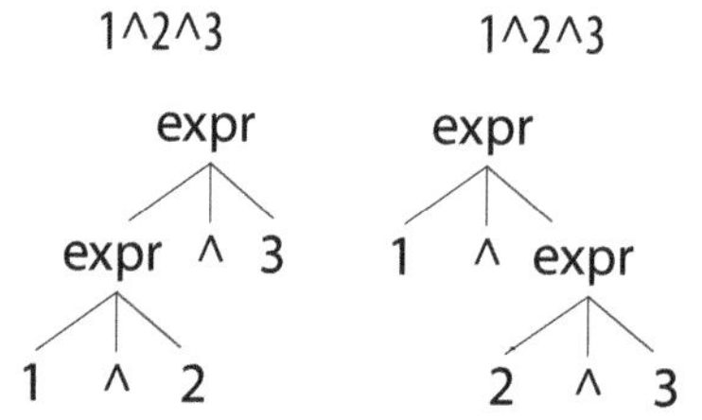

To combine all three operators in a single rule, we place the `^` alternative before the others because it has higher precedence than `*` and `+` (`1+2^3` is 9).

1. http://dinosaur.compilertools.net/bison/bison_8.html#SEC71

```
expr : expr '^'<assoc=right> expr  // ^ operator is right associative
     | expr '*' expr  // match subexpressions joined with '*' operator
     | expr '+' expr  // match subexpressions joined with '+' operator
     | INT            // matches simple integer atom
     ;
```

Readers familiar with ANTLR v3 have been waiting patiently for me to point out that ANTLR, like all conventional top-down parser generators, cannot handle left-recursive rules. However, one of ANTLR v4's major improvements is that it can now handle direct left recursion. A left-recursive rule is one that either directly or indirectly invokes itself on the left edge of an alternative. The expr rule is directly left recursive because everything but the INT alternative starts with a reference to the expr rule itself. (It's also *right recursive* because of the expr references on the right edges of some alternatives.)

While ANTLR v4 can handle *direct* left recursion, it can't handle *indirect* left recursion. That means we can't factor expr into the grammatically equivalent rules.

```
expr : expo  // indirectly invokes expr left recursively via expo
     | ...
     ;
expo : expr '^'<assoc=right> expr ;
```

Precedence Climbing Expression Parsing

Experienced compiler writers often build recursive-descent parsers by hand to squeeze out every last drop of performance and to allow complete control over error recovery. Instead of writing code for the long chain of expression rules, however, they often use *operator precedence parsers.*[a]

ANTLR uses a similar but more powerful strategy than operator precedence that follows work done by Keith Clarke[b] from 1986. Theodore Norvell subsequently coined the term *precedence climbing.*[c] Similarly, ANTLR replaces direct left recursion with a predicated loop that compares the precedence of the previous and next operators. We'll get into predicates in Chapter 11, *Altering the Parse with Semantic Predicates*, on page 191.

a. http://en.wikipedia.org/wiki/Operator-precedence_parser
b. http://antlr.org/papers/Clarke-expr-parsing-1986.pdf
c. http://www.engr.mun.ca/~theo/Misc/exp_parsing.htm

To recognize expressions with ANTLR v3, we had to unravel the left recursion we saw in the earlier expr into multiple rules, one for each precedence level. For example, we'd use rules like the following for expressions with multiplication and addition operators:

```
expr    : addExpr ;
addExpr : multExpr ('+' multExpr)* ;
multExpr: atom ('*' atom)* ;
atom    : INT ;
```

Expressions for languages such as C and Java end up with about fifteen such rules, which is a hassle whether we're building a top-down grammar or building a recursive-descent parser by hand.

ANTLR v4 makes short work of (directly) left-recursive expression rules. Not only is the new mechanism more efficient, expression rules are much smaller and easier to understand. For example, in a Java grammar, the number of lines dedicated to expressions dropped in half (from 172 to 91 lines).

In practice, we can handle all of the language structures we care about with direct left recursion. For example, here's a rule that matches a subset of the C declarator language including input such as `*(*a)[][]`:

```
decl : decl '[' ']'  // match [] suffixes using direct left-recursion
     | '*' decl      // *x, *x[], **x
     | '(' decl ')'  // (x), (x[]), (*x)[]
     | ID
     ;
```

To learn more about how ANTLR supports direct left recursion (using grammar transformations), please see Chapter 14, *Removing Direct Left Recursion*, on page 249.

At this point, we've studied the common patterns found in computer languages and figured out how to express them in ANTLR notation. But, before we can dive into some complete examples, we need to figure out how to describe the tokens referenced in our grammar rules. Just as there are a few key grammatical language patterns, we'll find that there are some extremely common lexical structures. Creating a complete grammar is a matter of combining grammatical rules from this section and lexical rules from the next section.

5.5 Recognizing Common Lexical Structures

Computer languages look remarkably similar lexically. For example, if I scramble up the order to obscure grammatical information, tokens `) 10 ( f` could be combined into valid phrases from the earliest languages to the most recent. Fifty years ago, we'd see `(f 10)` in LISP and `f(10)` in Algol. Of course, `f(10)` is also valid in virtually all programming languages from Prolog to Java to the new Go language.[2] Lexically, then, functional, procedural, declarative, and object-oriented languages look pretty much the same. Amazing!

2. http://golang.org/

That's great because we have to learn only how to describe identifiers and integers once and, with little variation, apply them to most programming languages. As with parsers, lexers use rules to describe the various language constructs. We get to use essentially the same notation. The only difference is that parsers recognize grammatical structure in a token stream and lexers recognize grammatical structure in a character stream.

Since lexing and parsing rules have similar structures, ANTLR allows us to combine both in a single grammar file. But since lexing and parsing are two distinct phases of language recognition, we must tell ANTLR which phase is associated with each rule. We do this by starting lexer rule names with uppercase letters and parser rule names with lowercase letters. For example, `ID` is a lexical rule name, and `expr` is a parser rule name.

When starting a new grammar, I typically cut and paste rules from an existing grammar, such as Java,[3] for the common lexical constructs: *identifiers*, *numbers*, *strings*, *comments*, and *whitespace*. A few tweaks, and I'm up and running. Almost all languages, even nonprogramming languages like XML and JSON, have a variation of those tokens. For example, despite being very distinct grammatically, a lexer for C would have no problem tokenizing the following JSON:

```
{
  "title":"Cat wrestling",
  "chapters":[ {"Intro":"..."}, ... ]
}
```

As another example, consider block comments. In Java, they are bracketed by `/* ... */`, and in XML, comments are bracketed by `<!-- ... -->`, but they are more or less the same lexical construct except for the start and stop symbols.

For keywords, operators, and punctuation, we don't need lexer rules because we can directly reference them in parser rules in single quotes like `'while'`, `'*'`, and `'++'`. Some developers prefer to use lexer rule references such as `MULT` instead of literal `'*'`. That way, they can change the multiply operator character without altering the references to `MULT` in the parser rules. Having both the literal and lexical rule `MULT` is no problem; they both result in the same token type.

To demonstrate what lexical rules look like, let's build simple versions of the common tokens, starting with our friend the humble identifier.

3. http://www.antlr.org/grammar/java

Matching Identifiers

In grammar pseudocode, a basic identifier is a nonempty sequence of uppercase and lowercase letters. Using our newfound skills, we know to express the sequence pattern using notation (...)+. Because the elements of the sequence can be either uppercase or lowercase letters, we also know that we'll have a choice operator inside the subrule.

```
ID : ('a'..'z'|'A'..'Z')+ ; // match 1-or-more upper or lowercase letters
```

The only new ANTLR notation here is the range operator: 'a'..'z' means any character from a to z. That is literally the ASCII code range from 97 to 122. To use Unicode code points, we need to use '\uXXXX' literals where XXXX is the hexadecimal value for the Unicode character code point value.

As a shorthand for character sets, ANTLR supports the more familiar regular expression set notation.

```
ID : [a-zA-Z]+ ; // match 1-or-more upper or lowercase letters
```

Rules such as ID sometimes conflict with other lexical rules or literals referenced in the grammar such as 'enum'.

```
grammar KeywordTest;
enumDef : 'enum' '{' ... '}' ;
...
FOR : 'for' ;
...
ID : [a-zA-Z]+ ; // does NOT match 'enum' or 'for'
```

Rule ID could also match keywords such as enum and for, which means there's more than one rule that could match the same string. To make this clearer, consider how ANTLR handles combined lexer/parser grammars such as this. ANTLR collects and separates all of the string literals and lexer rules from the parser rules. Literals such as 'enum' become lexical rules and go immediately after the parser rules but before the explicit lexical rules.

ANTLR lexers resolve ambiguities between lexical rules by favoring the rule specified first. That means your ID rule should be defined after all of your keyword rules, like it is here relative to FOR. ANTLR puts the implicitly generated lexical rules for literals before explicit lexer rules, so those always have priority. In this case, 'enum' is given priority over ID automatically.

Because ANTLR reorders the lexical rules to occur after the parser rules, the following variation on KeywordTest results in the same parser and lexer:

```
grammar KeywordTestReordered;
FOR : 'for' ;
ID : [a-zA-Z]+ ; // does NOT match 'enum' or 'for'
...
enumDef : 'enum' '{' ... '}' ;
...
```

This definition of an identifier doesn't allow numbers, but you can peek ahead to Section 6.3, *Parsing DOT*, on page 95, Section 6.4, *Parsing Cymbol*, on page 100, and Section 6.5, *Parsing R*, on page 104 for full-blown ID rules.

Matching Numbers

Describing integer numbers such as 10 is easy because it's just a sequence of digits.

```
INT : '0'..'9'+ ; // match 1 or more digits
```

or

```
INT : [0-9]+ ; // match 1 or more digits
```

Floating-point numbers are much more complicated, unfortunately, but we can make a simplified version easily if we ignore exponents. (See Section 6.5, *Parsing R*, on page 104 for lexical rules that match full floating-point numbers and even complex numbers like 3.2i.) A floating-point number is a sequence of digits followed by a period and then optionally a fractional part, or it starts with a period and continues with a sequence of digits. A period by itself is not legal. Our floating-point rule therefore uses a choice and a few sequence patterns.

```
FLOAT:  DIGIT+ '.' DIGIT*   // match 1. 39. 3.14159 etc...
    |          '.' DIGIT+   // match .1 .14159
    ;

fragment
DIGIT   :    [0-9] ;        // match single digit
```

Here we're also using a helper rule, DIGIT, so we don't have to write [0-9] everywhere. By prefixing the rule with fragment, we let ANTLR know that the rule will be used only by other lexical rules. It is not a token in and of itself. This means that we could not reference DIGIT from a parser rule.

Matching String Literals

The next token that computer languages tend to have in common is the string literal like "Hello". Most use double quotes, but some use single quotes or even both (Python). Regardless of the choice of delimiters, we match them using a rule that consumes everything between the delimiters. In grammar pseudocode, a string is a sequence of any characters between double quotes.

```
STRING : '"' .*? '"' ; // match anything in "..."
```

The dot *wildcard* operator matches any single character. Therefore, .* would be a loop that matches any sequence of zero or more characters. Of course, that would consume until the end of file, which is not very useful. Instead, ANTLR provides support for *nongreedy subrules* using standard regular expression notation (the ? suffix). Nongreedy means essentially to "scarf characters until you see what follows the subrule in the lexer rule." To be more precise, nongreedy subrules match the fewest number of characters while still allowing the entire surrounding rule to match. See Section 15.6, *Wildcard Operator and Nongreedy Subrules*, on page 285 for more details. In contrast, the .* is considered *greedy* because it greedily consumes characters that match the inside of the loop (wildcard in this case). If .*? is confusing, don't worry about it. Just remember it as a pattern for matching stuff inside quotes or other delimiters. We'll see nongreedy loops again shortly when we look at comments.

Our STRING rule isn't quite good enough yet because it doesn't allow double quotes inside strings. To support that, most languages define escape sequences starting with a backslash. To get a double quote inside a double-quoted string, we use \". To support the common escape characters, we need something like the following:

```
STRING: '"' (ESC|.)*? '"' ;
fragment
ESC : '\\"' | '\\\\' ; // 2-char sequences \" and \\
```

ANTLR itself needs to escape the escape character, so that's why we need \\ to specify the backslash character.

The loop in STRING now matches either an escape character sequence, by calling fragment rule ESC, or any single character via the dot wildcard. The *? subrule operator terminates the (ESC|.)*? loop upon seeing what follows, an unescaped double-quote character.

Matching Comments and Whitespace

When a lexer matches the tokens we've defined so far, it emits them via the token stream to the parser. The parser then checks the grammatical structure of the stream. But when the lexer matches comment and whitespace tokens, we'd like it to toss them out. That way, the parser doesn't have to worry about matching optional comments and whitespace everywhere. For example, the following parser rule would be very awkward and error-prone where WS is a whitespace lexical rule:

```
assign : ID (WS|COMMENT)? '=' (WS|COMMENT)? expr (WS|COMMENT)? ;
```

Defining these discarded tokens is the same as for nondiscarded tokens. We just have to indicate that the lexer should throw them out using the skip command. For example, here is how to match both single-line and multiline comments for C-derived languages:

```
LINE_COMMENT : '//' .*? '\r'? '\n' -> skip ; // Match "//" stuff '\n'
COMMENT      : '/*' .*? '*/'       -> skip ; // Match "/*" stuff "*/"
```

In LINE_COMMENT, .*? consumes everything after // until it sees a newline (optionally preceded by a carriage return to match Windows-style newlines). In COMMENT, .*? consumes everything after /* and before the terminating */.

The lexer accepts a number of commands following the -> operator; skip is just one of them. For example, we have the option to pass these tokens to the parser on a "hidden channel" by using the channel command. See Section 12.1, *Broadcasting Tokens on Different Channels*, on page 206 for more on token channels.

Let's deal with whitespace, our final common token. Most programming languages treat whitespace characters as token separators but otherwise ignore them. (Python is an exception because it uses whitespace for particular syntax purposes: newlines to terminate commands and indent level, with initial tabs or spaces to indicate nesting level.) Here is how to tell ANTLR to throw out whitespace:

```
WS : (' '|'\t'|'\r'|'\n')+ -> skip ; // match 1-or-more whitespace but discard
```

or

```
WS : [ \t\r\n]+ -> skip ; // match 1-or-more whitespace but discard
```

When newline is both whitespace to be ignored and the command terminator, we have a problem. Newline is context-sensitive. In one grammatical context, we should throw out newlines, and in another, we should pass it to the parser so that it knows a command has finished. For example, in Python, f() followed by newline executes the code, calling f(). But we could also insert an extra newline between the parentheses. Python waits until the newline after the) before executing the call.

```
⇒ $ python
⇒ >>> def f(): print "hi"
❮ ...
⇒ >>> f()
```

```
《 hi
⇒ >>> f(
⇒ ... )
《 hi
```

For a detailed discussion of the problem and solutions, see *Fun with Python Newlines*, on page 216.

So, now we know how to match basic versions of the most common lexical constructs: identifiers, numbers, strings, comments, and whitespace. Believe it or not, that's a great start on a lexer for even a big programming language. Here's a lexer starter kit we can use as a reference later:

Token Category | **Description and Examples**

Punctuation

The easiest way to handle operators and punctuation is to directly reference them in parser rules.

```
call : ID '(' exprList ')' ;
```

Some programmers prefer to define token labels such as LP (left parenthesis) instead.

```
call : ID LP exprList RP ;
LP : '(' ;
RP : ')' ;
```

Keywords

Keywords are reserved identifiers, and we can either reference them directly or define token types for them.

```
returnStat : 'return' expr ';'
```

Identifiers

Identifiers look almost the same in every language, with some variation about what the first character can be and whether Unicode characters are allowed.

```
ID : ID_LETTER (ID_LETTER | DIGIT)* ; // From C language
fragment ID_LETTER : 'a'..'z'|'A'..'Z'|'_' ;
fragment DIGIT : '0'..'9' ;
```

Numbers

These are definitions for integers and simple floating-point numbers.

```
INT : DIGIT+ ;
FLOAT
    : DIGIT+ '.' DIGIT*
    | '.' DIGIT+
    ;
```

Token Category	Description and Examples
Strings	Match double-quoted strings. `STRING : '"' ( ESC | . )*? '"' ;` `fragment ESC : '\\' [btnr"\\] ; // \b, \t, \n etc...`
Comments	Match and discard comments. `LINE_COMMENT : '//' .*? '\n' -> skip ;` `COMMENT : '/*' .*? '*/' -> skip ;`
Whitespace	Match whitespace in the lexer and throw it out. `WS : [ \t\n\r]+ -> skip ;`

At this point, we have a strategy to go from sample input files to parser and lexer rules and are ready to tackle the examples in the next chapter. Before we move on, though, there are two important issues to consider. First, it's not always obvious where to draw the line between what we match in the parser and what we match in the lexer. Second, ANTLR places a few constraints on our grammar rules that we should know about.

5.6 Drawing the Line Between Lexer and Parser

Because ANTLR lexer rules can use recursion, lexers are technically as powerful as parsers. That means we could match even grammatical structure in the lexer. Or, at the opposite extreme, we could treat characters as tokens and use a parser to apply grammatical structure to a character stream. (These are called *scannerless parsers*. See code/extras/CSQL.g4 for a grammar matching a small mix of C + SQL.)

Where to draw the line between the lexer and the parser is partially a function of the language but also a function of the intended application. Fortunately, a few rules of thumb will get us pretty far.

- Match and discard anything in the lexer that the parser does not need to see at all. Recognize and toss out things like whitespace and comments for programming languages. Otherwise, the parser would have to constantly check to see whether there are comments or whitespace in between tokens.

- Match common tokens such as identifiers, keywords, strings, and numbers in the lexer. The parser has more overhead than the lexer, so we shouldn't burden the parser with, say, putting digits together to recognize integers.

- Lump together into a single token type those lexical structures that the parser does not need to distinguish. For example, if our application treats integer and floating-point numbers the same, then lump them together as token type NUMBER. There's no point in sending separate token types to the parser.
- Lump together anything that the parser can treat as a single entity. For example, if the parser doesn't care about the contents of an XML tag, the lexer can lump everything between angle brackets into a single token type called TAG.
- On the other hand, if the parser needs to pull apart a lump of text to process it, the lexer should pass the individual components as tokens to the parser. For example, if the parser needs to process the elements of an IP address, the lexer should send individual tokens for the IP components (integers and periods).

When we say that the parser doesn't need to distinguish between certain lexical structures or doesn't care about what's inside a structure, we really mean that our application doesn't care. Our application performs the same action or translation on those lexical structures.

To see how the intended application affects what we match in the lexer vs. the parser, imagine processing a log file from a web server that has one record per line. We'll gradually increase the application requirements to see how it shifts the boundary between the lexer and the parser. Let's assume each row has a requesting IP address, HTTP protocol command, and result code. Here's a sample log entry:

```
192.168.209.85 "GET /download/foo.html HTTP/1.0" 200
```

Our brain naturally picks out the various lexical elements, but if all we want to do is count how many lines there are in the file, we can ignore everything but the sequence of newline characters.

```
file  : NL+ ;              // parser rule matching newline (NL) sequence
STUFF : ~'\n'+ -> skip ;   // match and discard anything but a '\n'
NL    : '\n' ;             // return NL to parser or other invoking code
```

The lexer doesn't have to recognize much in the way of structure, and the parser matches a sequence of newline tokens. (The ~x operator matches anything but x.)

Next, let's say that we need to collect a list of IP addresses from the log file. This means we need a rule to recognize the lexical structure of an IP address, and we might as well provide lexer rules for the other record elements.

```
IP    : INT '.' INT '.' INT '.' INT ; // 192.168.209.85
INT   : [0-9]+ ;        // match IP octet or HTTP result code
STRING: '"' .*? '"' ;   // matches the HTTP protocol command
NL    : '\n' ;          // match log file record terminator
WS    : ' ' -> skip ;   // ignore spaces
```

With a complete set of tokens, we can make parser rules that match the records in a log file.

```
file  : row+ ;                 // parser rule matching rows of log file
row   : IP STRING INT NL ;     // match log file record
```

Stepping up our processing requirements a little bit, let's say we need to convert the text IP addresses to 32-bit numbers. With convenient library functions like split('.'), we could pass IP addresses as strings to the parser and process them there. But, it's better to have the lexer match the IP address lexical structure and pass the components to the parser as tokens.

```
file  : row+ ;                 // parser rule matching rows of log file
row   : ip STRING INT NL ;     // match log file record
ip    : INT '.' INT '.' INT '.' INT ; // match IPs in parser

INT   : [0-9]+ ;        // match IP octet or HTTP result code
STRING: '"' .*? '"' ;   // matches the HTTP protocol command
NL    : '\n' ;          // match log file record terminator
WS    : ' ' -> skip ;   // ignore spaces
```

Switching lexer rule IP to parser rule ip shows how easily we can shift the dividing line. (Converting the four INT tokens to a 32-bit number would require some application code embedded in the grammar, which we haven't looked at yet in depth, so we'll leave them out.)

If the requirements call for processing the contents of the HTTP protocol command string, we would follow a similar thought process. If our application doesn't need to examine the parts of the string, then the lexer can pass the whole string to the parser as a single token. But, if we need to pull out the various pieces, it's better to have the lexer recognize those pieces and pass the components to the parser.

It doesn't take long to get a good feel for drawing the line according to a language's symbols and the needs of an application. The examples in the next chapter will help you internalize the rules of thumb from this section. Then, with that solid foundation, we'll examine a few nasty lexical problems in Chapter 12, *Wielding Lexical Black Magic*, on page 205. For example, Java compilers need to both ignore and process Javadoc comments, and XML files have different lexical structures inside and outside of tags.

In this chapter, we learned how to work from a representative sample of the language, or language documentation, to create grammar pseudocode and then a formal grammar in ANTLR notation. We also studied the common language patterns: sequence, choice, token dependency, and nested phrase. In the lexical realm, we looked at implementations for the most common tokens: identifiers, numbers, strings, comments, and whitespace. Now it's time to put this knowledge to work building grammars for some real-world languages.

CHAPTER 6

Exploring Some Real Grammars

In the previous chapter, we studied common lexical and grammatical structures and learned how to express them as snippets of ANTLR grammars. Now it's time to put that knowledge to use building some real-world grammars. Our primary goal is to learn how to assemble full grammars by sifting through reference manuals, sample input files, and existing non-ANTLR grammars. We'll tackle five languages, ramping up gradually in complexity. You don't have to build all of them now. Just work through the ones you're comfortable with and come back as you encounter more complicated problems in practice. Also feel free to pop back to look at the patterns and ANTLR snippets in the previous chapter.

The first language we'll look at is the comma-separated-value (CSV) format used by spreadsheets and databases. CSV is a great place to start because it's simple and yet widely applicable. The second language is also a data format, called JSON,[1] that has nested data elements, which lets us explore the use of rule recursion in a real language.

Next, we'll look at a declarative language called DOT[2] for describing graphs (networks). In a declarative language, we express logical constructions without specifying control flow. DOT lets us explore more complicated lexical structures, such as case-insensitive keywords.

Our fourth language is a simple non-object-oriented programming language called Cymbol (also discussed in Chapter 6 of *Language Implementation Patterns [Par09]*). It's a prototypical grammar we can use as a reference or starting point for other imperative programming languages (those composed of functions, variables, statements, and expressions).

---

1. http://www.json.org
2. http://www.graphviz.org

Finally, we'll build a grammar for the R functional programming language.[3] (Functional languages compute by evaluating expressions.) R is a statistical programming language increasingly used for data analysis. I chose R because its grammar consists primarily of a jumbo expression rule. It's a great opportunity to reinforce our understanding of operator precedence and associativity for a real language.

Once we have a firm grip on building grammars, we can move beyond recognition and get down to the business of triggering actions when the application sees input phrases of interest. In the next chapter, we'll create parser listeners that build data structures, manage symbol tables that track variable and function definitions, and perform language translations.

We begin with a grammar for CSV files.

6.1 Parsing Comma-Separated Values

While we have already seen a basic CSV grammar in *Pattern: Sequence*, on page 64, let's beef it up with the notion of a header row and allow empty columns. Here's a representative input file:

examples/data.csv
```
Details,Month,Amount
Mid Bonus,June,"$2,000"
,January,"""zippo"""
Total Bonuses,"","$5,000"
```

Header rows are no different from regular rows; we simply interpret the column value as the column header name. Rather than using a `row+` ANTLR fragment to match rows as well as the header row, we match it separately. When building a real application based upon this grammar, we'd probably want to treat the header differently. This way, we can get a handle on the first special row. Here's the first part of the grammar:

examples/CSV.g4
```
grammar CSV;

file : hdr row+ ;
hdr : row ;
```

Note that we've introduced an extra rule called `hdr` for clarity. Grammatically it's just a `row`, but we've made its role clearer by separating it out. Compare this to using just `row+` or `row row*` on the right-side rule `file`.

3. http://www.r-project.org

Rule row is the same as before: a list of fields separated by commas and terminated by a newline.

examples/CSV.g4
```
row : field (',' field)* '\r'? '\n' ;
```

To make our fields more flexible than they were in the previous chapter, let's allow arbitrary text, strings, and even empty fields in between commas.

examples/CSV.g4
```
field
    :   TEXT
    |   STRING
    |
    ;
```

The token definitions aren't too bad. TEXT tokens are a sequence of characters until we hit the next comma field separator or the end of the line. Strings are any characters in between double quotes. Here are the two token definitions we've used so far:

examples/CSV.g4
```
TEXT : ~[,\n\r"]+ ;
STRING : '"' ('""'|~'"')* '"' ; // quote-quote is an escaped quote
```

To get a double quote inside a double-quoted string, the CSV format generally uses two double quotes in a row. That's what the ('""'|~'"')* subrule does in rule STRING. We can't use a nongreedy loop with the wildcard, ('""'|.)*?, because it would stop at the first " it saw after the start of the string. Input like "x""y" would match two strings, not one string with "" inside it. Remember that nongreedy subrules match the fewest characters possible that still results in a match for the surrounding rule.

Before testing our parser rules, let's take a look at the token stream just to make sure that our lexer breaks up the character stream properly. Using TestRig via alias grun with option -tokens, we get the following:

```
⇒ $ antlr4 CSV.g4
⇒ $ javac CSV*.java
⇒ $ grun CSV file -tokens data.csv
❮ [@0,0:6='Details',<4>,1:0]
  [@1,7:7=',',<1>,1:7]
  [@2,8:12='Month',<4>,1:8]
  [@3,13:13=',',<1>,1:13]
  [@4,14:19='Amount',<4>,1:14]
  [@5,20:20='\n',<2>,1:20]
  [@6,21:29='Mid Bonus',<4>,2:0]
  [@7,30:30=',',<1>,2:9]
  [@8,31:34='June',<4>,2:10]
```

```
[@9,35:35=',',<1>,2:14]
[@10,36:43='"$2,000"',<5>,2:15]
[@11,44:44='\n',<2>,2:23]
[@12,45:45=',',<1>,3:0]
[@13,46:52='January',<4>,3:1]
...
```

Those tokens look fine. The punctuation, text, and strings all come through as expected.

Now, let's see how our grammar recognizes grammatical structure in the input stream. Using option -tree, the test rig prints out a text form of the parse tree (cleaned up for the book).

```
$ grun CSV file -tree data.csv
(file
 (hdr (row (field Details) , (field Month) , (field Amount) \n))
 (row (field Mid Bonus) , (field June) , (field "$2,000") \n)
 (row field , (field January) , (field """zippo""") \n)
 (row (field Total Bonuses) , (field "") , (field "$5,000") \n)
)
```

The root node represents everything that start rule file matched. It has a number of rows as children, starting with the header row. Here's what the parse tree looks like visually (obtained with the -ps file.ps option):

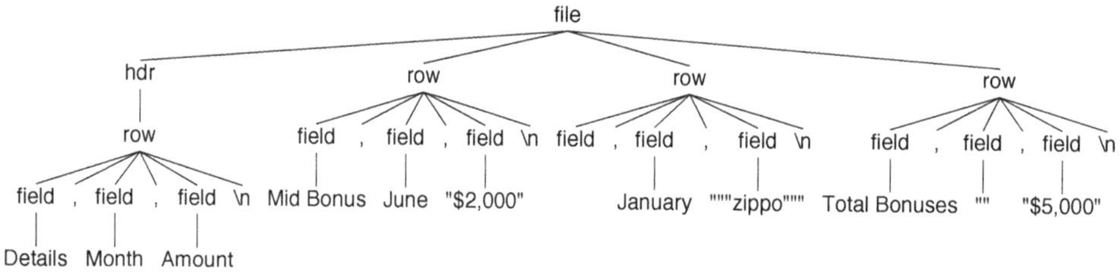

CSV is nice because of its simplicity, but it breaks down when we need a single field to hold multiple values. For that, we need a data format that allows nested elements.

6.2 Parsing JSON

JSON is a text data format that captures a collection of name-value pairs, and since values can themselves be collections, JSON can include nested structures. Designing a parser for JSON gives us an opportunity to derive a grammar from a language reference manual[4] and to work with some more complicated lexical rules. To make things more concrete, here's a simple JSON data file:

4. http://json.org

examples/t.json

```
{
	"antlr.org": {
		"owners" : [],
		"live" : true,
		"speed" : 1e100,
		"menus" : ["File", "Help\nMenu"]
	}
}
```

Our goal is to build an ANTLR grammar by reading the JSON reference manual and looking at its syntax diagram and existing grammar. We'll pull out key phrases from the manual and figure out how to encode them as ANTLR rules, starting with the grammatical structures.

JSON Grammatical Rules

The language reference says that a JSON file can be either an object, as shown earlier, or an array of values. Grammatically, that's just a choice pattern, which we can specify formally with this rule:

examples/JSON.g4

```
json:   object
    |   array
    ;
```

The next step is to drill down into the rule references in `json`. For objects, the reference says the following:

> An *object* is an unordered set of name-value pairs. An object begins with a left brace ({) and ends with a right brace (}). Each name is followed by a colon (:), and the name-value pairs are separated by a comma (,).

The syntax diagram at the JSON website also indicates that names have to be strings.

To convert this English description into grammar constructs, we break it apart looking for key phrases that represent one of our patterns: sequence, choice, token dependency, and nested phrase. The start of the sentence "An *object* is" clearly indicates we should create a rule called `object`. Next, an "unordered set of name-value pairs" is really just a sequence of pairs. The "unordered set" is referring to the semantics, or meaning, of the names; specifically, the order of the names has no meaning. That means we can just match any old list of pairs since we are just parsing.

The second sentence introduces a token dependency because an object starts and ends with curly braces. The final sentence refines our sequence of pairs to be a sequence with a comma separator. Altogether, we get something like this in ANTLR notation:

examples/JSON.g4

```
object
    :   '{' pair (',' pair)* '}'
    |   '{' '}' // empty object
    ;
pair:   STRING ':' value ;
```

For clarity and to reduce code duplication, it's a good idea to break out the name-value pairs into their own rule. Otherwise, the first alternative of `object` would look like this:

```
object : '{' STRING ':' value (',' STRING ':' value)* '}' | ... ;
```

Notice that we have `STRING` as a token and not a grammatical rule. It's almost certainly the case that an application reading JSON files would want to treat strings as complete entities, rather than character sequences. Per our rules of thumb from Section 5.6, *Drawing the Line Between Lexer and Parser*, on page 81, strings should be tokens.

The JSON reference also has some informal grammatical rules, so let's see how our ANTLR rules compare. Here's the grammar verbatim from the reference:

```
object
    {}
    { members }

members
    pair
    pair , members

pair
    string : value
```

The reference has also broken out the `pair` rule, but there's a `members` rule that we don't have. As described in the sidebar *Loops vs. Tail Recursion*, on page 91, it's how a grammar expresses sequences without `(...)*` loops.

Turning to arrays, the other high-level construct, the reference manual says this:

> An *array* is an ordered collection of values. An array begins with a left bracket (`[`) and ends with a right bracket (`]`). Values are separated by a comma (`,`).

Like rule `object`, `array` has a comma-separated sequence and a token dependency between the left and right square brackets.

Loops vs. Tail Recursion

Rule members from the JSON reference manual looks strange because there is nothing in the English description that seems to fit a choice of pair or pair followed by a comma and reference to itself.

```
members
    pair
    pair , members
```

The difference lies in that ANTLR supports Extended BNF (EBNF) grammars and the informal rules from the JSON reference manual use straight BNF. BNF does not support subrules like our (...)* loop so they simulate looping with tail recursion (a rule invocation to itself as the last element in an alternative).

To see the relationship between the English sequence description and this tail recursive rule, here's how members derives one, two, and three pairs:

```
members => pair

members => pair , members
        => pair , pair

members => pair , members
        => pair , pair , members
        => pair , pair , pair
```

This reinforces the warning in Section 5.2, *Using Existing Grammars as a Guide*, on page 62 that existing grammars should be used as a guide, not the gospel truth.

examples/JSON.g4

```
array
    :   '[' value (',' value)* ']'
    |   '[' ']' // empty array
    ;
```

Stepping down a level of granularity, we get to value, which is a choice pattern according to the reference.

> A *value* can be a *string* in double quotes or a *number* or true or false or null or an *object* or an *array*. These structures can be nested.

The term *nested* naturally indicates a nested phrase pattern for which we should expect some recursive rule references. In ANTLR notation, value looks like Figure 4, *value in ANTLR notation*, on page 92.

By referencing object or array, rule value becomes (indirectly) recursive. By invoking either rule from value, we would eventually get back to rule value.

examples/JSON.g4
```
value
    :   STRING
    |   NUMBER
    |   object  // recursion
    |   array   // recursion
    |   'true'  // keywords
    |   'false'
    |   'null'
    ;
```

Figure 4—value in ANTLR notation

Rule value directly references string literals to match the JSON keywords. We also treat numbers as tokens for the same reason as strings: applications will treat numbers as complete entities.

That's it for the grammatical rules. We've completely specified the structure of a JSON file. Here's how our grammar parses the sample input from earlier:

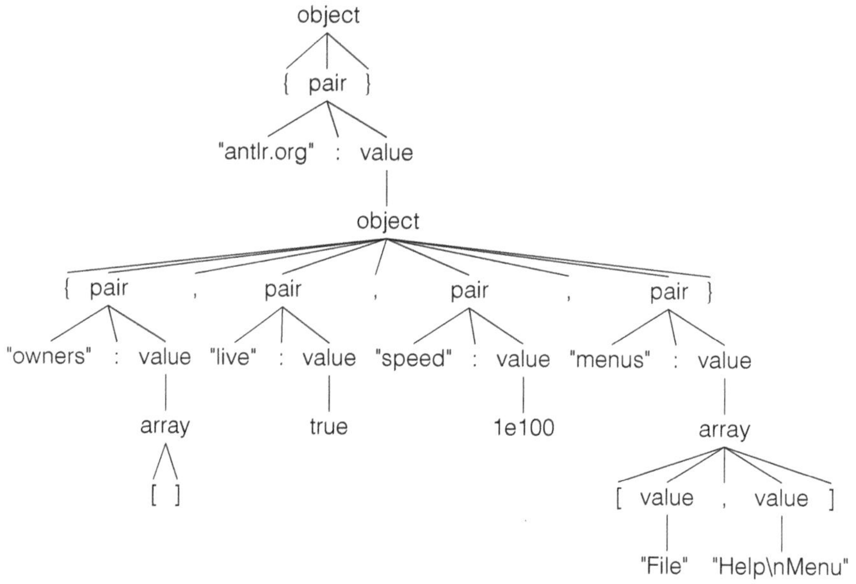

Of course, we can't yet run our program to generate the image in that figure until we've completed the lexer grammar. We need rules for the two key tokens: STRING and NUMBER.

JSON Lexical Rules

According to the JSON reference, strings are defined as follows:

> A *string* is a sequence of zero or more Unicode characters, wrapped in double quotes, using backslash escapes. A character is represented as a single character string. A string is very much like a C or Java string.

As we discussed in the previous chapter, strings in most languages are pretty much the same. JSON's strings are similar to what we did in *Matching String Literals*, on page 77, with the addition of Unicode escapes. Looking at the existing JSON grammar, we can tell that the written description is incomplete. The grammar says this:

```
char
    any-Unicode-character-except-"-or-\-or-control-character
    \"
    \\
    \/
    \b
    \f
    \n
    \r
    \t
    \u four-hex-digits
```

This specifies what all of the escapes are and that we should match any Unicode character except for the double quote and backslash, which we can specify with a `~["\\]` inverted character set. (Operator `~` means "not.") Our `STRING` definition looks like this:

examples/JSON.g4
```
STRING :  '"' (ESC | ~["\\])* '"' ;
```

The `ESC` rule matches either a predefined escape or a Unicode sequence.

examples/JSON.g4
```
fragment ESC :   '\\' (["\\/bfnrt] | UNICODE) ;
fragment UNICODE : 'u' HEX HEX HEX HEX ;
fragment HEX : [0-9a-fA-F] ;
```

Rather than repeat the definition of a hex digit multiple times in `UNICODE`, we use the `HEX` fragment rule as a shorthand. (Rules prefixed with `fragment` can be called only from other lexer rules; they are not tokens in their own right.)

The last token used by the parser is `NUMBER`. The JSON reference defines them as follows:

> A *number* is very much like a C or Java number, except that the octal and hexadecimal formats are not used.

The JSON reference's existing grammar has some fairly complicated rules for numbers, but we can pack it all into three main alternatives.

examples/JSON.g4
```
NUMBER
    :   '-'? INT '.' [0-9]+ EXP? // 1.35, 1.35E-9, 0.3, -4.5
    |   '-'? INT EXP             // 1e10 -3e4
    |   '-'? INT                 // -3, 45
    ;
fragment INT :   '0' | [1-9] [0-9]* ; // no leading zeros
fragment EXP :   [Ee] [+\-]? INT ; // \- since - means "range" inside [...]
```

Again, using fragment rules `INT` and `EXP` reduces duplication and makes the grammar easier to read.

We know that `INT` should not match integers beginning with digit 0 from the informal JSON grammar.

```
int
    digit
    digit1-9 digits
    - digit
    - digit1-9 digits
```

We deal with the `-` negation operator in `NUMBER` so we can focus on just the first two choices: `digit` and `digit1-9 digits`. The first choice matches any single digit, so `0` is cool all by itself. The second choice starts with `digit1-9`, which is any digit but 0.

Unlike the CSV example in the previous section, JSON has to worry about whitespace.

> Whitespace can be inserted between any pair of tokens.

That is the typical meaning of whitespace, so we can reuse a rule from the lexer "starter kit" found at the end of the previous chapter.

examples/JSON.g4
```
WS  :   [ \t\n\r]+ -> skip ;
```

Now that we have a complete set of grammatical and lexical rules, we can try it. Let's start by printing out the tokens from sample input `[1,"\u0049",1.3e9]`.

```
⇒ $ antlr4 JSON.g4
⇒ $ javac JSON*.java
⇒ $ grun JSON json -tokens
⇒ [1,"\u0049",1.3e9]
⇒ EOF
❮ [@0,0:0='[',<5>,1:0]
  [@1,1:1='1',<11>,1:1]
  [@2,2:2=',',<4>,1:2]
  [@3,3:10='"\u0049"',<10>,1:3]
  [@4,11:11=',',<4>,1:11]
  [@5,12:16='1.3e9',<11>,1:12]
```

```
[@6,17:17=']',<1>,1:17]
[@7,19:18='<EOF>',<-1>,2:0]
```

Our lexer correctly breaks up the input stream into tokens, so let's try the grammar rules.

```
⇒ $ grun JSON json -tree
⇒ [1,"\u0049",1.3e9]
⇒ EOF
❮ (json (array [ (value 1) , (value "\u0049") , (value 1.3e9) ]))
```

The grammar properly interprets the token stream as an array of three values, so everything looks great. For a more complicated grammar, we'd want to try lots of other input files to verify correctness.

At this point, we've seen grammars for two data languages (CSV and JSON), so let's move on to a declarative language called DOT that ratchets up the grammatical complexity and introduces us to a new lexical pattern: case-insensitive keywords.

6.3 Parsing DOT

DOT[5] is a declarative language for describing graphs such as network diagrams, trees, or state machines. (DOT is a declarative language because we say what the graph connections are, not how to build the graph.) It's a generically useful graphing tool, particularly if you have a program that needs to generate images. For example, ANTLR's -atn option uses DOT to generate state machine visualizations.

To get a feel for the language, imagine that we want to visualize a call tree graph for a program with four functions. We could draw this by hand, or we could specify the relationships with DOT as follows (either by hand or automatically by building a language application that computed the relationships from a program source):

examples/t.dot

```
digraph G {
    rankdir=LR;
    main [shape=box];
    main -> f -> g;         // main calls f which calls g
    f -> f [style=dotted] ; // f is recursive
    f -> h;                 // f calls h
}
```

Here's the resulting diagram created using the DOT visualizer, graphviz:[6]

5. http://www.graphviz.org/content/dot-language
6. http://www.graphviz.org

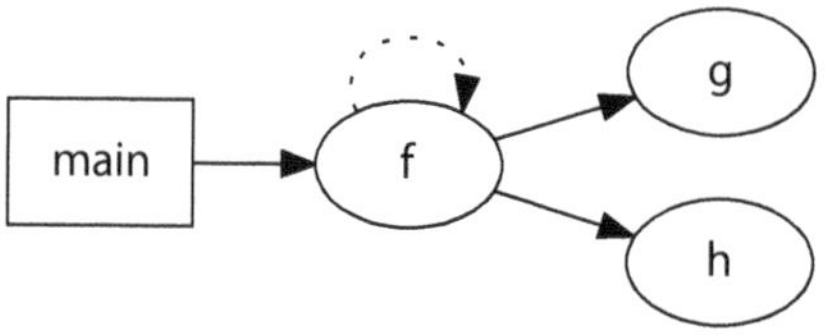

We're in a bit of luck because the DOT reference guide has syntax rules that we can reuse almost verbatim, if we convert them to ANTLR syntax. Unfortunately, we're on our own for the lexical rules. We'll have to read through the documentation and some examples to figure out the exact rules. Our easiest path is to start with the grammatical rules.

DOT Grammatical Rules

Here's the core grammar in ANTLR notation translated from the primary language reference:[7]

examples/DOT.g4

```
graph       :   STRICT? (GRAPH | DIGRAPH) id? '{' stmt_list '}' ;
stmt_list   :   ( stmt ';'? )* ;
stmt        :   node_stmt
            |   edge_stmt
            |   attr_stmt
            |   id '=' id
            |   subgraph
            ;
attr_stmt   :   (GRAPH | NODE | EDGE) attr_list ;
attr_list   :   ('[' a_list? ']')+ ;
a_list      :   (id ('=' id)? ','?)+ ;
edge_stmt   :   (node_id | subgraph) edgeRHS attr_list? ;
edgeRHS     :   ( edgeop (node_id | subgraph) )+ ;
edgeop      :   '->' | '--' ;
node_stmt   :   node_id attr_list? ;
node_id     :   id port? ;
port        :   ':' id (':' id)? ;
subgraph    :   (SUBGRAPH id?)? '{' stmt_list '}' ;
id          :   ID
            |   STRING
            |   HTML_STRING
            |   NUMBER
            ;
```

The only deviation we make from the reference grammar is rule port. The reference provides this.

```
port:   ':' ID [ ':' compass_pt ]
    |   ':' compass_pt
```

7. http://www.graphviz.org/pub/scm/graphviz2/doc/info/lang.html

```
compass_pt
    :   (n | ne | e | se | s | sw | w | nw)
```

These rules would normally be fine if the compass points were keywords and not legal as identifiers. But, the text in the reference alters the meaning of the grammar.

> Note also that the allowed compass point values are not keywords, so these strings can be used elsewhere as ordinary identifiers....

That means we have to accept edge statements such as `n -> sw;` where `n` and `sw` are identifiers, not compass points. The reference goes on to say this: "...conversely, the parser will actually accept any identifier." That's not entirely clear, but it sounds like the parser accepts any identifier for a compass point. If that's true, we don't have to worry about compass points at all in the grammar; we can replace references to rule `compass_pt` with `id`.

```
port:   ':' id (':' id)? ;
```

Just to be sure, it never hurts to try suppositions with a DOT viewer like those found on the Graphviz website.[8] DOT does, in fact, accept the following graph definition, so our `port` rule is OK:

```
digraph G { n -> sw; }
```

At this point, we have our grammatical rules in place. Pretending that our token definitions are finished, let's look at the parse tree for sample input `t.dot` (using `grun DOT graph -gui t.dot`).

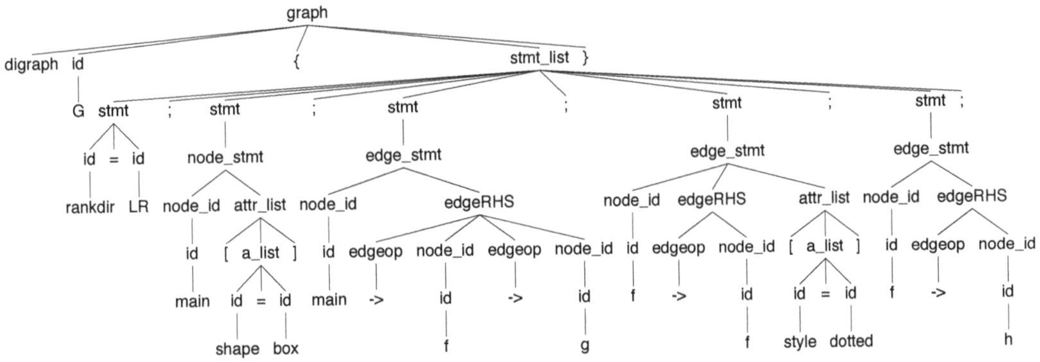

Now let's try to define those tokens.

8. http://www.graphviz.org

DOT Lexical Rules

Since the reference guide does not provide formal lexical rules, we have to derive them from the written description. The keywords are the simplest, so let's start with those.

The reference says that "the keywords node, edge, graph, digraph, subgraph, and strict are case-independent." If they weren't case insensitive, we could simply use literals in the grammar like 'node'. To allow variations such as nOdE, we need to lay out lexical rules with uppercase and lowercase variations at each character position.

examples/DOT.g4

```
STRICT      :   [Ss][Tt][Rr][Ii][Cc][Tt] ;
GRAPH       :   [Gg][Rr][Aa][Pp][Hh] ;
DIGRAPH     :   [Dd][Ii][Gg][Rr][Aa][Pp][Hh] ;
NODE        :   [Nn][Oo][Dd][Ee] ;
EDGE        :   [Ee][Dd][Gg][Ee] ;
SUBGRAPH    :   [Ss][Uu][Bb][Gg][Rr][Aa][Pp][Hh] ;
```

Identifiers are similar to most programming languages.

> Any string of alphabetic ([a-zA-Z\200-\377]) characters, underscores ('_'), or digits ([0-9]), not beginning with a digit.

The \200-\377 octal range is 80 through FF in hex, so our ID rule looks like this:

examples/DOT.g4

```
ID          :   LETTER (LETTER|DIGIT)*;
fragment
LETTER      :   [a-zA-Z\u0080-\u00FF_] ;
```

Helper rule DIGIT is one of the lexical rules we need to match numbers. The reference guide says numbers follow this regular expression:

> [-]?(.[0-9]+ | [0-9]+(.[0-9]*)?)

Replacing [0-9] with DIGIT, DOT numbers in ANTLR notation look like this:

examples/DOT.g4

```
NUMBER      :   '-'? ('.' DIGIT+ | DIGIT+ ('.' DIGIT*)? ) ;
fragment
DIGIT       :   [0-9] ;
```

DOT strings are pretty basic.

> any double-quoted string ("...") possibly containing escaped quotes (\")

To match anything inside the string, we use the dot wildcard operator to consume characters until it sees the final double quote. We can also match the escaped double quote as an alternative of the subrule loop.

examples/DOT.g4

```
STRING      :   '"' ('\\"'|.)*? '"' ;
```

DOT also has what it calls an HTML string, which is, as far as I can tell, exactly like a string except it uses angle brackets instead of double quotes. The reference uses notation <...> and goes on to say this:

> ... in HTML strings, angle brackets must occur in matched pairs, and unescaped newlines are allowed. In addition, the content must be legal XML, so that the special XML escape sequences for ", &, <, and > may be necessary in order to embed these characters in attribute values or raw text.

That description tells us most of what we need but doesn't answer whether we can have > inside an HTML comment. Also, it seems to imply we should wrap sequences of tags in angle brackets like this: <<i>hi</i>>. From experimentation with a DOT viewer, that is the case. DOT seems to accept anything between angle brackets as long as the brackets match. So, > inside HTML comments are not ignored like they would be by an XML parser. HTML string <foo<!--ksjdf > -->> gets treated like string "foo<!--ksjdf > --".

To accept anything in angle brackets, we can use ANTLR construct '<' .*? '>'. But that doesn't allow for angle brackets nested inside because it will associate the first > with the first < rather than the most recent <. The following rules do the trick:

examples/DOT.g4

```
/** "HTML strings, angle brackets must occur in matched pairs, and
 *  unescaped newlines are allowed."
 */
HTML_STRING :   '<' (TAG|~[<>])* '>' ;
fragment
TAG         :   '<' .*? '>' ;
```

The HTML_STRING rule allows a TAG within a pair of angle brackets, implementing the single level of nesting. The ~[<>] set takes care of matching XML character entities such as <. It matches anything other than a left or right angle bracket. We can't use wildcard and a nongreedy loop here. (TAG|.)*? would match invalid input such as <<foo> because the wildcard inside the loop can match <foo. HTML_STRING in that case wouldn't have to call TAG to match a tag or portion of a tag.

You might be tempted to use recursion to match up the angle brackets like this:

```
HTML_STRING : '<' (HTML_STRING|~[<>])* '>' ;
```

But, that matches nested tags instead of just balancing the start and stop angle brackets. A nested tag would look like <<i>
>>, which we don't want.

DOT has one last lexical structure we haven't seen before. DOT matches and discards lines starting with # because it considers them C preprocessor output. We can treat them just like the single-line comment rules we've seen.

examples/DOT.g4
```
PREPROC     :   '#' .*? '\n' -> skip ;
```

That's it for the DOT grammar (except for rules we're very familiar with). We've made it through our first moderately complex language! Aside from the more complex grammatical and lexical structures, this section emphasizes that we often have to look at multiple sources to unmask an entire language. The larger a language is, the more we need multiple references and multiple representative input samples. Sometimes poking and prodding an existing implementation is the only way to ferret out the edge cases. No language reference is ever perfectly comprehensive.

We also have to decide what is properly part of the parsing process and what should be processed later as a separate phase. For example, we treat the special port names, such as ne and sw, as simple identifiers in the parser. We also don't interpret the HTML inside <...> strings. A full DOT implementation would have to verify and process these elements at some point, but the parser gets to treat them as chunks.

Now it's time to tackle some programming languages. In the next section, we'll build a grammar for a traditional imperative programming language that looks like C. After that, we'll take on our biggest challenge yet with the R functional programming language.

6.4 Parsing Cymbol

To demonstrate how to parse a programming language with syntax derived from C, we're going to build a grammar for a language I conjured up called Cymbol. Cymbol is a simple non-object-oriented programming language that looks like C without structs. A grammar for this language serves as a good prototype for other new programming languages, if you'd like to build one. We won't see any new ANTLR syntax, but our grammar will demonstrate how to build a simple left-recursive expression rule.

When designing a language, there's no formal grammar or language reference manual to work from. Instead, we start by conjuring up representative samples of the language. From there, we derive a grammar as we did in Section 5.1, *Deriving Grammars from Language Samples*, on page 60. (This is also how we'd deal with an existing language for which we had no formal grammar or language reference.) Here's a program with a global variable and recursive function declaration that shows what Cymbol code looks like:

examples/t.cymbol
```
// Cymbol test
int g = 9;          // a global variable
int fact(int x) { // factorial function
    if x==0 then return 1;
    return x * fact(x-1);
}
```

Just like on a cooking show, let's see what the final product looks like so we have a target in mind. Here's the parse tree that illustrates how our grammar should interpret the input (via grun Cymbol file -gui t.cymbol):

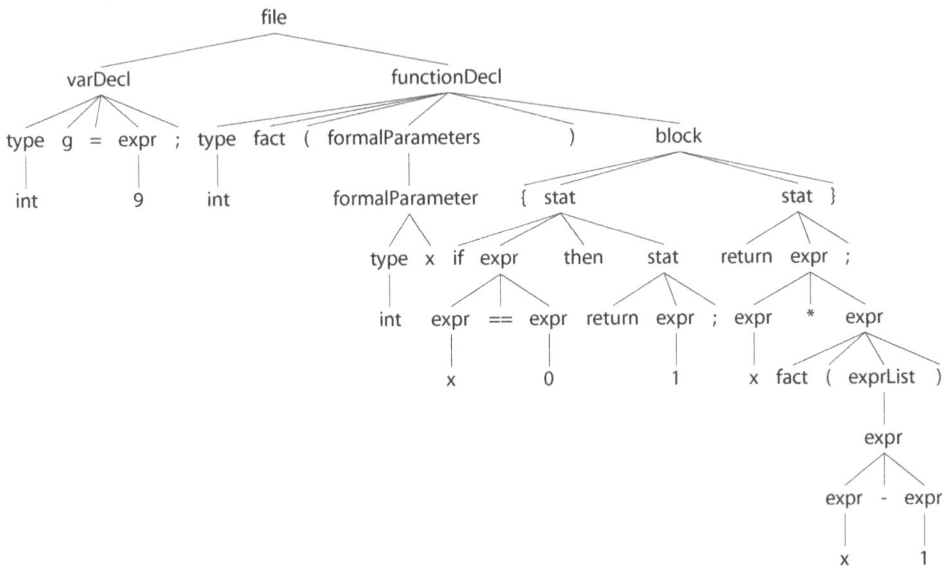

Looking at that Cymbol program at the coarsest level, we see a sequence of global variable and function declarations.

examples/Cymbol.g4
```
file:   (functionDecl | varDecl)+ ;
```

Variable declarations look like they do in all C derivatives, with a type followed by an identifier optionally followed by an initialization expression.

examples/Cymbol.g4
```
varDecl
    :   type ID ('=' expr)? ';'
    ;
type:   'float' | 'int' | 'void' ; // user-defined types
```

Functions are basically the same: a type followed by the function name followed by a parenthesized argument list followed by a function body.

examples/Cymbol.g4

```
functionDecl
    :   type ID '(' formalParameters? ')' block // "void f(int x) {...}"
    ;
formalParameters
    :   formalParameter (',' formalParameter)*
    ;
formalParameter
    :   type ID
    ;
```

A function body is a block of statements surrounded by curly braces. Let's make six kinds of statements: nested block, variable declaration, if statement, return statement, assignment, and function call. We can encode that in ANTLR syntax as follows:

examples/Cymbol.g4

```
block:  '{' stat* '}' ;   // possibly empty statement block
stat:   block
    |   varDecl
    |   'if' expr 'then' stat ('else' stat)?
    |   'return' expr? ';'
    |   expr '=' expr ';' // assignment
    |   expr ';'          // func call
    ;
```

The last major chunk of the language is the expression syntax. Because Cymbol is really just a prototype or stepping-stone for building other programming languages, it's OK to avoid a big list of operators. Let's say we have unary negate, Boolean not, multiplication, addition, subtraction, function calls, array indexing, equality comparison, variables, integers, and parenthesized expressions.

examples/Cymbol.g4

```
expr:   ID '(' exprList? ')'    // func call like f(), f(x), f(1,2)
    |   ID '[' expr ']'         // array index like a[i], a[i][j]
    |   '-' expr                // unary minus
    |   '!' expr                // boolean not
    |   expr '*' expr
    |   expr ('+'|'-') expr
    |   expr '==' expr          // equality comparison (lowest priority op)
    |   ID                      // variable reference
    |   INT
    |   '(' expr ')'
    ;
exprList : expr (',' expr)* ;   // arg list
```

The most important lesson here is that we generally have to list the alternatives in order from highest to lowest precedence. (For an in-depth discussion of how ANTLR removes left recursion and handles operator precedence, see Chapter 14, *Removing Direct Left Recursion*, on page 249.)

To see the precedence in action, take a look at the parse trees for input -x+y; and -a[i]; starting at rule stat (instead of file to reduce clutter).

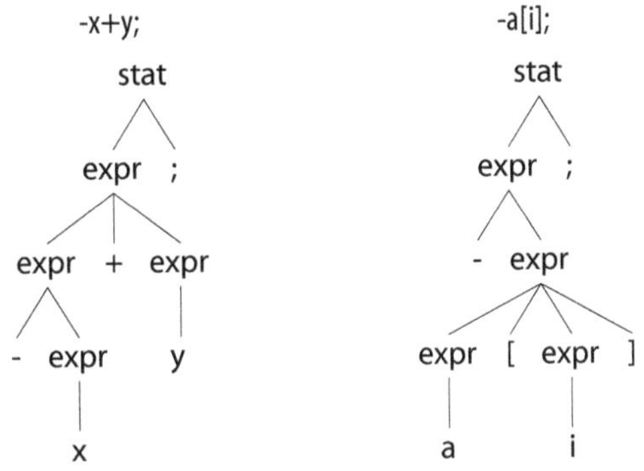

The parse tree on the left shows the unary minus binding most tightly to the x since it has higher priority than addition. The unary minus alternative appears before the addition alternative. On the other hand, unary minus has lower precedence than the array index suffix operator because the alternative with unary minus appears after the array index alternative. The parse tree on the right illustrates that the negation is applied to the a[i], not just identifier a. We'll see a more complicated expression rule in the next section.

We don't have to move on to the lexical rules like we usually do. Examining them wouldn't introduce anything new and interesting. The rules are pulled almost verbatim from the lexical patterns in the previous chapter. Our focus here is really on exploring the grammatical structure of an imperative programming language.

Using our intuitive sense of what a struct-less or class-less Java language might look like made building the Cymbol grammar pretty easy. And, if you've wrapped your head around this grammar, you're ready to build grammars for your own moderately complex imperative programming languages.

Next, we're going to tackle a language at the other extreme. To get a decent R grammar together, we'll have to deduce precise language structure by trudging through multiple references, examining sample programs, and testing the existing R implementation.

6.5 Parsing R

R is an expressive domain-specific programming language for describing statistical problems. For example, it's easy to create vectors, apply functions to them, and filter them (shown here using the R interactive shell).

```
⇒ x <- seq(1,10,.5)       # x = 1, 1.5, 2, 2.5, 3, 3.5, ..., 10
⇒ y <- 1:5                # y = 1, 2, 3, 4, 5
⇒ z <- c(9,6,2,10,-4)     # z = 9, 6, 2, 10, -4
⇒ y + z                   # add two vectors
《 [1] 10  8  5 14  1      # result is 1-dimensional vector
⇒ z[z<5]                  # all elements in z < 5
《 [1]  2 -4
⇒ mean(z)                 # compute the mean of vector z
《 [1] 4.6
⇒ zero <- function() { return(0) }
⇒ zero()
《 [1] 0
```

R is a medium-sized but complicated programming language, and most or all of us have a handicap: we don't know R. That means we can't just write down the grammar from our internal sense of the language structure like we could for Cymbol in the previous section. We must deduce R's structure by wading through reference manuals, examples, and a formal yacc grammar[9] from the existing implementation.

To get started, it's a good idea to skim through some language overviews.[10,11] We should also look at R examples to get a feel for the language and then pick some files to serve as an "acceptance test." Ajay Shah has built a fine set of examples[12] we can use. Covering those examples would mean that our grammar handles a large percentage of R code. (Getting a perfect grammar without knowing the language intimately is unlikely.) To help us in our quest to build an R grammar, there's a lot of documentation available at the main website,[13] but let's focus on R-intro[14] and language definition R-lang.[15]

Construction of our grammar begins at the coarsest level, as usual. From the language overviews, it's clear that R programs are a series of expressions or assignments. Even function definitions are assignments; we assign a function

---

9. http://svn.r-project.org/R/trunk/src/main/gram.y
10. http://www.stat.wisc.edu/~deepayan/SIBS2005/slides/language-overview.pdf
11. http://www.stat.lsa.umich.edu/~kshedden/Courses/Stat600/Notes/R_introduction.pdf
12. http://www.mayin.org/ajayshah/KB/R/index.html
13. http://www.r-project.org/
14. http://cran.r-project.org/doc/manuals/R-intro.pdf
15. http://cran.r-project.org/doc/manuals/R-lang.html

literal to a variable. The only unfamiliar thing is that there are three assignment operators: <-, =, and <<-. For our purposes, we don't have to care about their meaning because we're building only a parser, not an interpreter or compiler. Our first whack at the program structure looks something like this:

```
prog : (expr_or_assign '\n')* EOF ;

expr_or_assign
    :   expr ('<-' | '=' | '<<-' ) expr_or_assign
    |   expr
    ;
```

After reading some examples, though, it looks like we can also put more than one expression on a line by separating them with semicolons. R-intro confirms this. Also, while not in the manuals, the R shell allows and ignores blank lines. Tweaking our rules accordingly leads us to the beginning of our grammar.

examples/R.g4

```
prog:   (   expr_or_assign (';'|NL)
        |   NL
        )*
        EOF
    ;

expr_or_assign
    :   expr ('<-'|'='|'<<-') expr_or_assign
    |   expr
    ;
```

We use token NL rather than literal '\n' because we should allow Windows (\r\n) and Unix newlines (\n), which is easier to define as a lexical rule.

examples/R.g4

```
// Match both UNIX and Windows newlines
NL      :   '\r'? '\n' ;
```

Notice that NL doesn't say to discard those tokens as is customary. The parser uses them as expression terminators, like semicolons in Java, so the lexer must pass them to the parser.

The majority of R syntax relates to expressions, so that's what we'll focus on for the rest of the section. There are three main kinds: statement expressions, operator expressions, and function-related expressions. Since R statements are very similar to their imperative language counterparts, let's start with those to get them out of the way. Here are the alternatives dealing with statements from rule expr (which physically appear after the operator alternatives in expr):

examples/R.g4

```
|   '{' exprlist '}' // compound statement
|   'if' '(' expr ')' expr
|   'if' '(' expr ')' expr 'else' expr
|   'for' '(' ID 'in' expr ')' expr
|   'while' '(' expr ')' expr
|   'repeat' expr
|   '?' expr // get help on expr, usually string or ID
|   'next'
|   'break'
```

The first alternative matches the group of expressions per R-intro: "Elementary commands can be grouped together into one compound expression by braces ('{' and '}')." Here is exprlist:

examples/R.g4

```
exprlist
    :   expr_or_assign ((';'|NL) expr_or_assign?)*
    |
    ;
```

Most of the R expression language handles the plentiful operators. To get their correct forms, our best bet is to rely on the yacc grammar. Executable code is often, but not always, the best guide to a language author's intentions. To get the precedence, we need to look at the precedence table, which explicitly lays out the relative operator precedence. For example, here is what the yacc grammar says for the arithmetic operators (%left precedence commands listed first have lower priority):

```
%left           '+' '-'
%left           '*' '/'
```

The R-lang document also has a section called "Infix and prefix operators" that gives the operator precedence rules, but it seems to be missing the ::: operator found in the yacc grammar. Putting it all together, we can use the following alternatives for the binary, prefix, and suffix operators:

examples/R.g4

```
expr:   expr '[[' sublist ']' ']'  // '[[' follows R's yacc grammar
    |   expr '[' sublist ']'
    |   expr ('::'|':::') expr
    |   expr ('$'|'@') expr
    |   expr '^'<assoc=right> expr
    |   ('-'|'+') expr
    |   expr ':' expr
    |   expr USER_OP expr // anything wrappedin %: '%' .* '%'
    |   expr ('*'|'/') expr
    |   expr ('+'|'-') expr
    |   expr ('>'|'>='|'<'|'<='|'=='|'!=') expr
```

```
|    '!' expr
|    expr ('&'|'&&') expr
|    expr ('|'|'||') expr
|    '~' expr
|    expr '~' expr
|    expr ('->'|'->>'|':=') expr
```

We don't have to care about what the operators mean since we care only about recognition in this example. We just have to ensure that our grammar matches the precedence and associativity correctly.

The one unusual feature of the expr rule is the use of '[[' instead of '[' '[' in alternative expr '[[' sublist ']' ']'. ([[...]] selects a single element, whereas [...] yields a sublist.) I took '[[' directly from R's yacc grammar. This probably enforces a "no space between two left brackets" rule, but there was no obvious specification of this in the reference manual.

The ^ operator has token suffix <assoc=right> because R-lang indicates the following:

> The exponentiation operator '^' and the left assignment operators '<- = <<-' group right to left, all other operators group left to right. That is, 2 ^ 2 ^ 3 is 2 ^ 8, not 4 ^ 3.

With the statement and operator expressions out of the way, let's look at the last major chunk of the expr rule: defining and calling functions. We can use the following two alternatives:

examples/R.g4

```
|   'function' '(' formlist? ')' expr // define function
|   expr '(' sublist ')'              // call function
```

Rules formlist and sublist define the formal argument definition lists and call site argument expressions, respectively. The rule names mirror what the yacc grammar uses to make it easier to compare the two grammars.

The formal function arguments expressed by formlist follow the specification in R-lang.

> ... a comma-separated list of items each of which can be an identifier, or of the form '*identifier* = *default*', or the special token '...'. The *default* can be any valid expression.

We can encode that using an ANTLR rule that is similar to formlist in the yacc grammar (see Figure 5, *ANTLR rule for a formlist-like rule,* on page 108).

Now, to call a function instead of defining one, R-lang describes the argument syntax as shown in Figure 6, *R-lang argument syntax,* on page 108.

examples/R.g4
```
formlist : form (',' form)* ;

form:   ID
    |   ID '=' expr
    |   '...'
    ;
```

Figure 5—ANTLR rule for a formlist-like rule

> Each argument can be tagged (tag=expr), or just be a simple expression. It can also be empty or it can be one of the special tokens '...', '..2', etc.

Figure 6—R-lang argument syntax to call a function

A peek at the yacc grammar tightens this up a little bit for us; it indicates we can also have things like "n"=0, n=1, and NULL = 2. Combining specifications, we arrive at the following rules for function call arguments:

examples/R.g4
```
sublist : sub (',' sub)* ;
sub :   expr
    |   ID '='
    |   ID '=' expr
    |   STRING '='
    |   STRING '=' expr
    |   'NULL' '='
    |   'NULL' '=' expr
    |   '...'
    |
    ;
```

You might be wondering where in rule sub we match special tokens like ..2. It turns out we don't have to explicitly match them because our lexer can treat them as identifiers. According to R-lang:

> Identifiers consist of a sequence of letters, digits, the period ('.'), and the underscore. They must not start with a digit nor underscore, nor with a period followed by a digit. ... Notice that identifiers starting with a period [like] '...' and '..1', '..2', etc., are special.

To encode all of that, we use the following identifier rule:

examples/R.g4
```
ID  :   '.' (LETTER|'_'|'.') (LETTER|DIGIT|'_'|'.')*
    |   LETTER (LETTER|DIGIT|'_'|'.')*
    ;
fragment LETTER  : [a-zA-Z] ;
```

The first alternative separates out the first case, where an identifier starts with a period. We have to make sure that a digit is not the next character. We can ensure that with subrule (LETTER|'_'|'.'). To ensure that an identifier does not start with a digit or underscore, we start the second alternative with a reference to help rule LETTER. To match ..2, we use the first alternative. The initial '.' reference matches the first dot, the (LETTER|'_'|'.') subrule matches the second dot, and the last subrule matches digit 2.

The remainder of the lexer rules are direct copies or small extensions of rules we've seen before, so we can leave them out of our discussion here.

Let's take a look our handiwork now by using grun on the following input:

examples/t.R
```
addMe <- function(x,y) { return(x+y) }
addMe(x=1,2)
r <- 1:5
```

Here's how to build and bring up the parse tree visually (Figure 7, *Parse tree for input t.R*, on page 110) for input t.R:

```
$ antlr4 R.g4
$ javac R*.java
$ grun R prog -gui t.R
```

Our R grammar works well as long as each expression fits on a line, such as function addMe(). Unfortunately, that assumption is too restrictive because R allows functions and other expressions to span multiple lines. Nonetheless, we'll wrap up here because we've covered the R grammatical structure itself. In source directory code/extras, you'll find a solution to the persnickety problem of ignoring newlines within expressions; see R.g4, RFilter.g4, and TestR.java. It filters tokens from the lexer to keep or toss out newlines appropriately, according to syntax.

Our goal in this chapter was to solidify our knowledge of ANTLR syntax and to learn how to derive grammars from language reference manuals, examples, and existing non-ANTLR grammars. To that end, we looked at two data languages (CSV, JSON), a declarative language (DOT), an imperative language (Cymbol), and a functional language (R). These examples cover all of the skills you'll need to build grammars for most moderately complex languages. Before you move on, though, it's a good idea to lock in your new expertise by downloading the grammars and trying some simple modifications to alter the languages. For example, you might try adding more operators and statements to the Cymbol grammar. Use the TestRig to see the relationship between your altered grammars and sample inputs.

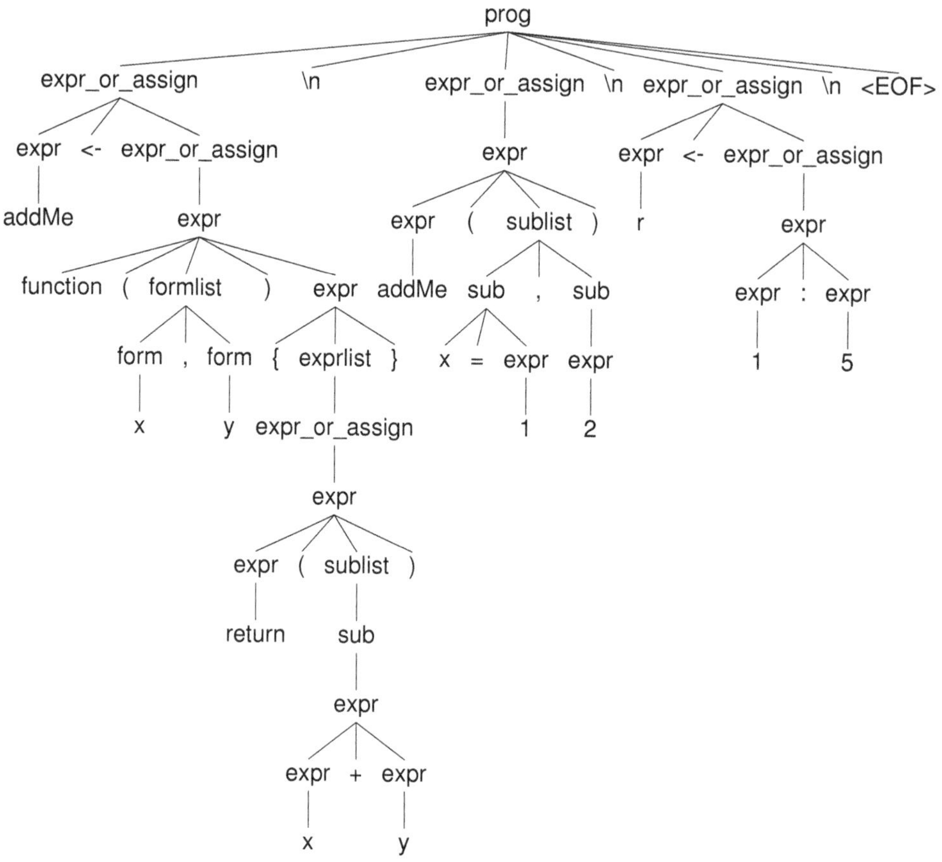

Figure 7—Parse tree for input t.R

So far in this book, we have focused on language recognition. But, grammars by themselves can indicate only whether the input conforms to the language. Now that we are parsing wizards, we're ready to learn about attaching application-specific code to the parsing mechanism, which we'll do in the next chapter. Following that, we'll build some real language applications.

CHAPTER 7

Decoupling Grammars from Application-Specific Code

Now that we know how to formally define languages using ANTLR grammar syntax, it's time to breathe some life into our grammars. By itself, a grammar isn't that useful because the associated parser tells us only whether an input sentence conforms to a language specification. To build language applications, we need the parser to trigger specific actions when it sees specific input sentences, phrases, or tokens. The collection of phrase → action pairs represents our language application or at least the interface between the grammar and a larger surrounding application.

In this chapter, we're going to learn how to use parse-tree *listeners* and *visitors* to build language applications. A listener is an object that responds to rule entry and exit events (phrase recognition events) triggered by a parse-tree walker as it discovers and finishes nodes. To support situations where an application must control how a tree is walked, ANTLR-generated parse trees also support the well-known tree visitor pattern.

The biggest difference between listeners and visitors is that listener methods aren't responsible for explicitly calling methods to walk their children. Visitors, on the other hand, must explicitly trigger visits to child nodes to keep the tree traversal going (as we saw in Section 2.5, *Parse-Tree Listeners and Visitors*, on page 18). Visitors get to control the order of traversal and how much of the tree gets visited because of these explicit calls to visit children. For convenience, I'll use the term *event method* to refer to either a listener callback or a visitor method.

Our goal in this chapter is to understand exactly what tree-walking facilities ANTLR builds for us and why. We'll start by looking at the origins of the listener mechanism and how we can keep application-specific code out of our grammars using listeners and visitors. Next, we'll learn how to get ANTLR to generate more precise events, one for each alternative in a rule. Once we know a little more about ANTLR's tree walking, we'll look at three calculator implementations that illustrate different ways to pass around subexpression results. Finally, we'll discuss the advantages and disadvantages of the three approaches. At that point, we'll be ready to tackle the real examples in the next chapter.

7.1 Evolving from Embedded Actions to Listeners

If you're used to previous versions of ANTLR or other parser generators, you'll be surprised to hear that we can build language applications without embedding actions (code) in the grammars. The listener and visitor mechanisms decouple grammars from application code, providing some compelling benefits. Such decoupling nicely encapsulates an application instead of fracturing it and dispersing the pieces across a grammar. Without embedded actions, we can reuse the same grammar in different applications without even recompiling the generated parser.

ANTLR can also generate parsers in different programming languages for the same grammar if it's bereft of actions. (I anticipate supporting different target languages after the 4.0 release.) Integrating grammar bug fixes or updates is also easy because we don't have to worry about merge conflicts because of embedded actions.

In this section, we're going to investigate the evolution from grammar with embedded actions to completely decoupled grammar and application. The following property file grammar with embedded actions sketched in with «...» reads property files, one property assignment per line. Actions like «*start file*» are just stand-ins for appropriate Java code.

```
grammar PropertyFile;
file : {«start file»} prop+ {«finish file»} ;
prop : ID '=' STRING '\n' {«process property»} ;
ID   : [a-z]+ ;
STRING : '"' .*? '"' ;
```

Such a tight coupling ties the grammar to one specific application. A better approach is to create a subclass of PropertyFileParser, the parser generated by ANTLR, and convert the embedded actions to methods. The refactoring leaves only trivial method call actions in the grammar that trigger the newly created methods. Then, by subclassing the parser, we can implement any number of different applications without altering the grammar. One such refactoring looks like this:

```
grammar PropertyFile;
@members {
    void startFile() { }  // blank implementations
    void finishFile() { }
    void defineProperty(Token name, Token value) { }
}
file : {startFile();} prop+ {finishFile();} ;
prop : ID '=' STRING '\n' {defineProperty($ID, $STRING)} ;
ID   : [a-z]+ ;
STRING : '"' .*? '"' ;
```

This decoupling makes the grammar reusable for different applications, but the grammar is still tied to Java because of the method calls. We'll deal with that shortly.

To demonstrate the reusability of the refactored grammar, let's build two different "applications," starting with one that just prints out the properties as it encounters them. The process is simply to extend the parser class generated by ANTLR and override one or more of the methods triggered by the grammar.

```
class PropertyFilePrinter extends PropertyFileParser {
    void defineProperty(Token name, Token value) {
        System.out.println(name.getText()+"="+value.getText());
    }
}
```

Notice that we don't have to override startFile() or finishFile() because of the default implementations in the PropertyFileParser superclass generated by ANTLR.

To launch this application, we need to create an instance of our special PropertyFilePrinter parser subclass instead of the usual PropertyFileParser.

```
PropertyFileLexer lexer = new PropertyFileLexer(input);
CommonTokenStream tokens = new CommonTokenStream(lexer);
PropertyFilePrinter parser = new PropertyFilePrinter(tokens);
parser.file(); // launch our special version of the parser
```

As a second application, let's load the properties into a map instead of printing them out. All we have to do is create a new subclass and put different functionality in defineProperty().

```
class PropertyFileLoader extends PropertyFileParser {
    Map<String,String> props = new OrderedHashMap<String, String>();
    void defineProperty(Token name, Token value) {
        props.put(name.getText(), value.getText());
    }
}
```

After the parser executes, field props will contain the name-value pairs.

This grammar still has the problem that the embedded actions restrict us to generating parsers only in Java. To make the grammar reusable and language neutral, we need to completely avoid embedded actions. The next two sections show how to do that with a listener and a visitor.

7.2 Implementing Applications with Parse-Tree Listeners

To build language applications without entangling the application and the grammar, the key is to have the parser create a parse tree and then walk it to trigger application-specific code. We can walk the tree using our favorite technique, or we can use one of the tree-walking mechanisms that ANTLR generates. In this section, we're going to use ANTLR's built-in ParseTreeWalker to build a listener-based version of the property file application from the previous section.

Let's start with a denuded version of the property file grammar.

listeners/PropertyFile.g4

```
file : prop+ ;
prop : ID '=' STRING '\n' ;
```

Here's a sample property file:

listeners/t.properties

```
user="parrt"
machine="maniac"
```

From the grammar, ANTLR generates PropertyFileParser, which automatically builds the following parse tree:

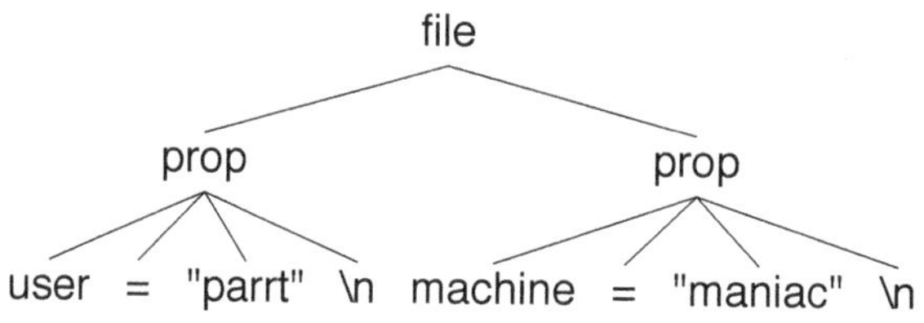

Once we have a parse tree, we can use ParseTreeWalker to visit all of the nodes, triggering enter and exit methods.

Let's take a look at listener interface PropertyFileListener that ANTLR generates from grammar PropertyFile. ANTLR's ParseTreeWalker triggers enter and exit methods for each rule subtree as it discovers and finishes nodes, respectively. Because there are only two parser rules in grammar PropertyFile, there are four methods in the interface.

listeners/PropertyFileListener.java

```
import org.antlr.v4.runtime.tree.*;
import org.antlr.v4.runtime.Token;

public interface PropertyFileListener extends ParseTreeListener {
	void enterFile(PropertyFileParser.FileContext ctx);
	void exitFile(PropertyFileParser.FileContext ctx);
	void enterProp(PropertyFileParser.PropContext ctx);
	void exitProp(PropertyFileParser.PropContext ctx);
}
```

The FileContext and PropContext objects are implementations of parse-tree nodes specific to each grammar rule. They contain useful methods that we'll explore as we go along.

As a convenience, ANTLR also generates class PropertyFileBaseListener with default implementations that mimic the blank methods we manually wrote in the @members area of the grammar in the previous section.

```
public class PropertyFileBaseListener implements PropertyFileListener {
    @Override public void enterFile(PropertyFileParser.FileContext ctx) { }
    @Override public void exitFile(PropertyFileParser.FileContext ctx) { }
    @Override public void enterProp(PropertyFileParser.PropContext ctx) { }
    @Override public void exitProp(PropertyFileParser.PropContext ctx) { }
    @Override public void enterEveryRule(ParserRuleContext ctx) { }
    @Override public void exitEveryRule(ParserRuleContext ctx) { }
    @Override public void visitTerminal(TerminalNode node) { }
    @Override public void visitErrorNode(ErrorNode node) { }
}
```

The default implementations let us override and implement only the methods we care about. For example, here's a reimplementation of the property file loader that has a single method like before, but using the listener mechanism:

listeners/TestPropertyFile.java

```
public static class PropertyFileLoader extends PropertyFileBaseListener {
    Map<String,String> props = new OrderedHashMap<String, String>();
    public void exitProp(PropertyFileParser.PropContext ctx) {
        String id = ctx.ID().getText(); // prop : ID '=' STRING '\n' ;
        String value = ctx.STRING().getText();
        props.put(id, value);
    }
}
```

The main differences? This version extends the base listener instead of the parser and the listener methods get triggered after the parser has completed.

There are a lot of interfaces and classes in flight here, so let's look at the inheritance relationship between the key players (interfaces in italics).

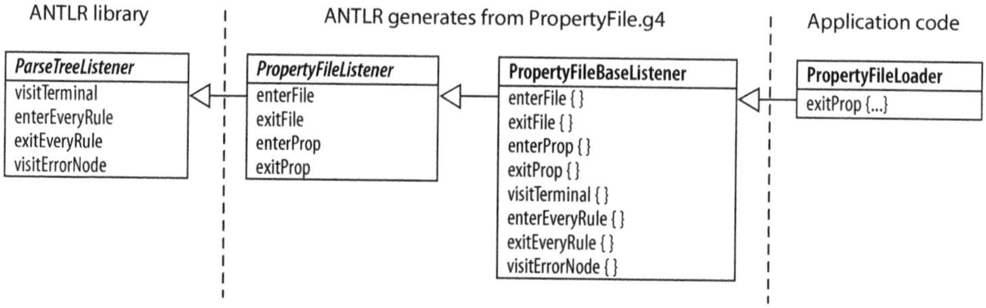

Interface ParseTreeListener is in the ANTLR runtime library and dictates that every listener respond to events visitTerminal(), enterEveryRule(), exitEveryRule(), and (upon syntax errors) visitErrorNode(). ANTLR generates interface PropertyFileListener from grammar PropertyFile and default implementations for all methods in class PropertyFileBaseListener. The only thing that we're building is the PropertyFileLoader, which inherits all of the blank functionality from PropertyFileBaseListener.

Method exitProp() has access to the rule context object, PropContext, associated with rule prop. That context object has methods for each of the elements mentioned in rule prop (ID and STRING). Because those elements are token references in the grammar, the methods return TerminalNode parse-tree nodes. We can either directly access the text of the token payload via getText(), as we've done here, or get the Token payload first via getSymbol().

And now for the exciting conclusion. Let's walk the tree, listening in with our new PropertyFileLoader.

listeners/TestPropertyFile.java

```
// create a standard ANTLR parse tree walker
ParseTreeWalker walker = new ParseTreeWalker();
// create listener then feed to walker
PropertyFileLoader loader = new PropertyFileLoader();
walker.walk(loader, tree);        // walk parse tree
System.out.println(loader.props); // print results
```

Here's a refresher on how to run ANTLR on a grammar, compile the generated code, and launch a test program to process an input file:

```
$ antlr4 PropertyFile.g4
$ ls PropertyFile*.java
PropertyFileBaseListener.java   PropertyFileListener.java
PropertyFileLexer.java          PropertyFileParser.java
$ javac TestPropertyFile.java PropertyFile*.java
$ cat t.properties
user="parrt"
machine="maniac"
$ java TestPropertyFile t.properties
{user="parrt", machine="maniac"}
```

Our test program successfully reconstitutes the property assignments from the file into a map data structure in memory.

A listener-based approach is great because all of the tree walking and method triggering is done automatically. Sometimes, though, automatic tree walking is also a weakness because we can't control the walk itself. For example, we might want to walk a parse tree for a C program, ignoring everything inside functions by skipping the function body subtrees. Listener event methods also can't use method return values to pass data around. When we need to control the walk or want to return values with event-method return values, we use a visitor pattern. Let's build a visitor-based version of this property file loader to compare the approaches.

7.3 Implementing Applications with Visitors

To use a visitor instead of a listener, we ask ANTLR to generate a visitor interface, implement that interface, and then create a test rig that calls visit() on the parse tree. We don't have to touch the grammar at all.

When we use the -visitor option on the command line, ANTLR generates interface PropertyFileVisitor and class PropertyFileBaseVisitor, which has the following default implementations:

```
public class PropertyFileBaseVisitor<T> extends AbstractParseTreeVisitor<T>
    implements PropertyFileVisitor<T>
{
    @Override public T visitFile(PropertyFileParser.FileContext ctx) { ... }
    @Override public T visitProp(PropertyFileParser.PropContext ctx) { ... }
}
```

We can copy the map functionality from exitProp() in the listener and paste it into the visitor method associated with rule prop.

listeners/TestPropertyFileVisitor.java

```
public static class PropertyFileVisitor extends
    PropertyFileBaseVisitor<Void>
{
    Map<String,String> props = new OrderedHashMap<String, String>();
    public Void visitProp(PropertyFileParser.PropContext ctx) {
        String id = ctx.ID().getText(); // prop : ID '=' STRING '\n' ;
        String value = ctx.STRING().getText();
        props.put(id, value);
        return null; // Java says must return something even when Void
    }
}
```

For comparison to the listener version in the previous section, here's the inheritance relationship between the visitor's interfaces and classes:

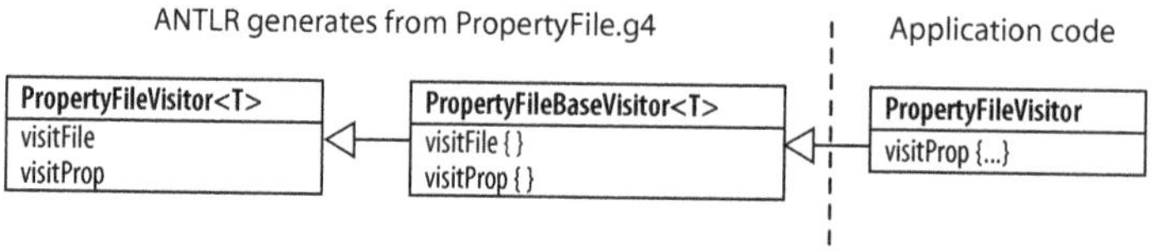

Visitors walk parse trees by explicitly calling interface ParseTreeVisitor's visit() method on child nodes. That method is implemented in AbstractParseTreeVisitor. In this case, the nodes created for prop invocations don't have children, so visitProp() doesn't have to call visit(). We'll look at visitor generic type parameters in *Traversing Parse Trees with Visitors*, on page 121.

The biggest difference between a visitor and listener test rig (such as TestPropertyFile) is that visitor test rigs don't need a ParseTreeWalker. They just ask the visitor to visit the tree created by the parser.

listeners/TestPropertyFileVisitor.java
```
PropertyFileVisitor loader = new PropertyFileVisitor();
loader.visit(tree);
System.out.println(loader.props); // print results
```

With all of that in place, here's the build and test sequence:

```
$ antlr4 -visitor PropertyFile.g4  # create visitor as well this time
$ ls PropertyFile*.java
PropertyFileBaseListener.java   PropertyFileListener.java
PropertyFileBaseVisitor.java    PropertyFileParser.java
PropertyFileLexer.java          PropertyFileVisitor.java
$ javac TestPropertyFileVisitor.java
$ cat t.properties
user="parrt"
machine="maniac"
$ java TestPropertyFileVisitor t.properties
{user="parrt", machine="maniac"}
```

We can build just about anything we want with visitors and listeners. Once we're in the Java space, there's no more ANTLR stuff to learn. All we have to know is the relationship between a grammar, its parse tree, and the visitor or listener event methods. Beyond that, it's just code. In response to recognizing input phrases, we can generate output, collect information (as we've done here), validate phrases in some way, or perform computations.

This property file example is small enough that we didn't run into an issue regarding rules with alternatives. By default, ANTLR generates a single kind of event for each rule no matter which alternative the parser matches. That's pretty inconvenient because the listener and visitor methods have to figure out which alternative was matched by the parser. In the next section, we'll see how to get events at a finer granularity.

7.4 Labeling Rule Alternatives for Precise Event Methods

To illustrate the event granularity problem, let's try to build a simple calculator with a listener for the following expression grammar:

listeners/Expr.g4

```
grammar Expr;
s : e ;
e : e op=MULT e    // MULT is '*'
  | e op=ADD e     // ADD is '+'
  | INT
  ;
```

As it stands, rule e yields a fairly unhelpful listener because all alternatives of e result in a tree walker triggering the same enterE() and exitE() methods.

```
public interface ExprListener extends ParseTreeListener {
    void enterE(ExprParser.EContext ctx);
    void exitE(ExprParser.EContext ctx);
    ...
}
```

The listener methods would have to test to see which alternative the parser matched for each e subtree using the op token label and the methods of ctx.

listeners/TestEvaluator.java

```
public void exitE(ExprParser.EContext ctx) {
    if ( ctx.getChildCount()==3 ) { // operations have 3 children
        int left = values.get(ctx.e(0));
        int right = values.get(ctx.e(1));
        if ( ctx.op.getType()==ExprParser.MULT ) {
            values.put(ctx, left * right);
        }
        else {
            values.put(ctx, left + right);
        }
    }
    else {
        values.put(ctx, values.get(ctx.getChild(0))); // an INT
    }
}
```

The MULT field referenced in exitE() is generated by ANTLR in ExprParser:

```
public class ExprParser extends Parser {
    public static final int MULT=1, ADD=2, INT=3, WS=4;
    ...
}
```

If we look at class EContext in class ExprParser, we can see that ANTLR packed all elements from all three alternatives into the same context object.

```
public static class EContext extends ParserRuleContext {
    public Token op;                          // derived from label op
    public List<EContext> e() { ... }         // get all e subtrees
    public EContext e(int i) { ... }          // get ith e subtree
    public TerminalNode INT() { ... }         // get INT node if alt 3 of e
    ...
}
```

To get more precise listener events, ANTLR lets us label the outermost alternatives of any rule using the # operator. Let's derive grammar LExpr from Expr and label e's alternatives. Here's the modified e rule:

listeners/LExpr.g4

```
e : e MULT e            # Mult
  | e ADD e             # Add
  | INT                 # Int
  ;
```

Now ANTLR generates a separate listener method for each alternative of e. Consequently, we don't need the op token label anymore. For alternative label X, ANTLR generates enterX() and exitX().

```
public interface LExprListener extends ParseTreeListener {
    void enterMult(LExprParser.MultContext ctx);
    void exitMult(LExprParser.MultContext ctx);
    void enterAdd(LExprParser.AddContext ctx);
    void exitAdd(LExprParser.AddContext ctx);
    void enterInt(LExprParser.IntContext ctx);
    void exitInt(LExprParser.IntContext ctx);
    ...
}
```

Note also that ANTLR generates specific context objects (subclasses of EContext) for the alternatives, named after the labels. The getter methods of the specialized context objects are limited to just those applicable to the associated alternatives. For example, IntContext has only an INT() method. We can ask for ctx.INT() in enterInt() but not in enterAdd().

Listeners and visitors are great. We get reusable and retargetable grammars as well as encapsulated language applications just by fleshing out event methods. ANTLR even automatically generates the skeleton code for us. It turns out, though, that the applications we've built so far are so simple we haven't run into a common implementation issue, which is that event methods sometimes need to pass around partial results or other information.

7.5 Sharing Information Among Event Methods

Whether we're collecting information or computing values, it's often most convenient and good programming practice to pass around arguments and return values, rather than using fields or other "global variables." The problem is that ANTLR automatically generates the signature of the listener methods without application-specific return values or arguments. ANTLR also generates visitor methods without application-specific arguments.

In this section, we're going to explore mechanisms that let event methods pass data around without altering the event method signatures. We'll build three different implementations of the same simple calculator based upon the LExpr expression grammar from the previous section. The first implementation uses visitor method return values, the second defines a field shared among event methods, and the third annotates parse tree nodes to squirrel away values of interest.

Traversing Parse Trees with Visitors

To build a visitor-based calculator, the easiest approach is to have the event methods associated with rule expr return subexpression values. For example, visitAdd() would return the result of adding two subexpressions. visitInt() would return the value of the integer. Conventional visitors don't specify return values for their visit methods. Adding a return type is easy when we implement a class for our specific application's needs, extending LExprBaseVisitor<T> and supplying Integer as the <T> type parameter. Here's what our visitor looks like:

listeners/TestLEvalVisitor.java

```
public static class EvalVisitor extends LExprBaseVisitor<Integer> {
    public Integer visitMult(LExprParser.MultContext ctx) {
        return visit(ctx.e(0)) * visit(ctx.e(1));
    }

    public Integer visitAdd(LExprParser.AddContext ctx) {
        return visit(ctx.e(0)) + visit(ctx.e(1));
    }

    public Integer visitInt(LExprParser.IntContext ctx) {
        return Integer.valueOf(ctx.INT().getText());
    }
}
```

EvalVisitor inherits the general visit() method from ANTLR's AbstractParseTreeVisitor class, which our visitor uses to concisely trigger subtree visits.

Notice that EvalVisitor doesn't have a visitor method for rule s. The default implementation of visitS() in LExprBaseVisitor calls predefined method ParseTreeVisitor.visitChildren(). visitChildren() returns the value returned from the visit of the last child. In this case, visitS() returns the value of the expression returned from visiting its only child (the e node). We can use this default behavior.

In test rig TestLEvalVisitor.java, we have the usual code to launch LExprParser and print the parse tree. Then we need code to launch EvalVisitor and print out the expression value computed while visiting the tree.

listeners/TestLEvalVisitor.java

```
EvalVisitor evalVisitor = new EvalVisitor();
int result = evalVisitor.visit(tree);
System.out.println("visitor result = "+result);
```

To build our calculator, we tell ANTLR to generate the visitor, using the -visitor option as we did for the property file grammar earlier. (If we no longer want to generate a listener, we also use option -no-listener.) Here's the complete build and test sequence:

```
⇒ $ antlr4 -visitor LExpr.g4
⇒ $ javac LExpr*.java TestLEvalVisitor.java
⇒ $ java TestLEvalVisitor
⇒ 1+2*3
⇒ EOF
❮ (s (e (e 1) + (e (e 2) * (e 3))))
  visitor result = 7
```

Visitors work very well if we need application-specific return values because we get to use the built-in Java return value mechanism. If we prefer not having to explicitly invoke visitor methods to visit children, we can switch to the listener mechanism. Unfortunately, that means giving up the cleanliness of using Java method return values.

Simulating Return Values with a Stack

ANTLR generates listener event methods that return no values (void return types). To return values to listener methods executing on nodes higher in the parse tree, we can store partial results in a field of our listener. A stack of values comes to mind, just as the Java runtime uses the CPU stack to store method return values temporarily. The idea is to push the result of computing a subexpression onto the stack. Methods for subexpressions further up the parse tree pop operands off the stack. Here's the full Evaluator calculator listener (physically in file TestLEvaluator.java):

listeners/TestLEvaluator.java

```
public static class Evaluator extends LExprBaseListener {
    Stack<Integer> stack = new Stack<Integer>();

    public void exitMult(LExprParser.MultContext ctx) {
        int right = stack.pop();
        int left = stack.pop();
        stack.push( left * right );
    }

    public void exitAdd(LExprParser.AddContext ctx) {
        int right = stack.pop();
        int left = stack.pop();
        stack.push(left + right);
    }

    public void exitInt(LExprParser.IntContext ctx) {
        stack.push( Integer.valueOf(ctx.INT().getText()) );
    }
}
```

To try this, we can create and use a ParseTreeWalker in test rig TestLEvaluator, following what we did in TestPropertyFile earlier in this chapter.

```
⇒ $ antlr4 LExpr.g4
⇒ $ javac LExpr*.java TestLEvaluator.java
⇒ $ java TestLEvaluator
⇒ 1+2*3
⇒ EOF
❮ (s (e (e 1) + (e (e 2) * (e 3))))
  stack result = 7
```

Using a stack field is a bit awkward but works fine. We have to make sure that the event methods push and pop things in the correct order across listener events. Visitors with return values do away with the awkwardness of the stack but require that we manually visit the nodes of the tree. The third option is to capture partial results by stashing them in tree nodes.

Annotating Parse Trees

Instead of using temporary storage to share data between event methods, we can store those values in the parse tree itself. We can use this tree annotation approach with both a listener and a visitor, but we'll demonstrate how it works using a listener here. Let's start by looking at the LExpr grammar parse tree for 1+2*3 annotated with partial results (Figure 8, *The LExpr grammar parse tree for 1+2*3*, on page 124).

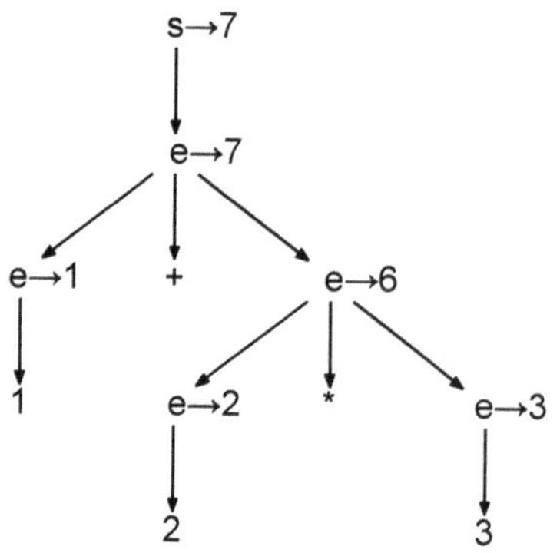

Figure 8—The LExpr grammar parse tree for 1+2*3

Each subexpression corresponds to a subtree root (and to an e rule invocation). The numbers pointed at by horizontal right arrows emanating from e nodes are the partial results we'd like to "return."

Adding Fields to Nodes via Rule Arguments and Return Values

If we didn't care about tying our grammar to a particular language, we could simply add a return value to the rule specification of interest.

```
e returns [int value]
  : e '*' e                      # Mult
  | e '+' e                      # Add
  | INT                          # Int
  ;
```

ANTLR places all parameters and return values of rules into the associated context object and so value ends up as a field of EContext.

```
public static class EContext extends ParserRuleContext {
    public int value;
    ...
}
```

Because the alternative-specific context is derived from EContext, all listener methods have access to this value. For example, listener methods could say ctx.value = 0;.

The approach shown here involves specifying that a rule method produces a result value, which is stored in the rule's context object. The specification uses target language syntax and consequently ties the grammar to a particular target language. However, the approach doesn't necessarily tie the grammar to a particular application, assuming that other applications can use the same rule result values. On the other hand, if we need more than one return value or a return value of a different type for a different application, this approach would not work.

Let's see how the node annotation strategy would work for rule e from our LExpr grammar.

listeners/LExpr.g4
```
e : e MULT e                # Mult
  | e ADD e                 # Add
  | INT                     # Int
  ;
```

The listener methods for the alternatives of e would each store a result in the corresponding e parse-tree node. Any subsequent add or multiply events on nodes higher up in the parse tree would grab subexpression values by looking at the values stored in their corresponding children.

If we assume, for the moment, that each parse-tree node (each rule context object) has a field called value, then exitAdd() would look like this:

```
public void exitAdd(LExprParser.AddContext ctx) {
    // e(0).value is the subexpression value of the first e in the alternative
    ctx.value = ctx.e(0).value + ctx.e(1).value; // e '+' e # Add
}
```

That looks pretty reasonable, but unfortunately, we can't extend class ExprContext to add field value dynamically in Java (like Ruby and Python can). To make parse-tree annotation work, we need a way to annotate the various nodes without manually altering the associated node classes generated by ANTLR. (Otherwise, ANTLR would overwrite our changes the next time it generated code.)

The easiest way to annotate parse-tree nodes is to use a Map that associates arbitrary values with nodes. For that reason, ANTLR provides a simple helper class called ParseTreeProperty. Let's build another calculator version called EvaluatorWithProps in file TestLEvaluatorWithProps.java that associates partial results with LExpr parse-tree nodes using a ParseTreeProperty instance. Here's the appropriate definition at the start of our listener:

listeners/TestLEvaluatorWithProps.java
```
public static class EvaluatorWithProps extends LExprBaseListener {
    /** maps nodes to integers with Map<ParseTree,Integer> */
    ParseTreeProperty<Integer> values = new ParseTreeProperty<Integer>();
```

Caution: If you want to use your own field of type Map instead of ParseTreeProperty, make sure to derive it from IdentityHashMap, not the usual HashMap. We need to annotate specific nodes, testing by identity instead of equals(). Two e nodes might be equals() but not the same physical node in memory.

To annotate a node, we say values.put(node, value). To get a value associated with a node, we say values.get(node). This is OK, but let's create some helper methods with obvious names to make the code easier to read.

listeners/TestLEvaluatorWithProps.java
```
public void setValue(ParseTree node, int value) { values.put(node, value); }
public int getValue(ParseTree node) { return values.get(node); }
```

Let's start the listener methods with the simplest expression alternative, Int. We want to annotate its parse-tree e node with the integer value of the INT token it matches.

listeners/TestLEvaluatorWithProps.java
```
public void exitInt(LExprParser.IntContext ctx) {
    String intText = ctx.INT().getText(); // INT   # Int
    setValue(ctx, Integer.valueOf(intText));
}
```

For addition subtrees, we get the value of the two subexpression children (operands) and annotate the subtree root with the sum.

listeners/TestLEvaluatorWithProps.java
```
public void exitAdd(LExprParser.AddContext ctx) {
    int left = getValue(ctx.e(0)); // e '+' e   # Add
    int right = getValue(ctx.e(1));
    setValue(ctx, left + right);
}
```

Method exitMult() is the same except that the calculation uses multiply instead of add.

Our test rig starts parsing at rule s, so we have to make sure that the parse-tree root has the value of the e subtree. (Or, we could start parsing at e instead of s.) To bubble up the value from the e node to the root s node, we implement exitS().

listeners/TestLEvaluatorWithProps.java
```
/** Need to pass e's value out of rule s : e ; */
public void exitS(LExprParser.SContext ctx) {
    setValue(ctx, getValue(ctx.e())); // like: int s() { return e(); }
}
```

Here's how to launch the listener and print out the expression value from the parse-tree root node:

listeners/TestLEvaluatorWithProps.java
```
ParseTreeWalker walker = new ParseTreeWalker();
EvaluatorWithProps evalProp = new EvaluatorWithProps();
walker.walk(evalProp, tree);
System.out.println("properties result = " +evalProp.getValue(tree));
```

And here's the build and test sequence:

```
⇒ $ antlr4 LExpr.g4
⇒ $ javac LExpr*.java TestLEvaluatorWithProps.java
⇒ $ java TestLEvaluatorWithProps
⇒ 1+2*3
⇒ EOF
❮ (s (e (e 1) + (e (e 2) * (e 3))))
  properties result = 7
```

Now we've seen three implementations of the same calculator, and we're almost ready to put our knowledge to use building real examples. Because each approach has its strengths and weaknesses, let's review what we've learned so far in this chapter and compare the different techniques.

Comparing Information Sharing Approaches

To get reusable and retargetable grammars, we need to keep them completely clear of user-defined actions. This means putting all of the application-specific code into some kind of listener or visitor external to the grammar. Listeners and visitors operate on parse trees, and ANTLR automatically generates appropriate tree-walking interfaces and default implementations. Since the event method signatures are fixed and not application specific, we looked at three ways event methods can share information.

- *Native Java call stack*: Visitor methods return a value of user-defined type. If a visitor needs to pass parameters, it must also use one of the next two techniques.
- *Stack-based*: A stack field simulates parameters and return values like the Java call stack.
- *Annotator*: A map field annotates nodes with useful values.

All three are completely decoupled from the grammar itself and nicely encapsulated in specialized objects. Beyond that, there are advantages and disadvantages to each. The needs of our problem and personal taste dictate which approach to take. There's also no reason that we can't use a variety of solutions even within the same application.

Visitor methods read nicely because they directly call other visitor methods to get partial results and can return values like any other method. That is also their negative. The visitor methods must explicitly visit their children, whereas the listeners do not. Because the visitor has a general interface, it can't define arguments. Visitors must use one of the other solutions to pass arguments to visitor methods it calls on children. A visitor's space efficiency is good because it has to keep around only a few partial results at any one time. There are no partial results hanging around after the tree walk. While visitor methods can return values, each value must be of the same type, unlike the other solutions.

The stack-based solution can simulate arguments and return values with a stack, but there's a chance of a disconnect when manually managing the stack. This can occur because the listener methods aren't calling each other directly. As programmers, we have to make sure that what we push is appropriately popped off by future event method calls. The stack can pass multiple values and multiple return values. The stack-based solution is also space efficient because it does not attach anything to the tree. All partial results storage goes away after the tree walk.

The annotator is my default solution because it allows me to arbitrarily provide information to event methods operating on nodes above and below in the parse tree. I can pass multiple values around, and they can be of arbitrary types. Annotation is better than using a stack with fleeting values in many cases. There is less chance of a disconnect between the data-passing expectations of the various methods. Annotating the tree with `setValue(ctx, value)` is less intuitive than saying `return value` in a programming language but is more general. The only disadvantage of this approach over the other two is that the partial results are kept around during the tree walk and so it has a larger memory footprint.

On the other hand, being able to annotate the tree is precisely what we need in some applications, such as Section 8.4, *Validating Program Symbol Usage*, on page 140. That application requires multiple passes over the tree, and it's convenient for the first pass to compute and squirrel away data in the tree. The second pass then has easy access to the data as the parse-tree walker rewalks the tree. All in all, tree annotation is extremely flexible and has an acceptable memory burden.

Now that we know how to implement some basic language applications using parse-tree listeners and visitors, it's time to build some real tools based upon these techniques. That's exactly what we'll do in the next chapter.

CHAPTER 8

Building Some Real Language Applications

Now that we know how to trigger application code via listeners and visitors, it's time to build some useful applications. We'll construct four listeners of increasing complexity based upon the CSV, JSON, and Cymbol grammars from Chapter 6, *Exploring Some Real Grammars*, on page 85. (We could just as easily use visitors.)

The first real application is a loader for CSV files that constructs a two-dimensional list data structure. Then, we'll figure out how to translate JSON text files into XML text files. Next, we'll read in Cymbol programs and visualize the function call dependency graph using DOT/graphviz. Finally, we'll build a real symbol table for Cymbol programs that checks for undefined variables or functions and verifies that variables and functions are used properly. The checker needs to make multiple passes over the parse tree and, therefore, demonstrates how to collect information in one pass and use it in the next.

Let's get started with the simplest application.

8.1 Loading CSV Data

Our goal is to build a listener that loads comma-separated-value (CSV) data into a nice "list of maps" data structure. This is the kind of thing that any data format reader or even a configuration file reader would do. We'll collect the fields of each row into a map that associates a header name with a value. So, given the following input:

listeners/t.csv
```
Details,Month,Amount
Mid Bonus,June,"$2,000"
,January,"""zippo"""
Total Bonuses,"","$5,000"
```

we'd like to see the following list of maps printed out:

```
[{Details=Mid Bonus, Month=June, Amount="$2,000"},
 {Details=, Month=January, Amount="""zippo"""},
 {Details=Total Bonuses, Month="", Amount="$5,000"}]
```

To get precise methods within our listener, let's label each of the alternatives in rule field from the CSV grammar we built in Section 6.1, *Parsing Comma-Separated Values*, on page 86.

listeners/CSV.g4

```
grammar CSV;

file : hdr row+ ;
hdr : row ;

row : field (',' field)* '\r'? '\n' ;

field
    :   TEXT     # text
    |   STRING   # string
    |            # empty
    ;

TEXT : ~[,\n\r"]+ ;
STRING : '"' ('""'|~'"')* '"' ;
```

Other than that, the CSV grammar is the same as before.

We can start the implementation of our listener by defining the data structures we'll need. First, we need the main data structure, a list of maps called rows. We also need a list of the column names found in the header row, header. To process a row, we'll read the field values into a temporary list, currentRowFieldValues, and then map the column names to those values as we finish each row.

Here is the start of our listener:

listeners/LoadCSV.java

```
public static class Loader extends CSVBaseListener {
    public static final String EMPTY = "";
    /** Load a list of row maps that map field name to value */
    List<Map<String,String>> rows = new ArrayList<Map<String, String>>();
    /** List of column names */
    List<String> header;
    /** Build up a list of fields in current row */
    List<String> currentRowFieldValues;
```

The following three rule methods process field values by computing the appropriate string and adding it to the currentRowFieldValues:

listeners/LoadCSV.java

```
public void exitString(CSVParser.StringContext ctx) {
    currentRowFieldValues.add(ctx.STRING().getText());
}

public void exitText(CSVParser.TextContext ctx) {
    currentRowFieldValues.add(ctx.TEXT().getText());
}

public void exitEmpty(CSVParser.EmptyContext ctx) {
    currentRowFieldValues.add(EMPTY);
}
```

Before we can process the rows, we need to get the list of column names from the first row. The header row is just another row syntactically, but we need to treat it differently than a regular row of data. That means we need to check context. For now, let's assume that after exitRow() executes, currentRowFieldValues contains a list of the column names. To fill in header, we just have to capture the field values of that first row.

listeners/LoadCSV.java

```
public void exitHdr(CSVParser.HdrContext ctx) {
    header = new ArrayList<String>();
    header.addAll(currentRowFieldValues);
}
```

Turning to the rows themselves, we need two operations: one when we start a row and one when we finish. When we start a row, we need to allocate (or clear) currentRowFieldValues to prepare for getting a fresh set of data.

listeners/LoadCSV.java

```
public void enterRow(CSVParser.RowContext ctx) {
    currentRowFieldValues = new ArrayList<String>();
}
```

At the end of a row, we have to consider context. If we just loaded the header row, we don't want to alter the rows field. The column names aren't data. In exitRow(), we can test context by looking at the getRuleIndex() value of our parent node in the parse tree (or by asking if the parent is of type HdrContext). If the current row is instead a data row, we create a map using values obtained by simultaneously walking the column names in header and the values in currentRowFieldValues.

listeners/LoadCSV.java

```
public void exitRow(CSVParser.RowContext ctx) {
    // If this is the header row, do nothing
    // if ( ctx.parent instanceof CSVParser.HdrContext ) return; OR:
    if ( ctx.getParent().getRuleIndex() == CSVParser.RULE_hdr ) return;
```

```
        // It's a data row
        Map<String, String> m = new LinkedHashMap<String, String>();
        int i = 0;
        for (String v : currentRowFieldValues) {
            m.put(header.get(i), v);
            i++;
        }
        rows.add(m);
    }
```

And that's all there is to loading the CSV data into a nice data structure. After using a ParseTreeWalker to traverse the tree, our main() in LoadCSV can print out the rows field.

listeners/LoadCSV.java

```
ParseTreeWalker walker = new ParseTreeWalker();
Loader loader = new Loader();
walker.walk(loader, tree);
System.out.println(loader.rows);
```

Here's the build and test sequence:

```
$ antlr4 CSV.g4
$ javac CSV*.java LoadCSV.java
$ java LoadCSV t.csv
[{Details=Mid Bonus, Month=June, Amount="$2,000"}, {Details=, Month=January,
 Amount="""zippo"""}, {Details=Total Bonuses, Month="", Amount="$5,000"}]
```

The other thing we might want to do after reading some data is to translate it to a different language, which is what we'll do in the next section.

8.2 Translating JSON to XML

Lots of web services return JSON data, and we might run into a situation where we want to feed some JSON data into existing code that accepts only XML. Let's use our JSON grammar from Section 6.2, *Parsing JSON*, on page 88 as a foundation to build a JSON to XML translator. Our goal is to read in JSON text like this:

listeners/t.json

```
{
    "description" : "An imaginary server config file",
    "logs" : {"level":"verbose", "dir":"/var/log"},
    "host" : "antlr.org",
    "admin": ["parrt", "tombu"],
    "aliases": []
}
```

and emit XML in an equivalent form, like this:

```
<description>An imaginary server config file</description>
<logs>
    <level>verbose</level>
    <dir>/var/log</dir>
</logs>
<host>antlr.org</host>
<admin>
    <element>parrt</element>
    <element>tombu</element>
</admin>
<aliases></aliases>
```

where <element> is a tag we need to conjure up during translation.

As we did with the CSV grammar, let's label some of the alternatives in the JSON grammar to get ANTLR to generate more precise listener methods.

listeners/JSON.g4

```
object
    :   '{' pair (',' pair)* '}'    # AnObject
    |   '{' '}'                     # EmptyObject
    ;

array
    :   '[' value (',' value)* ']'  # ArrayOfValues
    |   '[' ']'                     # EmptyArray
    ;
```

We'll do the same thing for rule value, but with a twist. All but three of the alternatives just have to return the text of the value matched by the alternative. We can use the same label for all of them, causing the parse-tree walker to trigger the same listener method for those alternatives.

listeners/JSON.g4

```
value
    :   STRING          # String
    |   NUMBER          # Atom
    |   object          # ObjectValue
    |   array           # ArrayValue
    |   'true'          # Atom
    |   'false'         # Atom
    |   'null'          # Atom
    ;
```

To implement our translator, it makes sense to have each rule return the XML equivalent of the input phrase matched by the rule. To track these partial results, we'll annotate the parse tree using field xml and two helper methods.

listeners/JSON2XML.java
```
public static class XMLEmitter extends JSONBaseListener {
    ParseTreeProperty<String> xml = new ParseTreeProperty<String>();
    String getXML(ParseTree ctx) { return xml.get(ctx); }
    void setXML(ParseTree ctx, String s) { xml.put(ctx, s); }
```

We'll attach the translated string for each subtree to the root of that subtree. Methods working on nodes further up the parse tree can grab those values to compute larger strings. The string attached to the root node is then the complete translation.

Let's start with the easiest translation. The Atom alternatives of value "return" (annotate the Atom node with) the text of the matched token (ctx.getText() gets the text matched by that rule invocation).

listeners/JSON2XML.java
```
public void exitAtom(JSONParser.AtomContext ctx) {
    setXML(ctx, ctx.getText());
}
```

Strings are basically the same except we have to strip off the double quotes (stripQuotes() is a helper method in the file).

listeners/JSON2XML.java
```
public void exitString(JSONParser.StringContext ctx) {
    setXML(ctx, stripQuotes(ctx.getText()));
}
```

If the value() rule method finds an object or array, it can copy the partial translation for that composite element to its own parse-tree node. Here's how to do it for objects:

listeners/JSON2XML.java
```
public void exitObjectValue(JSONParser.ObjectValueContext ctx) {
    // analogous to String value() {return object();}
    setXML(ctx, getXML(ctx.object()));
}
```

Once we can translate all of the values, we need to worry about name-value pairs and converting them to tags and text. The tag name for the resulting XML is derived from the STRING in the STRING ':' value alternative. The text in between the open and close tags is derived from the text attached to the value child.

listeners/JSON2XML.java
```
public void exitPair(JSONParser.PairContext ctx) {
    String tag = stripQuotes(ctx.STRING().getText());
    JSONParser.ValueContext vctx = ctx.value();
    String x = String.format("<%s>%s</%s>\n", tag, getXML(vctx), tag);
    setXML(ctx, x);
}
```

JSON objects consist of name-value pairs. So, for every pair found by object in the alternative marked by AnObject, we append the results computed here in the parse tree:

listeners/JSON2XML.java

```
public void exitAnObject(JSONParser.AnObjectContext ctx) {
    StringBuilder buf = new StringBuilder();
    buf.append("\n");
    for (JSONParser.PairContext pctx : ctx.pair()) {
        buf.append(getXML(pctx));
    }
    setXML(ctx, buf.toString());
}
public void exitEmptyObject(JSONParser.EmptyObjectContext ctx) {
    setXML(ctx, "");
}
```

Processing arrays follows a similar pattern, simply joining the list of results from child nodes and then wrapping them in <element> tags.

listeners/JSON2XML.java

```
public void exitArrayOfValues(JSONParser.ArrayOfValuesContext ctx) {
    StringBuilder buf = new StringBuilder();
    buf.append("\n");
    for (JSONParser.ValueContext vctx : ctx.value()) {
        buf.append("<element>"); // conjure up element for valid XML
        buf.append(getXML(vctx));
        buf.append("</element>");
        buf.append("\n");
    }
    setXML(ctx, buf.toString());
}

public void exitEmptyArray(JSONParser.EmptyArrayContext ctx) {
    setXML(ctx, "");
}
```

Finally, we need to annotate the root of the parse tree with the overall translation, collected from an object or array.

listeners/JSON.g4

```
json:   object
    |   array
    ;
```

We can do that in our listener with a simple set operation.

listeners/JSON2XML.java

```
public void exitJson(JSONParser.JsonContext ctx) {
    setXML(ctx, getXML(ctx.getChild(0)));
}
```

Here's the build and test sequence:

```
$ antlr4 JSON.g4
$ javac JSON*.java
$ java JSON2XML t.json

<description>An imaginary server config file</description>
<logs>
<level>verbose</level>
...
```

Translations are not always as straightforward as JSON to XML. But, this example shows us how to approach the problem of sentence translation by piecing together partially translated phrases. (If you look in the source code directory, you'll also see a version that uses StringTemplate,[1] JSON2XML_ST.java, to generate output and another that builds XML DOM trees, JSON2XML_DOM.java.)

OK, enough playing around with data. Let's do something interesting with a programming language.

8.3 Generating a Call Graph

Software is hard to write and maintain, which is why we try to build tools to increase our productivity and effectiveness. For example, over the past decade we've seen an explosion of testing frameworks, code coverage tools, and code analyzers. It's also nice to see a class hierarchy visually as a tree, and most development environments support this. The other visualization I like is called a *call graph*, which has functions as nodes and function calls as directed edges between the nodes.

In this section, we're going to build a call graph generator using the Cymbol grammar from Section 6.4, *Parsing Cymbol*, on page 100. I think you'll be surprised at how simple it is, especially given how cool the results are. To give you an idea of what we're trying to achieve, consider the following set of functions and function calls:

listeners/t.cymbol

```
int main() { fact(); a(); }

float fact(int n) {
  print(n);

  if ( n==0 ) then return 1;
  return n * fact(n-1);
}
```

1. http://www.stringtemplate.org

```
void a() { int x = b(); if false then {c(); d();} }
void b() { c(); }
void c() { b(); }
void d() { }
void e() { }
```

We'd like to visualize the call graph like this:

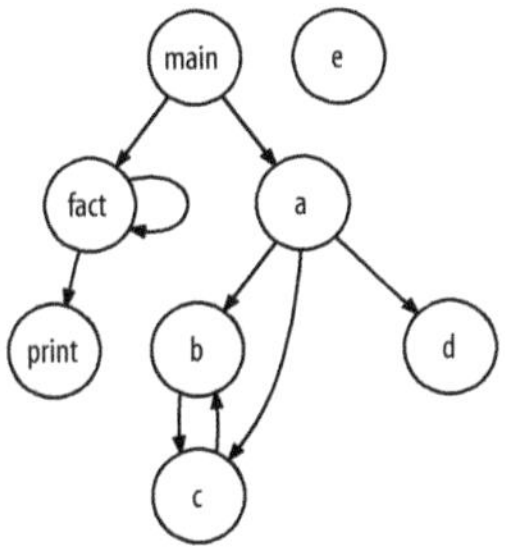

The good thing about visualizations is that the human eye can easily pick out aberrations. For example, the e() node is an orphan, which means that no one calls it and it is therefore dead code. At a glance, we found a function to jettison. We can also detect recursion very easily by looking for cycles in the graph such as fact() → fact() and b() → c() → b().

To visualize a call graph, we need to read in a Cymbol program and create a DOT file (and then view it with graphviz). For example, here is the DOT we need to generate for file t.cymbol from the earlier example:

```
digraph G {
  ranksep=.25;
  edge [arrowsize=.5]
  node [shape=circle, fontname="ArialNarrow",
        fontsize=12, fixedsize=true, height=.45];
  main; fact; a; b; c; d; e;
  main -> fact;
  main -> a;
  fact -> print;
  fact -> fact;
  a -> b;
  a -> c;
  a -> d;
  b -> c;
  c -> b;
}
```

The output consists of boilerplate setup statements such as ranksep=.25; and then a list of nodes and edges. To catch orphan nodes, we need to make sure to generate a node definition for each function name, even if it has no incoming or outgoing edges. It would not appear in the graph otherwise. Note the e on the end of the node definition line.

```
main; fact; a; b; c; d; e;
```

Our strategy is straightforward. When the parser finds a function declaration, our application will add the name of the current function to a list and set a field called currentFunctionName. When the parser sees a function call, our application will record an edge from the currentFunctionName to the callee's function name.

To get started, let's label some rule alternatives in Cymbol.g4 to get more precise listener methods.

listeners/Cymbol.g4

```
expr:   ID '(' exprList? ')'    # Call
    |   expr '[' expr ']'       # Index
    |   '-' expr                # Negate
    |   '!' expr                # Not
    |   expr '*' expr           # Mult
    |   expr ('+'|'-') expr     # AddSub
    |   expr '==' expr          # Equal
    |   ID                      # Var
    |   INT                     # Int
    |   '(' expr ')'            # Parens
    ;
```

Then, as a foundation for our language application, let's encapsulate all of the graph-related stuff into a class.

listeners/CallGraph.java

```
static class Graph {
    // I'm using org.antlr.v4.runtime.misc: OrderedHashSet, MultiMap
    Set<String> nodes = new OrderedHashSet<String>(); // list of functions
    MultiMap<String, String> edges =                  // caller->callee
        new MultiMap<String, String>();
    public void edge(String source, String target) {
        edges.map(source, target);
    }
```

From the collection of nodes and edges, we can dump out the appropriate DOT code using a little bit of Java in toDOT() of class Graph.

listeners/CallGraph.java

```
public String toDOT() {
    StringBuilder buf = new StringBuilder();
    buf.append("digraph G {\n");
```

```
        buf.append("  ranksep=.25;\n");
        buf.append("  edge [arrowsize=.5]\n");
        buf.append("  node [shape=circle, fontname=\"ArialNarrow\",\n");
        buf.append("        fontsize=12, fixedsize=true, height=.45];\n");
        buf.append("  ");
        for (String node : nodes) { // print all nodes first
            buf.append(node);
            buf.append("; ");
        }
        buf.append("\n");
        for (String src : edges.keySet()) {
            for (String trg : edges.get(src)) {
                buf.append("  ");
                buf.append(src);
                buf.append(" -> ");
                buf.append(trg);
                buf.append(";\n");
            }
        }
        buf.append("}\n");
        return buf.toString();
    }
```

Now all we have to do is fill in those data structures using a listener. The listener needs two fields for bookkeeping.

listeners/CallGraph.java

```
static class FunctionListener extends CymbolBaseListener {
    Graph graph = new Graph();
    String currentFunctionName = null;
```

And our application only needs to listen for two events. First, it has to record the current function name as the parser finds function declarations.

listeners/CallGraph.java

```
public void enterFunctionDecl(CymbolParser.FunctionDeclContext ctx) {
    currentFunctionName = ctx.ID().getText();
    graph.nodes.add(currentFunctionName);
}
```

Then, when the parser detects a function call, the application records an edge from the current function to the invoked function.

listeners/CallGraph.java

```
public void exitCall(CymbolParser.CallContext ctx) {
    String funcName = ctx.ID().getText();
    // map current function to the callee
    graph.edge(currentFunctionName, funcName);
}
```

Notice that the function calls can't hide inside nested code blocks or declarations such as in a().

```
void a() { int x = b(); if false then {c(); d();} }
```

The tree walker triggers listener method exitCall() regardless of where it finds function calls.

With the parse tree and class FunctionListener, we can launch a walker with our listener to generate output.

listeners/CallGraph.java
```
ParseTreeWalker walker = new ParseTreeWalker();
FunctionListener collector = new FunctionListener();
walker.walk(collector, tree);
System.out.println(collector.graph.toString());
System.out.println(collector.graph.toDOT());
```

Before dumping the DOT string, that code prints out the list of functions and edges.

```
$ antlr4 Cymbol.g4
$ javac Cymbol*.java CallGraph.java
$ java CallGraph t.cymbol
edges: {main=[fact, a], fact=[print, fact], a=[b, c, d], b=[c], c=[b]},
functions: [main, fact, a, b, c, d, e]
digraph G {
  ranksep=.25;
  edge [arrowsize=.5]
...
```

Naturally, to view the call graph, cut and paste just the output starting with digraph G {.

With very little code, we were able to build a call graph generator in this section. To demonstrate that our Cymbol grammar is reusable, we're going to use it again without modification in the next section to build a totally different application. Not only that, but we'll make two passes over the same tree with two different listeners.

8.4 Validating Program Symbol Usage

To build an interpreter, compiler, or translator for a programming language such as Cymbol, we'd need to verify that Cymbol programs used symbols (identifiers) properly. In this section, we're going to build a Cymbol validator that checks the following conditions:

- Variable references have corresponding definitions that are visible to them (in scope).

- Function references have corresponding definitions (functions can appear in any order).
- Variables are not used as functions.
- Functions are not used as variables.

To check all these conditions, we have a bit of work to do, so this example is going to take a little bit longer than the others to absorb. But, our reward will be a great base from which to build real language tools.

Let's get started by taking a look at some sample Cymbol code with lots of different references, some of which are invalid.

listeners/vars.cymbol
```
int f(int x, float y) {
    g();   // forward reference is ok
    i = 3; // no declaration for i (error)
    g = 4; // g is not variable (error)
    return x + y; // x, y are defined, so no problem
}

void g() {
    int x = 0;
    float y;
    y = 9; // y is defined
    f();   // backward reference is ok
    z();   // no such function (error)
    y();   // y is not function (error)
    x = f; // f is not a variable (error)
}
```

To verify that everything is OK within a program according to the previous conditions, we should print out the list of functions and their local variables plus the list of global symbols (functions and global variables). Further, we should emit an error when we find a problem. For example, for the previous input, let's build an application called CheckSymbols that generates the following:

```
$ java CheckSymbols vars.cymbol
locals:[]
function<f:tINT>:[<x:tINT>, <y:tFLOAT>]
locals:[x, y]
function<g:tVOID>:[]
globals:[f, g]
line 3:4 no such variable: i
line 4:4 g is not a variable
line 13:4 no such function: z
line 14:4 y is not a function
line 15:8 f is not a variable
```

The key to implementing this kind of problem is an appropriate data structure called a *symbol table*. Our application will store symbols in the symbol table and then check identifier references for correctness by looking them up in the symbol table. In the next section, we'll take a peek at what the data structure looks like and then use it to solve the validation problem at hand.

A Crash Course in Symbol Tables

Language implementers typically call the data structure that holds symbols a *symbol table*. The language being implemented dictates a symbol table's structure and complexity. If a programming language allows the same identifier to mean different things in different contexts, the symbol table groups symbols into *scopes*. A scope is just a set of symbols such as a list of parameters for a function or the list of variables and functions in a global scope.

The symbol table by itself is just a repository of symbol definitions—it doesn't do any checking. To validate code, we need to check the variable and function references in expressions against the rules we set up earlier. There are two fundamental operations for symbol validation: *defining* symbols and *resolving* symbols. Defining a symbol means adding it to a scope. Resolving a symbol means figuring out which definition the symbol refers to. In some sense, resolving a symbol means finding the "closest" matching definition. The closest scope is the closest enclosing scope. For example, let's look at another Cymbol example that has symbol definitions in different scopes (labeled with circumscribed numbers).

listeners/vars2.cymbol

```
① int x;
  int y;
② void a()
③ {
      int x;
      x = 1;  // x resolves to current scope, not x in global scope
      y = 2;  // y is not found in current scope, but resolves in global
④     { int y = x; }
  }
⑤ void b(int z)
⑥ { }
```

The global scope, ❶, contains variables x and y as well as the functions a() and b(). Functions live in the global scope, but they also constitute new scopes that hold the functions' parameters, if any: ❷ and ❺. Also nested within a function scope is the function's local code block (❸ and ❻), which constitutes another new scope. Local variables are held in local scopes (❸, ❹, and ❻) nested within the function scopes.

Because symbol x is defined twice, we can't just stuff all of our identifiers into a single set without collision. That's where scopes come in. We keep a set of scopes and allow only a single definition for each identifier in a scope. We also keep a pointer to the parent scope so that we can find symbol definitions in outer scopes. The scopes form a tree.

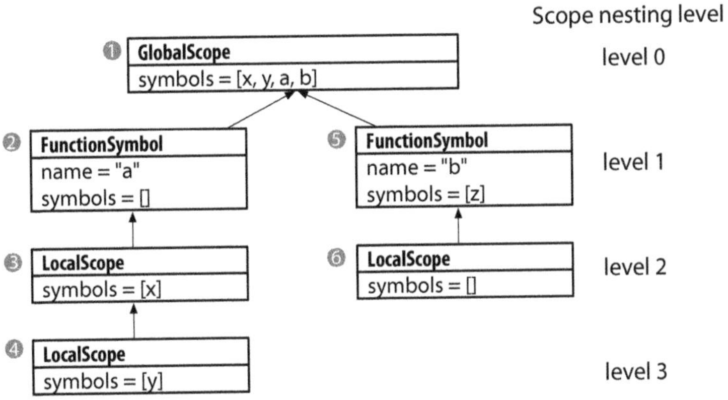

The circled numbers refer to the scope from the source code. The nodes along the path from any scope to the root (global scope) form a stack of scopes. To find a symbol's definition, we start in the scope surrounding the reference and walk up the scope tree until we find its definition.

Rather than reimplement an appropriate symbol table just for this example, I've copied the symbol table source code[2] from Chapter 6 of *Language Implementation Patterns [Par09]*. I encourage you to look through the source for BaseScope, GlobalScope, LocalScope, Symbol, FunctionSymbol, and VariableSymbol to get a feel for the implementation. Together, those classes embody the symbol table, and we'll assume that they just work. With a symbol table in place, we're ready to build our validator.

Validator Architecture

To begin building our validator, let's think about the big picture and form an overall strategy. We can break this problem down according to the key operations: *define* and *resolve*. For definitions, we need to listen for variable and function definition events and insert Symbol objects into the scope surrounding that definition. At the start of a function, we need to "push" a new scope and then pop it at the end of that function definition.

2. http://pragprog.com/book/tpdsl/language-implementation-patterns

To resolve and check symbol references, we need to listen for variable and function name references within expressions. For each reference, we'll verify that there is a matching definition and that the reference uses the symbol properly.

That seems straightforward, but there's a complication: a Cymbol program can call a function defined after it in the source file. We call that a *forward reference*. To support them, we need to make two passes over the parse tree. The first pass, or phase, defines the symbols including the functions, and the second pass does the resolutions. In this way, the second pass can see all functions in the file. Here's the code in the test rig that triggers both passes over the parse tree:

listeners/CheckSymbols.java

```
ParseTreeWalker walker = new ParseTreeWalker();
DefPhase def = new DefPhase();
walker.walk(def, tree);
// create next phase and feed symbol table info from def to ref phase
RefPhase ref = new RefPhase(def.globals, def.scopes);
walker.walk(ref, tree);
```

During the definition phase, we'll be creating lots of scopes. Unless we keep references to them, the garbage collector will throw the scopes out. For the symbol table to survive the transition from the definition to the resolution phase, we need to track those scopes. The most logical place to squirrel them away is in the parse tree itself (or, technically, using an annotation map that associates values with tree nodes). The reference phase can then simply pick up the current scope pointer as it descends the parse tree. Tree nodes associated with functions and local blocks will get pointers to their scopes.

Defining and Resolving Symbols

With our general strategy in mind, let's build our validator, starting with the DefPhase. Our phase classes need three fields: a reference to a global scope, a parse tree annotator to track the scopes we create, and a pointer to the current scope. The listener code for enterFile() starts off the activity, creating the global scope. At the end, exitFile() is responsible for printing the results.

listeners/DefPhase.java

```
public class DefPhase extends CymbolBaseListener {
    ParseTreeProperty<Scope> scopes = new ParseTreeProperty<Scope>();
    GlobalScope globals;
    Scope currentScope; // define symbols in this scope
    public void enterFile(CymbolParser.FileContext ctx) {
        globals = new GlobalScope(null);
        currentScope = globals;
    }
```

```
    public void exitFile(CymbolParser.FileContext ctx) {
        System.out.println(globals);
    }
```

When the parser finds a function declaration, our application needs to create a FunctionSymbol object. FunctionSymbol objects do double duty as a symbol and as the scope containing the arguments. To nest the function scope within the global scope, we "push" the function scope. We do that by setting the function's enclosing scope to be the current scope and resetting the current scope.

listeners/DefPhase.java

```
public void enterFunctionDecl(CymbolParser.FunctionDeclContext ctx) {
    String name = ctx.ID().getText();
    int typeTokenType = ctx.type().start.getType();
    Symbol.Type type = CheckSymbols.getType(typeTokenType);

    // push new scope by making new one that points to enclosing scope
    FunctionSymbol function = new FunctionSymbol(name, type, currentScope);
    currentScope.define(function); // Define function in current scope
    saveScope(ctx, function);      // Push: set function's parent to current
    currentScope = function;       // Current scope is now function scope
}

void saveScope(ParserRuleContext ctx, Scope s) { scopes.put(ctx, s); }
```

Method saveScope() annotates the functionDecl rule node with the function scope so our reference phase can pick it up later. As we leave a function, we pop the function scope so that the current scope is again the global scope.

listeners/DefPhase.java

```
public void exitFunctionDecl(CymbolParser.FunctionDeclContext ctx) {
    System.out.println(currentScope);
    currentScope = currentScope.getEnclosingScope(); // pop scope
}
```

Local scopes work in a similar way. We push a scope in listener method enterBlock() and pop it in exitBlock().

Now that we've taken care of the scopes and function definitions, let's define the arguments and variables.

listeners/DefPhase.java

```
public void exitFormalParameter(CymbolParser.FormalParameterContext ctx) {
    defineVar(ctx.type(), ctx.ID().getSymbol());
}

public void exitVarDecl(CymbolParser.VarDeclContext ctx) {
    defineVar(ctx.type(), ctx.ID().getSymbol());
}
```

```
void defineVar(CymbolParser.TypeContext typeCtx, Token nameToken) {
    int typeTokenType = typeCtx.start.getType();
    Symbol.Type type = CheckSymbols.getType(typeTokenType);
    VariableSymbol var = new VariableSymbol(nameToken.getText(), type);
    currentScope.define(var); // Define symbol in current scope
}
```

That finishes up the definition phase.

To build our reference phase, let's start by setting the current scope to the global scope passed to us from the definition phase.

listeners/RefPhase.java

```
public RefPhase(GlobalScope globals, ParseTreeProperty<Scope> scopes) {
    this.scopes = scopes;
    this.globals = globals;
}
public void enterFile(CymbolParser.FileContext ctx) {
    currentScope = globals;
}
```

Then, as the tree walker triggers enter and exit events for Cymbol functions and blocks, our listener methods keep currentScope up-to-date by accessing values stored in the tree during the definition phase.

listeners/RefPhase.java

```
public void enterFunctionDecl(CymbolParser.FunctionDeclContext ctx) {
    currentScope = scopes.get(ctx);
}
public void exitFunctionDecl(CymbolParser.FunctionDeclContext ctx) {
    currentScope = currentScope.getEnclosingScope();
}

public void enterBlock(CymbolParser.BlockContext ctx) {
    currentScope = scopes.get(ctx);
}
public void exitBlock(CymbolParser.BlockContext ctx) {
    currentScope = currentScope.getEnclosingScope();
}
```

With the scopes set appropriately as the walker proceeds, we can resolve symbols by implementing listener methods for variable references and function calls. When the walker encounters a variable reference, it calls exitVar(), which uses resolve() to try to find the name in the current scope's symbol table. If resolve() doesn't find the symbol in the current scope, it looks up the enclosing scope chain. If necessary, resolve() will look all the way up to the global scope. It returns null if it can't find a suitable definition. If, however, resolve() finds a symbol but it's a function, not a variable, we need to generate an error message.

listeners/RefPhase.java

```
public void exitVar(CymbolParser.VarContext ctx) {
    String name = ctx.ID().getSymbol().getText();
    Symbol var = currentScope.resolve(name);
    if ( var==null ) {
        CheckSymbols.error(ctx.ID().getSymbol(), "no such variable: "+name);
    }
    if ( var instanceof FunctionSymbol ) {
        CheckSymbols.error(ctx.ID().getSymbol(), name+" is not a variable");
    }
}
```

Handling function calls is basically the same. We emit an error if we can't find a definition or we find a variable, not a function.

Finally, here's the build and test sequence that shows the desired output from earlier:

```
$ antlr4 Cymbol.g4
$ javac Cymbol*.java CheckSymbols.java *Phase.java *Scope.java *Symbol.java
$ java CheckSymbols vars.cymbol
locals:[]
function<f:tINT>:[<x:tINT>, <y:tFLOAT>]
...
```

With both passes complete, we've finished our symbol validator. We had to cover a lot ground, but the effort is worthwhile because this example is a great starting point for creating your own language tools. The implementation of the listeners is only about 150 lines of Java, with the symbol table support code coming in at another 100. If you're not actively building a tool that needs a symbol table at the moment, don't sweat the details here. The takeaway is that there is a well-known solution to tracking and validating symbols that's not rocket science. To learn more about symbol table management, I shamelessly suggest you purchase and dig through *Language Implementation Patterns [Par09]*.

If you've been following along pretty well so far in this section of the book, you're in great shape! Not only can you build grammars by digging through language reference manuals, you can bring those grammars to life to perform useful tasks by implementing listeners. Certainly there are language problems out there you might have difficulty with at this point, but your kung fu is very strong.

This chapter finishes Part II of the book. Once you have some experience using these key ANTLR skills, you'll want to jump into the next part to learn about advanced ANTLR usage.

Part III

Advanced Topics

In Part II, we learned how to abstract language structure (syntax) from language samples and reference manuals and then how to formally describe syntax with ANTLR grammars. To develop language applications, we built several tree listeners and visitors that operated on automatically generated parse trees. Now we have the keys to effectively use ANTLR for most problems.

Part III is about advanced usages of ANTLR. First, we'll examine ANTLR's automatic error handling mechanism. Then, we'll explore how to embed code snippets directly within a grammar in order to generate output or perform computations on-the-fly during the parse. Then we'll see how to dynamically turn alternatives in the grammar on and off based upon runtime information using semantic predicates. Finally, we'll perform some lexical black magic.

CHAPTER 9

Error Reporting and Recovery

As we develop a grammar, there will be lots of mistakes to fix just like any piece of software. The resulting parser won't recognize all valid sentences until we finish (and debug) our grammar. In the meantime, informative error messages help us track down grammar problems. Once we have a correct grammar, we then have to deal with ungrammatical sentences entered by users or even ungrammatical sentences generated by other programs gone awry.

In both situations, the manner in which our parser responds to ungrammatical input is an important productivity consideration. In other words, a parser that responds with "Eh?" and bails out upon the first syntax error isn't very useful for us during development or for our users during deployment.

Developers using ANTLR get a good error reporting facility and a sophisticated error recovery strategy for free. ANTLR generates parsers that automatically emit rich error messages upon syntax error and successfully resynchronize much of the time. The parsers even avoid generating more than a single error message for each syntax error.

In this chapter, we'll learn about the automatic error reporting and recovery strategy used by ANTLR-generated parsers. We'll also see how to alter the default error handling mechanism to suit atypical needs and how to customize error messages for a specific application domain.

9.1 A Parade of Errors

The best way to describe ANTLR's error recovery strategy is to watch an ANTLR-generated parser respond to erroneous input. Let's look at a grammar for a simple Java-like language containing class definitions with field and method members. The methods have simple statements and expressions.

We'll use it as the core of the examples in this section and the remainder of the chapter.

errors/Simple.g4
```
grammar Simple;

prog:   classDef+ ; // match one or more class definitions

classDef
    :   'class' ID '{' member+ '}' // a class has one or more members
        {System.out.println("class "+$ID.text);}
    ;

member
    :   'int' ID ';'                       // field definition
        {System.out.println("var "+$ID.text);}
    |   'int' f=ID '(' ID ')' '{' stat '}' // method definition
        {System.out.println("method: "+$f.text);}
    ;

stat:   expr ';'
        {System.out.println("found expr: "+$stat.text);}
    |   ID '=' expr ';'
        {System.out.println("found assign: "+$stat.text);}
    ;

expr:   INT
    |   ID '(' INT ')'
    ;

INT :   [0-9]+ ;
ID  :   [a-zA-Z]+ ;
WS  :   [ \t\r\n]+ -> skip ;
```

The embedded actions print out elements as the parser finds them. We're using embedded actions instead of a parse-tree listener for simplicity and brevity. We'll learn more about actions in Chapter 10, *Attributes and Actions*, on page 177.

First, let's run the parser with some valid input to observe the normal output.

```
⇒ $ antlr4 Simple.g4
⇒ $ javac Simple*.java
⇒ $ grun Simple prog
⇒ class T { int i; }
⇒ EOF
❮ var i
  class T
```

We get no errors from the parser, and it executes the print statements to report proper recognition of variable i and class definition T.

Now, let's try a class with a method definition containing a bogus assignment expression.

```
⇒ $ grun Simple prog -gui
⇒ class T {
⇒   int f(x) { a = 3 4 5; }
⇒ }
⇒ EOF
❮ line 2:19 mismatched input '4' expecting ';'
  method: f
  class T
```

At the 4 token, the parser doesn't find the ; it was expecting and reports an error. The line 2:19 indicates that the offending token was found on the second line at the twentieth character position (character positions start from zero). Because of the -gui option, we also see the parse tree with error nodes highlighted (more on this in a moment).

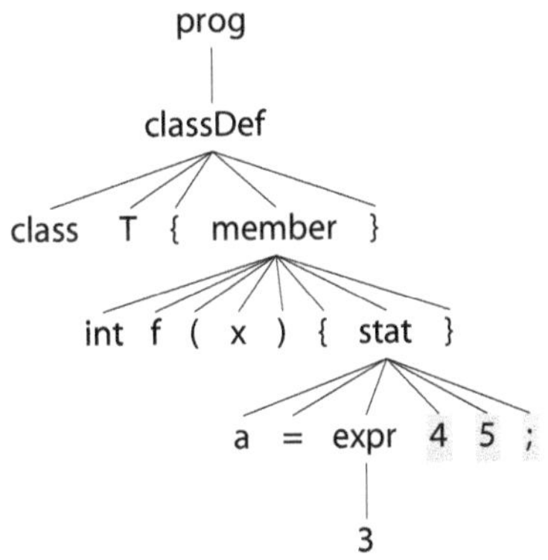

In this case, there are two extra tokens, and the parser gives a generic error message about the mismatch. If there is just a single extra token, however, the parser can be a little bit smarter, indicating it's an extraneous token. In the following test run, there is an extraneous ; after the class name and before the start of the class body:

```
⇒ $ grun Simple prog
⇒ class T ; { int i; }
⇒ EOF
❮ line 1:8 extraneous input ';' expecting '{'
  var i
  class T
```

The parser reports an error at the ; but gives a slightly more informative answer because it knows that the next token is what it was actually looking for. This feature is called *single-token deletion* because the parser can simply pretend the extraneous token isn't there and keep going.

Language Theory Humor

Apparently, the great Niklaus Wirth[a] had an excellent sense of humor. He used to joke that in Europe people called him by "reference" (properly pronouncing his name "Ni-klaus Virt") and that in America people called him by "value" (pronouncing his name "Nickle-less Worth").

At the Compiler Construction 1994 conference, Kristen Nygaard[b] (inventor of Simula) told a story about how, while teaching a language theory course, he commented that "Strong typing is fascism," referring to his preference for languages that are loose with types. A student came up to him afterward and asked why typing hard on the keyboard was fascism.

a. See http://en.wikipedia.org/wiki/Niklaus_Wirth.
b. See http://en.wikipedia.org/wiki/Kristen_Nygaard.

Similarly, the parser can do *single-token insertion* when it detects a missing token. Let's chop off the closing } to see what happens.

```
$ grun Simple prog
class T {
  int f(x) { a = 3; }
EOF
found assign: a=3;
method: f
line 3:0 missing '}' at '<EOF>'
class T
```

The parser reports that it couldn't find the required ending } token.

Another common syntax error occurs when the parser is at a decision point and the remaining input isn't consistent with any of the alternatives of that rule or subrule. For example, if we forget the variable name in a field declaration, neither of the alternatives in rule member will match. The parser reports that there is no viable alternative.

```
$ grun Simple prog
class T { int ; }
EOF
line 1:14 no viable alternative at input 'int;'
class T
```

There is no space between int and ; because we told the lexer to skip() in the whitespace WS() rule.

If there are lexical errors, ANTLR also emits an error message indicating the character or characters it could not match as part of a token. For example, if we send in a completely unknown character, we get a token recognition error.

```
$ grun Simple prog
class # { int i; }
EOF
line 1:6 token recognition error at: '#'
line 1:8 missing ID at '{'
var i
class <missing ID>
```

Since we did not give a valid class name, the single-token insertion mechanism conjured up the name missing ID so that the class name token was non-null. To take control of how the parser conjures up tokens, override getMissingSymbol() in DefaultErrorStrategy (see Section 9.5, *Altering ANTLR's Error Handling Strategy*, on page 173).

You might have noticed that the sample runs in this section show the actions executing as expected, despite the presence of errors. Aside from producing good error messages and resynchronizing the input by consuming tokens, parsers also have to bounce to an appropriate location in the generated code.

For example, when matching members via rule member in rule classDef, the parser should not bail out of classDef upon a bad member definition. That's why the parser is still able to execute those actions—a syntax error does not cause the parser to exit the rule. The parser tries really hard to keep looking for a valid class definition. We'll learn all about this topic in Section 9.3, *Automatic Error Recovery Strategy*, on page 160. But first, let's look at altering standard error reporting to help with grammar debugging and to provide better messages for our users.

9.2 Altering and Redirecting ANTLR Error Messages

By default, ANTLR sends all errors to standard error, but we can change the destination and the content by providing an implementation of interface ANTLRErrorListener. The interface has a syntaxError() method that applies to both lexers and parsers. Method syntaxError() receives all sorts of information about the location of the error as well as the error message. It also receives a reference to the parser, so we can query it about the state of recognition.

For example, here's an error listener (in test rig TestE_Listener.java) that prints out the rule invocation stack followed by the usual error message augmented with offending token information:

errors/TestE_Listener.java

```
public static class VerboseListener extends BaseErrorListener {
    @Override
    public void syntaxError(Recognizer<?, ?> recognizer,
                            Object offendingSymbol,
                            int line, int charPositionInLine,
                            String msg,
                            RecognitionException e)
    {
        List<String> stack = ((Parser)recognizer).getRuleInvocationStack();
        Collections.reverse(stack);
        System.err.println("rule stack: "+stack);
        System.err.println("line "+line+":"+charPositionInLine+" at "+
                           offendingSymbol+": "+msg);
    }

}
```

With this definition, our application can easily add an error listener to the parser before invoking the start rule.

errors/TestE_Listener.java

```
SimpleParser parser = new SimpleParser(tokens);
parser.removeErrorListeners(); // remove ConsoleErrorListener
parser.addErrorListener(new VerboseListener()); // add ours
parser.prog(); // parse as usual
```

Right before we add our error listener, we need to remove the standard console error listener so that we don't get repeated error messages.

Let's see what the error messages look like now for a class definition containing an extra class name and missing field name.

```
⇒ $ javac TestE_Listener.java
⇒ $ java TestE_Listener
⇒ class T T {
⇒   int ;
⇒ }
⇒ EOF
❮ rule stack: [prog, classDef]
  line 1:8 at [@2,8:8='T',<9>,1:8]: extraneous input 'T' expecting '{'
  rule stack: [prog, classDef, member]
  line 2:6 at [@5,18:18=';',<8>,2:6]: no viable alternative at input 'int;'
  class T
```

Stack [prog, classDef] indicates that the parser is in rule classDef, which was called by prog. Notice that the token information contains the character position within the input stream. This is useful for highlighting errors in the input like development environments do. For example, token [@2,8:8='T',<9>,1:8] indicates that it is the third token in the token stream (index 2 from 0), ranges from characters 8 to 8, has token type 9, resides on line 1, and is at character position 8 (counting from 0 and treating tabs as one character).

We can just as easily send that message to a dialog box using Java Swing by altering the syntaxError() method.

errors/TestE_Dialog.java
```
public static class DialogListener extends BaseErrorListener {
    @Override
        public void syntaxError(Recognizer<?, ?> recognizer,
                                Object offendingSymbol,
                                int line, int charPositionInLine,
                                String msg,
                                RecognitionException e)
    {
        List<String> stack = ((Parser)recognizer).getRuleInvocationStack();
        Collections.reverse(stack);
        StringBuilder buf = new StringBuilder();
        buf.append("rule stack: "+stack+" ");
        buf.append("line "+line+":"+charPositionInLine+" at "+
                   offendingSymbol+": "+msg);

        JDialog dialog = new JDialog();
        Container contentPane = dialog.getContentPane();
        contentPane.add(new JLabel(buf.toString()));
        contentPane.setBackground(Color.white);
        dialog.setTitle("Syntax error");
        dialog.pack();
        dialog.setLocationRelativeTo(null);
        dialog.setDefaultCloseOperation(JFrame.DISPOSE_ON_CLOSE);
        dialog.setVisible(true);
    }
}
```

Running test rig TestE_Dialog on input class T { int int i; } pops up a dialog box such as the following:

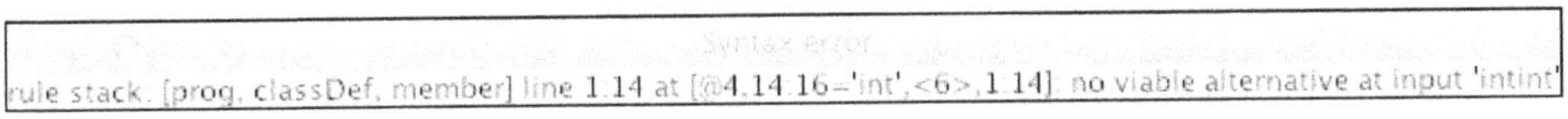

As another example, let's build an error listener, TestE_Listener2.java, that prints out the line with the offending token underlined, as in the following sample run:

```
$ javac TestE_Listener2.java
$ java TestE_Listener2
class T XYZ {
  int ;
}
EOF
line 1:8 extraneous input 'XYZ' expecting '{'
class T XYZ {
        ^^^
line 2:6 no viable alternative at input 'int;'
  int ;
      ^
class T
```

To make things easier, we'll ignore tabs—charPositionInLine isn't the column number because tab size isn't universally defined. Here's an error listener implementation that underlines error locations in the input like we just saw:

errors/TestE_Listener2.java

```
public static class UnderlineListener extends BaseErrorListener {
        public void syntaxError(Recognizer<?, ?> recognizer,
                                Object offendingSymbol,
                                int line, int charPositionInLine,
                                String msg,
                                RecognitionException e)
    {
        System.err.println("line "+line+":"+charPositionInLine+" "+msg);
        underlineError(recognizer,(Token)offendingSymbol,
                       line, charPositionInLine);
    }

    protected void underlineError(Recognizer recognizer,
                                  Token offendingToken, int line,
                                  int charPositionInLine) {
        CommonTokenStream tokens =
            (CommonTokenStream)recognizer.getInputStream();
        String input = tokens.getTokenSource().getInputStream().toString();
        String[] lines = input.split("\n");
        String errorLine = lines[line - 1];
        System.err.println(errorLine);
        for (int i=0; i<charPositionInLine; i++) System.err.print(" ");
        int start = offendingToken.getStartIndex();
        int stop = offendingToken.getStopIndex();
        if ( start>=0 && stop>=0 ) {
            for (int i=start; i<=stop; i++) System.err.print("^");
        }
        System.err.println();
    }
}
```

There's one final thing to know about error listeners. When the parser detects an ambiguous input sequence, it notifies the error listener. The default error listener, ConsoleErrorListener, however, doesn't print anything to the console. As we saw in Section 2.3, *You Can't Put Too Much Water into a Nuclear Reactor*, on page 14, ambiguous input likely indicates an error in our grammar; the parser should not inform our users. Let's look back at the ambiguous grammar from that section that can match input f(); in two different ways.

errors/Ambig.g4

```
grammar Ambig;

stat: expr ';'        // expression statement
    | ID '(' ')' ';'  // function call statement
    ;

expr: ID '(' ')'
    | INT
    ;

INT :   [0-9]+ ;
ID  :   [a-zA-Z]+ ;
WS  :   [ \t\r\n]+ -> skip ;
```

If we test the grammar, we don't see a warning for the ambiguous input.

```
⇒ $ antlr4 Ambig.g4
⇒ $ javac Ambig*.java
⇒ $ grun Ambig stat
⇒ f();
⇒ EOF
```

To hear about it when the parser detects an ambiguity, tell the parser to use an instance of DiagnosticErrorListener using addErrorListener().

```
parser.removeErrorListeners(); // remove ConsoleErrorListener
parser.addErrorListener(new DiagnosticErrorListener());
```

You should also inform the parser that you're interested in all ambiguity warnings, not just those it can detect quickly. In the interest of efficiency, ANTLR's decision-making mechanism doesn't always chase down full ambiguity information. Here's how to make the parser report all ambiguities:

```
parser.getInterpreter()
    .setPredictionMode(PredictionMode.LL_EXACT_AMBIG_DETECTION);
```

If you're using TestRig via the grun alias, use option -diagnostics to have it use DiagnosticErrorListener instead of the default console error listener (and turn on LL_EXACT_AMBIG_DETECTION).

```
⇒ $ grun Ambig stat -diagnostics
⇒ f();
⇒ EOF
❮ line 1:3 reportAttemptingFullContext d=0, input='f();'
  line 1:3 reportAmbiguity d=0: ambigAlts={1, 2}, input='f();'
```

The output shows that the parser also calls reportAttemptingFullContext(). ANTLR calls this method when *SLL(*)* parsing fails and the parser engages the more powerful full *ALL(*)* mechanism. See Section 13.7, *Maximizing Parser Speed*, on page 245.

It's a good idea to use the diagnostics error listener during development since the ANTLR tool can't warn you about ambiguous grammar constructs statically (when generating parsers). Only the parser can detect ambiguities in ANTLR v4. It's the difference between static typing in Java, say, and the dynamic typing in Python.

Improvements in ANTLR v4

There are two error-related important improvements in v4: ANTLR does much better inline error recovery and makes it much easier for programmers to alter the error handling strategy. When Sun Microsystems was building a parser for JavaFX with ANTLR v3, it noticed that a single misplaced semicolon could force the parser to stop looking for a list of, say, class members (via member+). Now, v4 parsers attempt to resynchronize before and during subrule recognition instead of gobbling tokens and exiting the current rule. The second improvement lets programmers specify an error handling mechanism following the Strategy pattern.

Now that we have a good idea about the kinds of messages ANTLR parsers generate and how to tweak and redirect them, let's explore error recovery.

9.3 Automatic Error Recovery Strategy

Error recovery is what allows the parser to continue after finding a syntax error. In principle, the best error recovery would come from the human touch in a handwritten recursive-descent parser. In my experience, though, it's really tough to get good error recovery by hand because it's so tedious and easy to screw up. In this latest version of ANTLR, I've incorporated every bit of jujitsu I've learned and picked up over the years to provide good error recovery automatically for ANTLR grammars.

ANTLR's error recovery mechanism is based upon Niklaus Wirth's early ideas in *Algorithms + Data Structures = Programs [Wir78]* (as well as Rodney Topor's *A Note on Error Recovery in Recursive Descent Parsers [Top82]*) but also includes

Josef Grosch's good ideas from his CoCo parser generator (*Efficient and Comfortable Error Recovery in Recursive Descent Parsers [Gro90]*).

Here is how ANTLR uses those ideas together in a nutshell: parsers perform *single-token insertion* and *single-token deletion* upon mismatched token errors if possible. If not, parsers gobble up tokens until they find a token that could reasonably follow the current rule and then return, continuing as if nothing had happened. In this section, we'll see what those terms mean and explore how ANTLR recovers from errors in various situations. Let's begin with the fundamental recovery strategy that ANTLR uses.

Recovery by Scanning for Following Tokens

When faced with truly borked-up input, the current rule can't continue, so the parser recovers by gobbling up tokens until it thinks that it has resynchronized and then returns to the calling rule. We can call this the *sync-and-return* strategy. Some people call this "panic mode," but it works remarkably well. The parser knows it can't match the current input with the current rule. It can throw out tokens only until the lookahead is consistent with something that should match after the parser exits from the rule. For example, if there is a syntax error within an assignment statement, it makes a great deal of sense to throw out tokens until the parser sees a semicolon or other statement terminator. Drastic, but effective. As we'll see, ANTLR tries to recover within the rule before falling back on this basic strategy.

Each ANTLR-generated rule method is wrapped in a `try-catch` that responds to syntax errors by reporting the error and attempting to recover before returning.

```
try {
    ...
}
catch (RecognitionException re) {
    _errHandler.reportError(this, re);
    _errHandler.recover(this, re);
}
```

We'll look at the error handling strategy in more detail in Section 9.5, *Altering ANTLR's Error Handling Strategy*, on page 173, but, for now, we can summarize `recover()` as consuming tokens until it finds one in the *resynchronization set*. The resynchronization set is the union of rule reference *following sets* for all the rules on the invocation stack. The following set for a rule reference is the set of tokens that can match immediately following that reference and without leaving the current rule. So, for example, given alternative `assign ';'`, the following set for rule reference assign is {';'}. If the alternative were just assign, the following set would be empty.

It's worthwhile going through an example to lock in what resynchronization sets contain. Consider the following grammar, and imagine that, at each rule invocation, the parser tracks the following set for every rule invocation:

errors/F.g4

```
grammar F;
group
    : '[' expr ']'      // Tokens following ref to expr: {']'}
    | '(' expr ')'      // Tokens following ref to expr: {')'}
    ;
expr: atom '^' INT ;    // Tokens following ref to atom: {'^'}
atom: ID
    | INT
    ;

INT :   [0-9]+ ;
ID  :   [a-zA-Z]+ ;
WS  :   [ \t\r\n]+ -> skip ;
```

Consider the parse tree on the left for input [1^2] in the following diagram:

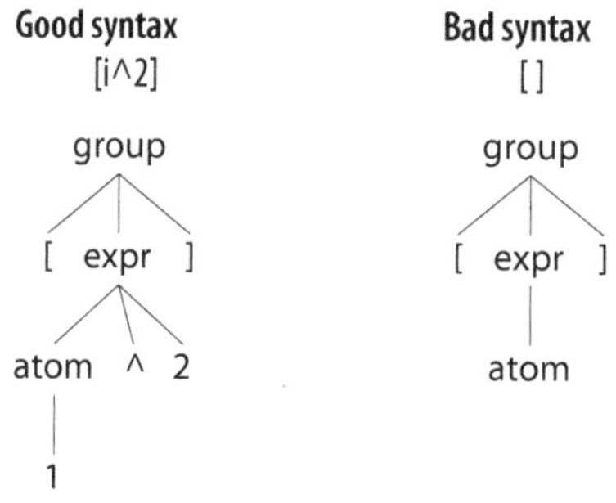

When matching token 1 in rule atom, the call stack is [group, expr, atom] (group called expr, which called atom). By looking at the call stack, we know precisely the set of tokens that can follow every rule the parser has called to get us to the current position. Following sets consider tokens only within the current rule so that, at runtime, we can combine just the sets associated with the current call stack. In other words, we can't get to rule expr from both alternatives of group at the same time.

Combining the following sets pulled from the comments in grammar F, we get a resynchronization set of {'^', ']'}. To see why this is the set we want, let's watch what happens when the parser encounters erroneous input []. We get the parse tree shown on the right in the earlier side-by-side diagram. In atom, the parser discovers that the current token,], isn't consistent with either alternative of atom. To resynchronize, the parser consumes tokens until it finds a token from the resynchronization set. In this case, current token] starts out as a member of the resynchronization set so the parser doesn't actually consume any tokens to resynchronize in atom.

After finishing the recovery process in rule atom, the parser returns to rule expr but immediately discovers that it doesn't have the ^ token. The process repeats itself, and the parser consumes tokens until it finds something in the resynchronization set for rule expr. The resynchronization set for expr is the following set for the expr reference in the first alternative of group: { ']' }. Again, the parser does not consume anything and exits expr, returning to the first alternative of rule group. Now, the parser finds exactly what it is looking for following the reference to expr. It successfully matches the ']' in group, and the parser is now properly resynchronized.

During recovery, ANTLR parsers avoid emitting cascading error messages (an idea borrowed from Grosch). That is, parsers emit a single error message for each syntax error until they successfully recover from that error. Through the use of a simple Boolean variable, set upon syntax error, the parser avoids emitting further errors until the parser successfully matches a token and resets the variable. (See field errorRecoveryMode in class DefaultErrorStrategy.)

FOLLOW Sets vs. Following Sets

Those familiar with language theory will wonder whether the resynchronization set for rule atom is just *FOLLOW*(atom), the set of all viable tokens that can follow references to atom in some context. It isn't that simple, unfortunately, and the resynchronization sets must be computed dynamically to get the set of tokens that can follow the rule in a particular context rather than in all contexts. *FOLLOW*(expr) is { ')', ']' }, which includes all tokens that can follow references to expr in both contexts (alternatives 1 and 2 of group). Clearly, though, at runtime the parser can call expr from only one location at a time. Note that *FOLLOW*(atom) is '^', and if the parser resynchronized to that token instead of resynchronization set {'^', ']'}, it would consume until the end of file because there is no '^' on the input stream.

In many cases, ANTLR can recover more intelligently than consuming until the resynchronization set and returning from the current rule. It pays to attempt to "repair" the input and continue within the same rule. Over the next few sections, we'll look at how the parser recovers from mismatched tokens and errors within subrules.

Recovering from Mismatched Tokens

One of the most common operations during parsing is "match token." For every token reference, T, in the grammar, the parser invokes match(T). If the current token isn't T, match() notifies the error listener(s) and attempts to resynchronize. To resynchronize, it has three choices. It can delete a token, it can conjure one up, or it can punt and throw an exception to engage the basic sync-and-return mechanism.

Deleting the current token is the easiest way to resynchronize, if it makes sense to do so. Let's revisit rule classDef from our simple class definition language in grammar Simple.

errors/Simple.g4

```
classDef
    :   'class' ID '{' member+ '}' // a class has one or more members
        {System.out.println("class "+$ID.text);}
    ;
```

Given input class 9 T { int i; }, the parser will delete 9 and keep going within the rule to match the class body. The following image illustrates the state of the input after the parser has consumed class:

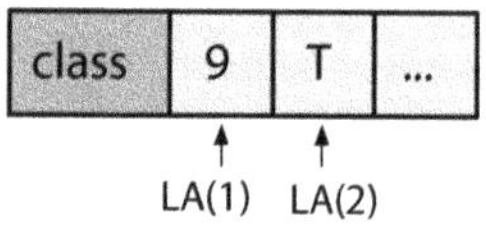

The LA(1) and LA(2) labels mark the first token of lookahead (the current token) and the second token of lookahead. The match(ID) expects LA(1) to be an ID, but it's not. However, the next token, LA(2), is in fact an ID. To recover, we just have to delete the current token (as noise), consume the ID we were expecting, and exit match().

If the parser can't resynchronize by deleting a token, it attempts to insert a token instead. Let's say we forgot the ID so that classDef sees input class { int i; }. After matching class, the input state looks like this:

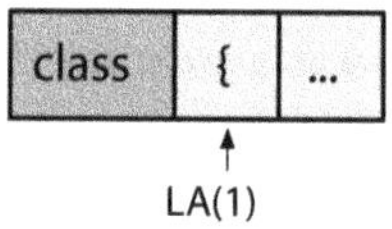

The parser invokes match(ID) but instead of an identifier finds {. In this situation, the parser knows that the { is what it will need next since that is what follows the ID reference in classDef. To resynchronize, the match() can pretend to see the identifier and return, thus allowing the next match('{') call to succeed.

That works great if we ignore embedded actions, such as the print statement that references the class name identifier. The print statement references the missing token via $ID.text and will cause an exception if the token is null. Rather than simply pretending the token exists, the error handler conjures one up; see getMissingSymbol() in DefaultErrorStrategy. The conjured token has the token type that the parser expected and takes line and character position information from the current input token, LA(1). This conjured token also prevents exceptions in listeners and visitors that reference the missing token.

The easiest way to see what's going on is to look at the parse tree, which shows how the parser recognizes all the tokens. In the case of errors, the parse tree highlights in red the tokens that the parser deletes or conjures up during resynchronization. For input class { int i; } and grammar Simple, we get the following parse tree:

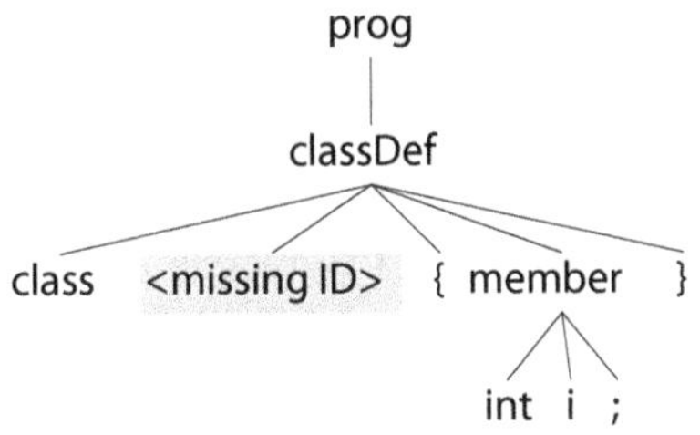

The parser also executes the embedded print actions without throwing an exception since error recovery conjures up a valid Token object for $ID.

```
⇒ $ grun Simple prog -gui
⇒ class { int i; }
⇒ EOF
❮ line 1:6 missing ID at '{'
  var i
  class <missing ID>
```

Naturally, an identifier with text <missing ID> isn't really useful for whatever goal we're trying to accomplish, but at least error recovery doesn't induce a bunch of null pointer exceptions.

Now that we know how ANTLR does in-rule recovery for simple token references, let's explore how it recovers from errors before and during subrule recognition.

Recovering from Errors in Subrules

Years ago the JavaFX group at Sun contacted me because their ANTLR-generated parser didn't recover well in certain cases. It turns out that the parser was bailing out of subrule loops like member+ at the first whiff of trouble, forcing sync-and-return recovery for the surrounding rule. A small error in a member declaration like var width Number; (missing a colon after width) would force the parser to skip all of the remaining members.

Jim Idle, an ANTLR mailing list contributor and consultant, came up with what I call "Jim Idle's magic sync" error recovery. His solution was to manually insert references to an empty rule into the grammar that contained a special action that triggered error recovery when necessary. ANTLR v4 now automatically inserts synchronization checks at the start and at the loop continuation test to avoid such drastic recovery. The mechanism looks like this:

Subrule start At the start of any subrule, parsers attempt single-token deletion. But, unlike token matches, parsers don't attempt single-token insertion. ANTLR would have a hard time conjuring up a token because it would have to guess which of several alternatives would ultimately be successful.

Looping subrule continuation test If the subrule is a looping construct, (...)* or (...)+, the parser tries to recover aggressively upon error to stay in the loop. After successfully matching an alternative of the loop, the parser consumes until it finds a token consistent with one of these sets:

(a) Another iteration of the loop

(b) What follows the loop

(c) The resynchronization set of the current

Let's look at single-token deletion in front of a subrule first. Consider the looping member+ construct in rule classDef of grammar Simple. If we stutter and type an extra {, the member+ subrule will delete the extra token before jumping into member, as shown in the following parse tree:

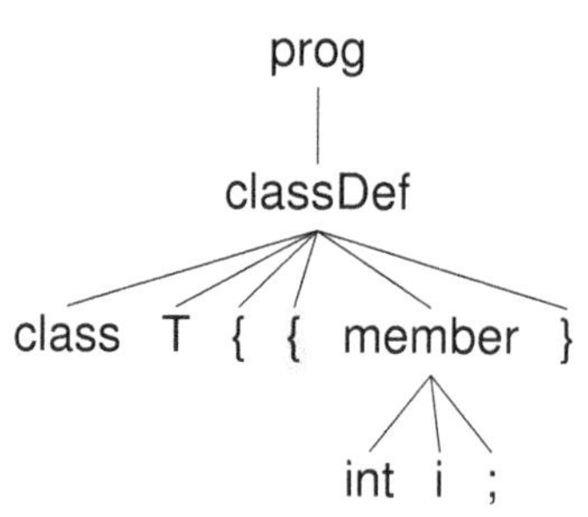

The following session confirms proper recovery because it correctly identifies variable i:

```
⇒ $ grun Simple prog
⇒ class T {{ int i; }
⇒ EOF
❮ line 1:9 extraneous input '{' expecting 'int'
  var i
  class T
```

Now let's try some really messed up input and see whether the member+ loop can recover and continue looking for members.

```
⇒ $ grun Simple prog
⇒ class T {{
⇒   int x;
⇒   y;;;
⇒   int z;
⇒ }
⇒ EOF
❮ line 1:9 extraneous input '{' expecting 'int'
  var x
  line 3:2 extraneous input 'y' expecting {'int', '}'}
  var z
  class T
```

We know that the parser resynchronized and stayed within the loop because it identified variable z. The parser gobbles up y;;; until it sees the start of another member (set *(c)* earlier) and then loops back to member. If the input did not include int z;, the parser would have gobbled until it had seen } (set *(b)* above) and exited the loop. The parse tree highlights the deleted tokens and illustrates that the parser still interpreted int z; as a valid member.

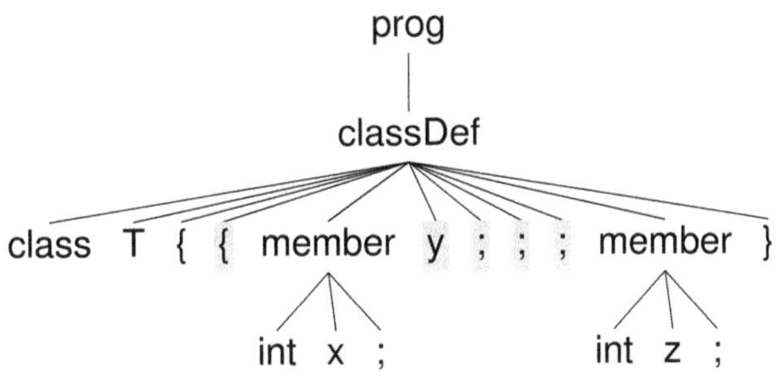

If the user provides rule member with bad syntax and also forgets the closing } of a class, we wouldn't want the parser to scan until it finds }. Parser resynchronization could throw out an entire following class definition looking for }. Instead, the parser stops gobbling if it sees a token in set *(c)*, as shown the following session:

```
$ grun Simple prog
class T {
  int x;
  ;
class U { int y; }
EOF
var x
line 3:2 extraneous input ';' expecting {'int', '}'}
class T
var y
class U
```

The parser stops resynchronization when it sees keyword class, as we can see from the parse tree.

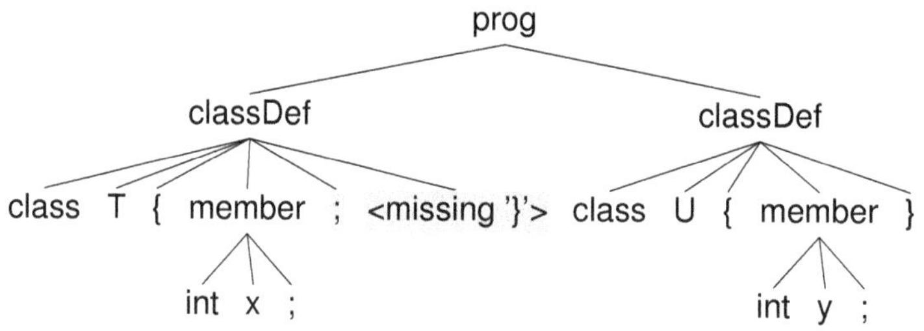

Besides the recognition of tokens and subrules, parsers can also fail to match semantic predicates.

Catching Failed Semantic Predicates

We've gotten only a taste of semantic predicates at this point, but it's appropriate to discuss what happens upon failed predicates in this error handling chapter. We'll look at predicates in depth in Chapter 11, *Altering the Parse with Semantic Predicates*, on page 191. For now, let's treat semantic predicates like assertions. They specify conditions that must be true at runtime for the parser to get past them. If a predicate evaluates to false, the parser throws a FailedPredicateException exception, which is caught by the catch of the current rule. The parser reports an error and does the generic sync-and-return recovery.

Let's look at an example that uses a semantic predicate to restrict the number of integers in a vector, very similar to the grammar in *Altering the Parse with Semantic Predicates*, on page 50. Rule ints matches up to max integers.

errors/Vec.g4

```
vec4:   '[' ints[4] ']' ;
ints[int max]
locals [int i=1]
    :   INT ( ',' {$i++;} {$i<=$max}? INT )*
    ;
```

Given one too many integers, as in the following session, we see an error message and get error recovery that throws out the extra comma and integers:

```
⇒ $ antlr4 Vec.g4
⇒ $ javac Vec*.java
⇒ $ grun Vec vec4
⇒ [1,2,3,4,5,6]
⇒ EOF
❮ line 1:9 rule ints failed predicate: {$i<=$max}?
```

The parse tree shows that the parser detected the error at the fifth integer.

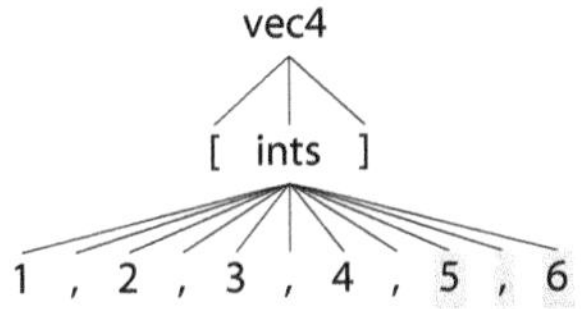

The {$i<=$max} error message might be helpful to us as grammar designers, but it's certainly not helpful to our users. We can change the message from a chunk of code to something a little more readable by using the fail option on the semantic predicate. For example, here is the ints rule again but with an action that computes a readable string:

errors/VecMsg.g4

```
ints[int max]
locals [int i=1]
    :   INT ( ',' {$i++;} {$i<=$max}?<fail={"exceeded max "+$max}> INT )*
    ;
```

Now we get a better message for the same input.

```
⇒ $ antlr4 VecMsg.g4
⇒ $ javac VecMsg*.java
⇒ $ grun VecMsg vec4
⇒ [1,2,3,4,5,6]
⇒ EOF
❮ line 1:9 rule ints exceeded max 4
```

The fail option takes either a string literal in single quotes or an action that evaluates to a string. The action is handy if you'd like to execute a function when a predicate fails. Just use an action that calls a function such as {...}?<fail={failedMaxTest()}>.

A word of caution about using semantic predicates to test for input validity. In the vector example, the predicate enforces syntactic rules, so it's OK to throw an exception and try to recover. If, on the other hand, we have a syntactically valid but semantically invalid construct, it's not a good idea to use a semantic predicate.

Imagine that, in some language, we can assign any value to a variable except 0. That means assignment x = 0; is syntactically valid but semantically invalid. Certainly we have to emit an error to the user, but we should not trigger error recovery. x = 0; is perfectly legal syntactically. In a sense, the parser will automatically "recover" from the error. Here's a simple grammar that demonstrates the issue:

errors/Pred.g4
```
assign
    : ID '=' v=INT {$v.int>0}? ';'
      {System.out.println("assign "+$ID.text+" to ");}
    ;
```

If the predicate in rule assign throws an exception, the sync-and-return behavior will throw out the ; after the predicate. This might work out just fine, but we risk an imperfect resynchronization. A better solution is to emit an error manually and let the parser continue matching the correct syntax. So, instead of the predicate, we should use a simple action with a conditional.

```
{if ($v.int==0) notifyListeners("values must be > 0");}
```

Now that we've looked at all the situations that can trigger error recovery, it's worth pointing out a potential flaw in the mechanism. Given that the parser sometimes doesn't consume any tokens during a single recovery attempt, it's possible that overall recovery could go into an infinite loop. If we recover without consuming a token and get back to the same location in the parser, we will recover again without consuming a token. In the next section, we'll see how ANTLR avoids this pitfall.

Error Recovery Fail-Safe

ANTLR parsers have a built-in fail-safe to guarantee error recovery terminates. If we reach the same parser location and have the same input position, the parser forces a token consumption before attempting recovery. Returning to the simple Simple grammar from the start of this chapter, let's look at a sample input that trips the fail-safe. If we add an extra int token in a field definition, the parser detects an error and tries to recover. As we'll see in the next test run, the parser will call recover() and try to restart parsing multiple times before correctly resynchronizing (Figure 9, *Parser resynchronization*, on page 171).

The right parse tree in the diagram in Figure 10, *Parse trees for good and bad syntax*, on page 171 shows that there are three invocations of member from classDef.

```
⇒ $ grun Simple prog
⇒ class T {
⇒   int int x;
⇒ }
⇒ EOF
❮ line 2:6 no viable alternative at input 'intint'
  var x
  class T
```

Figure 9—Parser resynchronization

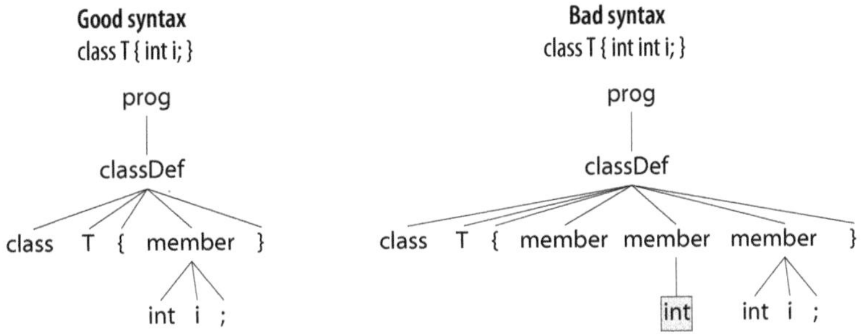

Figure 10—Parse trees for good and bad syntax

The first reference doesn't match anything, but the second one matches the extraneous int token. The third attempt at matching a member matches the proper int x; sequence.

Let's walk through the exact sequence of events. The parser is in rule member when it detects the first error.

errors/Simple.g4

```
member
    :   'int' ID ';'                        // field definition
        {System.out.println("var "+$ID.text);}
    |   'int' f=ID '(' ID ')' '{' stat '}' // method definition
        {System.out.println("method: "+$f.text);}
    ;
```

Input int int doesn't fit either alternative of member, so the parser engages the sync-and-return error recovery strategy. It emits the first error message and consumes until it sees a token in the resynchronization set for call stack [prog, classDef, member].

Because of the classDef+ and member+ loops in the grammar, computing the resynchronization set is a little complicated. Following the call to member, the parser could loop back and find another member or exit the loop and find the '}' that closes the class definition. Following the call to classDef, the parser could loop back to see the start of another class or simply exit prog. So, for call stack [prog, classDef, member], the resynchronization set is {'int', '}', 'class'}.

At this point, the parser recovers without consuming a token because the current input token, int, is in the resynchronization set. It simply returns to the caller: the member+ loop in classDef. The loop then tries to match another member. Unfortunately, since it has not consumed any tokens, the parser detects another error when it returns to member (though it hushes the spurious error message, by virtue of the errorRecovery flag).

During recovery for this second error, the parser trips the fail-safe because it has arrived at the same parser location and input position. The fail-safe forces a token consumption before attempting resynchronization. Since int is in the resynchronization set, it doesn't consume a second token. Fortunately, that's exactly what we want because the parser is now properly resynchronized. The next three tokens represent a valid member definition: int x;. The parser returns once again from member to the loop in classDef. For the third time, we go back to member, but now parsing will succeed.

So, that's the story with ANTLR's automatic error recovery mechanism. Now let's look at a manual mechanism that can sometimes provide better error recovery.

9.4 Error Alternatives

Some syntax errors are so common that it's worth treating them specially. For example, programmers often have the wrong number of parentheses at the end of a function call with nested arguments. To handle these cases specially, all we have to do is add alternatives to match the erroneous but common syntax. The following grammar recognizes function calls with a single argument, possibly with nested parentheses in the argument. Rule fcall has two so-called *error alternatives*.

errors/Call.g4

```
stat:   fcall ';' ;
fcall
    :   ID '(' expr ')'
    |   ID '(' expr ')' ')' {notifyErrorListeners("Too many parentheses");}
    |   ID '(' expr         {notifyErrorListeners("Missing closing ')'");}
    ;

expr:   '(' expr ')'
    |   INT
    ;
```

While these error alternatives can make an ANTLR-generated parser work a little harder to choose between alternatives, they don't in any way confuse the parser. Just like any other alternative, the parser matches them if they are consistent with the current input. For example, let's try some input sequences that match the error alternatives, starting with a valid function call.

```
⇒ $ antlr4 Call.g4
⇒ $ javac Call*.java
⇒ $ grun Call stat
⇒ f(34);
⇒ EOF
⇒ $ grun Call stat
⇒ f((34);
⇒ EOF
❮ line 1:6 Missing closing ')'
⇒ $ grun Call stat
⇒ f((34)));
⇒ EOF
❮ line 1:8 Too many parentheses
```

At this point, we've learned quite a bit about the error messages that ANTLR parsers can generate and also how parsers recover from errors in lots of different situations. We've also seen how to customize error messages and redirect them to different error listeners. All of this functionality is controlled and encapsulated in an object that specifies ANTLR's error handling strategy. In the next section, we'll look at that strategy in detail to learn more about customizing how parsers respond to errors.

9.5 Altering ANTLR's Error Handling Strategy

The default error handling mechanism works very well, but there are a few atypical situations in which we might want to alter it. First, we might want to disable some of the in-line error handling because of its runtime overhead. Second, we might want to bail out of the parser upon the first syntax error. For example, when parsing a command line for a shell like bash, there's no point in trying to recover from errors. We can't risk executing that command anyway, so the parser can bail out at the first sign of trouble.

To explore the error handling strategy, take a look at interface ANTLRErrorStrategy and its concrete implementation class DefaultErrorStrategy. That class holds everything associated with the default error handling behavior. ANTLR parsers signal that object to report errors and recover. For example, here's the catch block inside of each ANTLR-generated rule function:

```
_errHandler.reportError(this, re);
_errHandler.recover(this, re);
```

_errHandler is a variable holding a reference to an instance of DefaultErrorStrategy. Methods reportError() and recover() embody the error reporting and sync-and-return functionality. reportError() delegates error reporting to one of three methods, according to the type of exception thrown.

Turning to our first atypical situation, let's decrease the runtime burden that error handling places on the parser. Take a look at this code that ANTLR generates for the member+ subrule in grammar Simple:

```
_errHandler.sync(this);
_la = _input.LA(1);
do {
    setState(22); member();
    setState(26);
    _errHandler.sync(this);
    _la = _input.LA(1);
} while ( _la==6 );
```

For applications where it's safe to assume the input is syntactically correct, such as network protocols, we might as well avoid the overhead of detecting and recovering from errors in subrules. We can do that by subclassing DefaultErrorStrategy and overriding sync() with an empty method. The Java compiler would likely then inline and eliminate the _errHandler.sync(this) calls. We'll see how to notify the parser to use a different error strategy through the next example.

The other atypical situation is bailing out of the parser upon the first syntax error. To make this work, we have to override three key recovery methods, as shown in the following code:

errors/BailErrorStrategy.java

```
import org.antlr.v4.runtime.*;

public class BailErrorStrategy extends DefaultErrorStrategy {
    /** Instead of recovering from exception e, rethrow it wrapped
     *  in a generic RuntimeException so it is not caught by the
     *  rule function catches.  Exception e is the "cause" of the
     *  RuntimeException.
     */

    @Override
    public void recover(Parser recognizer, RecognitionException e) {
        throw new RuntimeException(e);
    }
```

```
    /** Make sure we don't attempt to recover inline; if the parser
     *  successfully recovers, it won't throw an exception.
     */
    @Override
    public Token recoverInline(Parser recognizer)
        throws RecognitionException
    {
        throw new RuntimeException(new InputMismatchException(recognizer));
    }

    /** Make sure we don't attempt to recover from problems in subrules. */
    @Override
    public void sync(Parser recognizer) { }
}
```

For a test rig, we can reuse our typical boilerplate code. In addition to creating and launching the parser, we need to create a new BailErrorStrategy instance and tell the parser to use it instead of the default strategy.

errors/TestBail.java

```
parser.setErrorHandler(new BailErrorStrategy());
```

While we're at it, we should also bail out at the first lexical error. To do that, we have to override method recover() in Lexer.

errors/TestBail.java

```
public static class BailSimpleLexer extends SimpleLexer {
    public BailSimpleLexer(CharStream input) { super(input); }
    public void recover(LexerNoViableAltException e) {
        throw new RuntimeException(e); // Bail out
    }
}
```

Let's try a lexical error first by inserting a wacky # character at the beginning of the input. The lexer throws an exception that blasts control flow all the way out to the main program.

```
⇒ $ antlr4 Simple.g4
⇒ $ javac Simple*.java TestBail.java
⇒ $ java TestBail
⇒ # class T { int i; }
⇒ EOF
❮ line 1:1 token recognition error at: '#'
  Exception in thread "main"
  java.lang.RuntimeException: LexerNoViableAltException('#')
  at TestBail$BailSimpleLexer.recover(TestBail.java:9)
  at org.antlr.v4.runtime.Lexer.nextToken(Lexer.java:165)
  at org.antlr.v4.runtime.BufferedTokenStream.fetch(BufferedT...Stream.java:139)
  at org.antlr.v4.runtime.BufferedTokenStream.sync(BufferedT...Stream.java:133)
  at org.antlr.v4.runtime.CommonTokenStream.setup(CommonTokenStream.java:129)
  at org.antlr.v4.runtime.CommonTokenStream.LT(CommonTokenStream.java:111)
```

```
at org.antlr.v4.runtime.Parser.enterRule(Parser.java:424)
at SimpleParser.prog(SimpleParser.java:68)
at TestBail.main(TestBail.java:23)
...
```

The parser also bails out at the first syntax error (a missing class name, in this case).

```
⇒ $ java TestBail
⇒ class { }
⇒ EOF
❮ Exception in thread "main" java.lang.RuntimeException:
    org.antlr.v4.runtime.InputMismatchException
  ...
```

To demonstrate the flexibility of the ANTLRErrorStrategy interface, let's finish up by altering how the parser reports errors. To alter the standard message, "no viable alternative at input X," we can override reportNoViableAlternative() and change the message to something different.

errors/MyErrorStrategy.java

```
import org.antlr.v4.runtime.*;
public class MyErrorStrategy extends DefaultErrorStrategy {
    @Override
    public void reportNoViableAlternative(Parser parser,
                                          NoViableAltException e)
        throws RecognitionException
    {
        // ANTLR generates Parser subclasses from grammars and
        // Parser extends Recognizer. Parameter parser is a
        // pointer to the parser that detected the error
        String msg = "can't choose between alternatives"; // nonstandard msg
        parser.notifyErrorListeners(e.getOffendingToken(), msg, e);
    }
}
```

Remember, though, that if all we want to do is change *where* error messages go, we can specify an ANTLRErrorListener as we did in Section 9.2, *Altering and Redirecting ANTLR Error Messages*, on page 155. To learn how to completely override how ANTLR generates code for catching exceptions, see *Catching Exceptions*, on page 268.

We've covered all of the important error reporting and recovery facilities within ANTLR. Because of ANTLRErrorListener and ANTLRErrorStategy interfaces, we have great flexibility over where error messages go, what those messages are, and how the parser recovers from errors.

In the next chapter, we're going to learn how to embed code snippets called *actions* directly within the grammar.

CHAPTER 10

Attributes and Actions

So far, we've isolated our application-specific code to parse-tree walkers, which means that our code has always executed after parsing is complete. As we'll see in the next few chapters, some language applications require executing application-specific code while parsing. To do that, we need the ability to inject code snippets, called *actions*, directly into the code ANTLR generates. Our first goal, then, is to learn how to embed actions in parsers and lexers and to figure out what we can put in those actions.

Keep in mind that, in general, it's a good idea to avoid entangling grammars and application-specific code. Grammars without actions are easier to read, aren't tied to a particular target language, and aren't tied to a specific application. Still, embedded actions can be useful for three reasons.

- *Simplicity*: Sometimes it's easier just to stick in a few actions and avoid creating a tree listener or visitor.
- *Efficiency*: In resource-critical applications, we might not want to waste the time or memory needed to build a parse tree.
- *Predicated parsing*: In rare cases, we can't parse properly without referencing data collected previously in the input stream. Some grammars need to build up a symbol table and then recognize future input differently, depending on whether an identifier is, say, a type or a method. We'll explore this in Chapter 11, *Altering the Parse with Semantic Predicates*, on page 191.

Actions are arbitrary chunks of code written in the target language (the language in which ANTLR generates code) enclosed in {...}. We can do whatever we want in these actions as long as they are valid target language statements. Typically, actions operate on the attributes of tokens and rule references. For example, we can ask for the text of a token or the text matched by an entire rule invocation. Using data derived from token and rule references, we can print things out and perform arbitrary computations. Rules also allow parameters and return values so we can pass data around between rules.

We're going to learn about grammar actions by exploring three examples. First, we're going to build a calculator with the same functionality as that in Section 7.4, *Labeling Rule Alternatives for Precise Event Methods*, on page 119. Second, we'll add some actions to the CSV grammar (from Section 6.1, *Parsing Comma-Separated Values*, on page 86) to explore rule and token attributes. In the third example, we'll learn about actions in lexer rules by building a grammar for a language whose keywords aren't known until runtime.

It's time to get our hands dirty, starting with an action-based calculator implementation.

10.1 Building a Calculator with Grammar Actions

Let's revisit the expression grammar from Section 4.2, *Building a Calculator Using a Visitor*, on page 40 to learn about actions. In that section, we built a calculator using a tree visitor that evaluated expressions such as the following:

actions/t.expr

```
x = 1
x
x+2*3
```

Our goal here is to reproduce that same functionality, but without using a visitor and without even building a parse tree. Moreover, we'll employ a little trick to make it interactive, meaning we get results when we hit Return, not at the end of the input. Our examples so far have scarfed up the entire input and then processed the resulting parse trees.

As we go through this section, we're going to learn how to put generated parsers into packages, define parser fields and methods, insert actions within rule alternatives, label grammar elements for use within actions, and define rule return values.

Using Actions Outside of Grammar Rules

Outside of grammar rules, there are two kinds of things we want to inject into generated parsers and lexers: package/import statements and class members like fields and methods.

Here is an idealized code generation template that illustrates where we want to inject code snippets for, say, the parser:

```
<header>
public class <grammarName>Parser extends Parser {
        <members>
        ...
}
```

To specify a header action, we use @header {...} in our grammar. To inject fields or methods into the generated code, we use @members {...}. In a combined parser/lexer grammar, these named actions apply to both the parser and the lexer. (ANTLR option -package lets us set the package without a header action.) To restrict an action to the generated parser or lexer, we use @parser::*name* or @lexer::*name*.

Let's see what these look like for our calculator. The expression grammar starts with a grammar declaration like before, but now we're going to declare that the generated code lives in a Java package. We'll also need to import some standard Java utility classes.

actions/tools/Expr.g4

```
grammar Expr;

@header {
package tools;
import java.util.*;
}
```

The previous calculator's EvalVisitor class had a memory field that stored name-value pairs to implement variable assignments and references. We'll put that in our members action. To reduce clutter in the grammar, let's also define a convenience method called eval() that performs an operation on two operands. Here's what the complete members action looks like:

actions/tools/Expr.g4

```
@parser::members {
    /** "memory" for our calculator; variable/value pairs go here */
    Map<String, Integer> memory = new HashMap<String, Integer>();

    int eval(int left, int op, int right) {
        switch ( op ) {
            case MUL : return left * right;
            case DIV : return left / right;
            case ADD : return left + right;
            case SUB : return left - right;
        }
        return 0;
    }
}
```

With that infrastructure in place, let's see how to use these parser class members inside actions among the rule elements.

Embedding Actions Within Rules

In this section, we're going to learn how to embed actions in the grammar in order to generate some output, update data structures, and set rule return values. We'll also look at how ANTLR wraps up rule parameters, return values, and other attributes of a rule invocation into instances of ParserRuleContext subclasses.

The Basics

Rule stat recognizes expressions, variable assignments, and blank lines. Because we do nothing upon a blank line, stat needs only two actions.

actions/tools/Expr.g4

```
stat:   e NEWLINE           {System.out.println($e.v);}
    |   ID '=' e NEWLINE    {memory.put($ID.text, $e.v);}
    |   NEWLINE
    ;
```

Actions execute after the preceding grammar element and before the next one. In this case, the actions appear at the end of the alternatives, so they execute after the parser matches the entire statement. When stat sees an expression followed by NEWLINE, it should print the value of the expression. When stat sees a variable assignment, it should store the name-value pair in field memory.

The only unfamiliar syntax in those actions are $e.v and $ID.text. In general, $x.y refers to attribute *y* of element *x*, where *x* is either a token reference or a rule reference. Here, $e.v refers to the return value from calling rule e. (We'll see why it's called v in a second.) $ID.text refers to the text matched by the ID reference.

If ANTLR doesn't recognize the *y* component, it doesn't translate it. In this case, text is a known attribute of a token, and ANTLR translates it to getText(). We could also use $ID.getText() to get the same thing. For a complete list of the attributes for rules and tokens, see Section 15.4, *Actions and Attributes*, on page 273.

Turning to rule e now, let's see what it looks like with embedded actions. The basic idea is to mimic the EvalVisitor functionality by inserting code snippets directly into the grammar as actions.

actions/tools/Expr.g4

```
e returns [int v]
    : a=e op=('*'|'/') b=e  {$v = eval($a.v, $op.type, $b.v);}
    | a=e op=('+'|'-') b=e  {$v = eval($a.v, $op.type, $b.v);}
    | INT                   {$v = $INT.int;}
    | ID
      {
      String id = $ID.text;
      $v = memory.containsKey(id) ? memory.get(id) : 0;
      }
    | '(' e ')'             {$v = $e.v;}
    ;
```

A number of interesting things are going on in this example. The first thing we see is the return value specification for an integer, v. That's why stat's actions refer to $e.v. ANTLR return values differ from Java return values in that we get to name them and we can have more than one.

Next, we see labels on e rule references and on the operator subrules such as op=('*'|'/'). Labels refer to Token or ParserRuleContext objects derived from matching a token or invoking a rule.

Before turning to the action contents, it's worth looking at where ANTLR stores things like return values and labels. It'll make following the ANTLR-generated code easier when source-level debugging.

One Rule Context Object to Bind Them All

In Section 2.4, *Building Language Applications Using Parse Trees*, on page 16, we learned that ANTLR implements parse-tree nodes with rule context objects. Each rule invocation creates and returns a rule context object, which holds all of the important information about the recognition of a rule at a specific location in the input stream. For example, rule e creates and returns EContext objects.

```
public final EContext e(...) throws RecognitionException {...}
```

Naturally, a rule context object is a very handy place to put rule-specific entities. The first part of EContext looks like this:

```
public static class EContext extends ParserRuleContext {
        public int v;         // rule e return value from "returns [int v]"
        public EContext a;    // label a on (recursive) rule reference to e
        public Token op;      // label on operator sub rules like ('*'|'/')
        public EContext b;    // label b on (recursive) rule reference to e
        public Token INT;     // reference to INT matched by 3rd alternative
        public Token ID;      // reference to ID matched by 4th alternative
        public EContext e;    // reference to context object from e invocation
        ...
}
```

Labels always become fields in the rule context object, but ANTLR doesn't always generate fields for alternative elements such as ID, INT, and e. ANTLR generates fields for them only if they're referenced by actions in the grammar (as e's actions do). ANTLR tries to reduce the number of context object fields.

Now we have all the pieces in place, so let's analyze the contents of the actions among the alternatives of rule e.

Computing Return Values

All of the actions in e set the return value with assignment $v = ...;. This sets the return value but does not perform a return from the rule function. (Don't use a return statement in your actions because it will make the parser go insane.) Here is the action used by the first two alternatives:

```
$v = eval($a.v, $op.type, $b.v);
```

This action computes the value of the subexpression and sets the return value for e. The arguments to eval() are the return values from the two references to e, $a.v and $b.v, and the token type of the operator matched by the alternative, $op.type. $op.type will always be the token type for one of the arithmetic operators. Notice that we can reuse labels (as long as they refer to the same kind of thing). The second alternative reuses labels a, b, and op.

The third alternative's action uses $INT.int to access the integer value of the text matched by the INT token. This is just shorthand for Integer.valueOf($INT.text). The embedded action is much simpler than the equivalent visitor visitInt() method (but at the cost of entangling application-specific code with the grammar).

tour/EvalVisitor.java

```
/** INT */
@Override
public Integer visitInt(LabeledExprParser.IntContext ctx) {
    return Integer.valueOf(ctx.INT().getText());
}
```

The fourth alternative recognizes a variable reference and sets e's return value to the value stored in memory, if we've stored a value for that name. This action uses the Java ?: operator, but we could've just as easily used an if-then-else Java statement. We can put anything into an action that would work as a body of a Java method.

Finally, the $v = $e.v; action in the last alternative sets the return value to the result of the expression matched in parentheses. We're just passing the return value through. The value of (3) is 3.

That's it for the grammar and action code. Now, let's figure out how to build an interactive driver for our calculator.

Building an Interactive Calculator

Before exploring the details of building an interactive tool, let's give it a whirl by building and testing the grammar and Calc.java test rig. Because we put statement package tools; in the header action, we need to put the generated Java code in a directory called tools. (This reflects the standard Java relationship between package and directory structure.) That means we need to either run ANTLR from tools or run it from the directory above tools with path tools/Expr.g4 instead of just Expr.g4.

```
$ antlr4 -no-listener tools/Expr.g4  # gen parser w/o listener into tools
$ javac -d . tools/*.java            # compile, put .class files in tools
```

To try it, we run Calc using its fully qualified name.

```
⇒ $ java tools.Calc
⇒ x = 1
⇒ x
❮ 1
⇒ x+2*3
❮ 7
⇒ EOF
```

You'll notice that the calculator immediately responds with an answer when you hit Return. Because ANTLR reads the entire input (usually into a big buffer) by default, we have to pass input line by line to the parser to make it interactive. Each line represents a complete expression. (If you need to handle expressions that can span multiple lines, see *Fun with Python Newlines*, on page 216.) In the main() method, here's how we get the first expression:

actions/tools/Calc.java

```
BufferedReader br = new BufferedReader(new InputStreamReader(is));
String expr = br.readLine();              // get first expression
int line = 1;                             // track input expr line numbers
```

To maintain memory field values across expressions, we need a single shared parser for all input lines.

actions/tools/Calc.java

```
ExprParser parser = new ExprParser(null); // share single parser instance
parser.setBuildParseTree(false);          // don't need trees
```

As we read in a line, we'll create a new token stream and pass it to the shared parser.

actions/tools/Calc.java

```
while ( expr!=null ) {            // while we have more expressions
    // create new lexer and token stream for each line (expression)
    ANTLRInputStream input = new ANTLRInputStream(expr+"\n");
    ExprLexer lexer = new ExprLexer(input);
    lexer.setLine(line);           // notify lexer of input position
    lexer.setCharPositionInLine(0);
    CommonTokenStream tokens = new CommonTokenStream(lexer);
    parser.setInputStream(tokens); // notify parser of new token stream
    parser.stat();                 // start the parser
    expr = br.readLine();          // see if there's another line
    line++;
}
```

So, now we know how to build an interactive tool, and we have a pretty good idea about how to place and use embedded actions. Our calculator used a header action to specify a package and a members action to define two parser class members. We used actions within the rules to compute and return subexpression values as a function of token and rule attributes. In the next section, we're going to see some more attributes and identify a few more action locations.

10.2 Accessing Token and Rule Attributes

Let's use the CSV grammar from Section 6.1, *Parsing Comma-Separated Values*, on page 86 as a foundation for exploring some more action-related features. We're going to build an application that creates a map from column name to field for each row and prints out information gained from parsing the data. Our goal here is really just to learn more about rule-related actions and attributes.

First, let's take a look at how to define local variables using the locals section. As with parameters and return values, the declarations in a locals section become fields in the rule context object. Because we get a new rule context object for every rule invocation, we get a new copy of the locals as we'd expect. The following augmented version of rule file does a number of interesting things, but let's start by focusing on what it does with locals.

actions/CSV.g4

```
/** Derived from rule "file : hdr row+ ;" */
file
locals [int i=0]
     : hdr ( rows+=row[$hdr.text.split(",")] {$i++;} )+
       {
       System.out.println($i+" rows");
       for (RowContext r : $rows) {
           System.out.println("row token interval: "+r.getSourceInterval());
       }
       }
     ;
```

Rule file defines a local variable, i, and uses it to count how many rows there are in the input using action $i++;. To reference local variables, don't forget the $ character prefix, or the compiler will complain about undefined variables. ANTLR translates $i to _localctx.i; there is no i local variable in the rule function generated for file.

Next, let's take a look at the call to rule row. Rule invocation row[$hdr.text.split(",")] illustrates that we use square brackets instead of parentheses to pass parameters to rules (ANTLR uses parentheses for subrule syntax). Argument expression $hdr.text.split(",") splits the text matched by the hdr rule invocation to get an array of strings needed by row.

Let's break that apart. $hdr is a reference to the sole hdr invocation and evaluates to its HdrContext object. We don't need to label the hdr reference in this case (like h=hdr) because $hdr is unique. $hdr.text, then, is the text matched for the header row. We split the comma-separated header columns using the standard Java String.split() method, which returns an array of strings. We'll see shortly that rule row takes an array-of-string parameter.

The call to row also introduces a new kind of label that uses += instead of the = label operator. Rather than tracking a single value, label rows is a list of all RowContext objects returned from all row invocations. After printing out the number of rows, the final action in file has a loop that iterates through the RowContext objects. Each time through the loop, it prints out the range of token indexes matched by the row invocation (using getSourceInterval()).

That loop uses r, not $r, because r is a local variable created within a Java action. ANTLR can see only those local variables defined with the locals keyword, not in arbitrary user-defined embedded actions. The difference is that the parse tree node for rule file would define field i but not r.

Turning to rule hdr now, let's just print out the header row. We could do that by referencing $row.text, which is the text matched by the row rule reference. Alternatively, we can ask for the text of the surrounding rule with $text.

actions/CSV.g4
```
hdr : row[null] {System.out.println("header: '"+$text.trim()+"'");} ;
```

In this case, it will also be the text matched by row because that is all there is in that rule.

Now let's figure out how to convert every row of data into a map from column name to value with actions in rule row. To begin with, row takes the array of column names as a parameter and returns the map. Next, to move through the column names array, we'll need a local variable, col. Before parsing the row, we need to initialize the return value map, and, for fun, let's print out the map after row finishes. All of that goes into the header for the rule.

actions/CSV.g4

```
/** Derived from rule "row : field (',' field)* '\r'? '\n' ;" */
row[String[] columns] returns [Map<String,String> values]
locals [int col=0]
@init {
    $values = new HashMap<String,String>();
}
@after {
    if ($values!=null && $values.size()>0) {
        System.out.println("values = "+$values);
    }
}
```

The init action happens before anything is matched in the rule, regardless of how many alternatives there are. Similarly, the after action happens after the rule matches one of the alternatives. In this case, we could express the after action functionality by putting the print statement in an action at the end of row's outer alternative.

With everything set up, we can collect the data and fill the map.

actions/CSV.g4

```
// rule row cont'd...
    :   field
        {
        if ($columns!=null) {
            $values.put($columns[$col++].trim(), $field.text.trim());
        }
        }
        (   ',' field
            {
            if ($columns!=null) {
                $values.put($columns[$col++].trim(), $field.text.trim());
            }
            }
        )* '\r'? '\n'
    ;
```

The meaty parts of the actions store the field value at the column name in the values map using $values.put(...). The first parameter gets the column name, increments the column count, and trims away the whitespace from the name: $columns[$col++].trim(). The second parameter trims the text of the most recently matched field: $field.text.trim(). (Both actions in row are identical, so it might be a good idea to factor that out into a method in a members action.)

Everything else in CSV.g4 is familiar to us, so let's move on to building this thing and giving it a try. We don't need to write a special test rig because of grun, so we can just generate the parser and compile it.

```
$ antlr4 -no-listener CSV.g4   # again, we won't use a listener
$ javac CSV*.java
```

Here's some CSV data we can use:

actions/users.csv

```
User,  Name,     Dept
parrt, Terence, 101
tombu, Tom,     020
bke, Kevin,     008
```

And, here is the output:

```
$ grun CSV file users.csv
header: 'User,  Name,     Dept'
values = {Name=Terence, User=parrt, Dept=101}
values = {Name=Tom, User=tombu, Dept=020}
values = {Name=Kevin, User=bke, Dept=008}
3 rows
row token interval: 6..11
row token interval: 12..17
row token interval: 18..23
```

Rule hdr prints out the first line of output, and the three calls to row print out the values = ... lines. Back in rule file, the action prints out the number of rows and the token intervals associated with each row of data.

At this point, we have a very good handle on the use of embedded actions, both inside and outside of rules. We also know quite a bit about rule attributes. On the other hand, both the calculator and CSV example use actions exclusively in the parser rules. It turns out actions can be very useful in lexer rules as well. We'll explore that next by seeing how to handle a large or dynamic set of keywords.

10.3 Recognizing Languages Whose Keywords Aren't Fixed

To explore actions embedded in lexer rules, let's build a grammar for a contrived programming language whose keywords can change dynamically (from run to run). This is not as unusual as it sounds. For example, in version 5, Java added the keyword enum, so the same compiler must be able to enable and disable a keyword depending on the -version option.

Perhaps a more common use would be dealing with languages that have huge keyword sets. Rather than making the lexer match all of the keywords individually (as separate rules), we can make a catchall ID rule and then look up the identifier in a keywords table. If the lexer finds a keyword, we can specifically set the token type from a generic ID to the token type for that keyword.

Before we get to the ID rule and the keyword lookup mechanism, let's take a look at a statement rule that references keywords.

actions/Keywords.g4

```
stat:   BEGIN stat* END
    |   IF expr THEN stat
    |   WHILE expr stat
    |   ID '=' expr ';'
        ;

expr:   INT | CHAR ;
```

ANTLR will implicitly define token types for the keywords BEGIN, END, and so on. But, ANTLR will warn us that there is no corresponding lexical definition for these token types.

```
$ antlr4 Keywords.g4
warning(125): Keywords.g4:31:8: implicit definition of token BEGIN in parser
...
```

To hush this warning, let's be explicit.

actions/Keywords.g4

```
// explicitly define keyword token types to avoid implicit def warnings
tokens { BEGIN, END, IF, THEN, WHILE }
```

In the generated KeywordsParser, ANTLR defines token types like this:

```
public static final int ID=3, BEGIN=4, END=5, IF=6, ... ;
```

Now that we've defined our token types, let's look at the grammar declaration and a header action, which imports Map and HashMap.

actions/Keywords.g4

```
grammar Keywords;
@lexer::header {    // place this header action only in lexer, not the parser
import java.util.*;
}
```

We'll use a Map from keyword name to integer token type for the keywords table, and we can define the mappings inline using a Java instance initializer (the inner set of curly braces).

actions/Keywords.g4

```
@lexer::members {  // place this class member only in lexer
Map<String,Integer> keywords = new HashMap<String,Integer>() {{
    put("begin", KeywordsParser.BEGIN);
    put("end",   KeywordsParser.END);
    put("if",    KeywordsParser.IF);
```

```
    put("then",  KeywordsParser.THEN);
    put("while", KeywordsParser.WHILE);
}};
}
```

With all of our infrastructure in place, let's match identifiers as we've done many times before, but with an action that flips the token type appropriately.

actions/Keywords.g4

```
ID  :   [a-zA-Z]+
        {
        if ( keywords.containsKey(getText()) ) {
            setType(keywords.get(getText())); // reset token type
        }
        }
    ;
```

Here we use Lexer's getText() method to get the text of the current token. We use it to see whether the identifier exists within keywords. If it does, then we reset the token type from ID to the keyword's token type value.

While we're having fun in the lexer, let's figure out how to change the text of a token. This is useful for stripping single and double quotes from character and string literals. Usually, a language application would want just the text inside the quotes. Here's how to override the text of a token using setText():

actions/Keywords.g4

```
/** Convert 3-char 'x' input sequence to string x */
CHAR:   '\'' . '\'' {setText( String.valueOf(getText().charAt(1)) );} ;
```

If we wanted to get really crazy, we could even specify the Token object to return from the lexer using setToken(). This is a way to return custom token implementations. Another way is to override Lexer's emit() method.

We're ready to try our little language. The behavior we expect is to have keywords differentiated from regular identifiers. In other words, x = 34; should work, but if = 34; should not because if is a keyword. Let's run ANTLR, compile the generated code, and try it on the valid assignment.

```
⇒ $ antlr4 -no-listener Keywords.g4
⇒ $ javac Keywords*.java
⇒ $ grun Keywords stat
⇒ x = 34;
⇒ EOF
```

No problem; there are no errors. However, the parser gives a syntax error for the assignment that tries to use if as an identifier. It also accepts a valid if statement without error.

```
$ grun Keywords stat
if = 34;
EOF
line 1:3 extraneous input '=' expecting {CHAR, INT}
line 2:0 mismatched input '<EOF>' expecting THEN
$ grun Keywords stat
if 1 then i = 4;
EOF
```

If you are unlucky enough to be building a parser for a language that, in some contexts, allows keywords as identifiers, see *Treating Keywords As Identifiers*, on page 211.

Actions are less commonly needed in the lexer than the parser, but they are still useful in situations like this where we need to alter token types or the token text. We could also alter tokens by looking at the token stream after the fact instead of with actions while tokenizing the input.

In this chapter, we learned how to embed application code within grammars using actions among the rule elements and outside rules using named actions such as `header` and `members`. We also saw how to define and reference rule parameters and return values. Along the way, we also used token attributes such as `text` and `type`. Taken together, these action-related features let us customize the code ANTLR generates.

Again, try to avoid grammar actions when you can because actions tie a grammar to a particular programming language target. Actions also tie a grammar to a specific application. That said, you might not care about these issues because your company always programs in a single language and your grammar is specific to a particular application anyway. In that situation, it could make sense to embed actions directly in the grammar for simplicity or efficiency reasons (no parse tree construction). Most importantly, some parsing problems require runtime tests to recognize the input properly. In the next chapter, we're going to explore arbitrary Boolean expressions called *semantic predicates* that can dynamically turn alternatives on and off.

CHAPTER 11

Altering the Parse with Semantic Predicates

In the previous chapter, we learned how to embed actions within a grammar in order to execute application-specific code on-the-fly during the parse. Those actions did not affect the operation of the parser in any way, much as log statements do not affect the surrounding program. Our embedded actions just computed values or printed things out. In rare cases, however, altering the parse with embedded code is the only way to reasonably recognize the input sentences of a language.

In this chapter, we're going to learn about special actions, `{...}?`, called *semantic predicates* that let us selectively deactivate portions of a grammar at runtime. Predicates are Boolean expressions that have the effect of reducing the number of choices that the parser sees. Believe it or not, selectively reducing choice actually increases the power of the parser!

There are two common use cases for semantic predicates. First, we might need a parser to handle multiple, slightly different versions (dialects) of the same language. For example, the syntax of a database vendor's SQL evolves over time. To build a database front end for that vendor, we'd need to support different versions of the same SQL. Similarly, the Gnu C compiler, `gcc`, has to deal with ANSI C as well as its own dialect that adds things like the awesome computed goto. Moreover, semantic predicates let us choose between dialects at runtime with a command-line switch or other dynamic mechanism.

The second use case involves resolving grammar ambiguities (discussed in Section 2.2, *Implementing Parsers*, on page 12). In some languages, the same syntactic construct can mean different things, and predicates give us a way to choose between multiple interpretations of the same input phrase. For example, in good ol' Fortran, `f(i)` could be an array reference or a function call, depending on what `f` was defined to be—the syntax was the same. A compiler had to look up the identifier in a symbol table to properly interpret the input.

Semantic predicates give us a way to turn off improper interpretations based upon what we find in a symbol table. This leaves the parser with only a single choice, the proper interpretation.

We're going to learn about semantic predicates by working through examples taken from Java and C++. Along the way, we'll pick up most of the details, but you can check Section 15.7, *Semantic Predicates*, on page 288 in the reference chapter for a discussion of the fine print. Armed with embedded actions and predicates, we'll be sufficiently prepared to tackle some formidable language problems in the next chapter.

11.1 Recognizing Multiple Language Dialects

For our first lesson, we're going to learn how to use semantic predicates to deactivate parts of a Java grammar. The effect will be to recognize different dialects, according to results of evaluating Boolean expressions on-the-fly. In particular, we're going to see how the same parser can switch between allowing and disallowing enumerated types.

The Java language has been extended over the years to include new constructs. For example, prior to Java 5, the following declaration was invalid:

predicates/Temp.java
```
enum Temp { HOT, COLD }
```

Rather than building separate compilers for the slightly different dialects, the Java compiler javac has a -source option. Here's what happens when we try to compile that enum with Java version 1.4:

```
$ javac -source 1.4 Temp.java
Temp.java:1: enums are not supported in -source 1.4
(use -source 5 or higher to enable enums)
enum Temp { HOT, COLD }
^
1 error
$ javac Temp.java  # javac assumes the latest dialect; compiles fine.
```

Introducing enumerated types flipped enum from an identifier to a keyword, causing a backward-compatibility issue. Lots of legacy code uses enum as a variable like this: int enum;. With an option on the compiler to recognize the earlier dialect, we don't have to alter ancient code just to compile it again.

To get a taste for how javac handles multiple dialects, let's build a grammar that recognizes a tiny piece of Java: just enum declarations and assignment statements. The goal is to create a grammar that properly recognizes pre- and post–Java 5 languages, but *not both* at the same time. For example, using enum as both a keyword and an identifier should be invalid.

```
enum enum { HOT, COLD }    // syntax error in any Java version
```

Let's start our solution by looking at the core of a grammar that recognizes our minimal Java subset and then figure out how to handle the enum keyword.

predicates/Enum.g4

```
grammar Enum;
@parser::members {public static boolean java5;}

prog:   (   stat
        |   enumDecl
        )+
    ;

stat:   id '=' expr ';' {System.out.println($id.text+"="+$expr.text);} ;

expr
    :   id
    |   INT
    ;
```

We're already familiar with these grammatical constructs and actions, so let's move on to enum declarations.

```
enumDecl
    :   'enum' name=id '{' id (',' id)* '}'
        {System.out.println("enum "+$name.text);}
    ;
```

That rule recognizes the (simplified) syntax of an enumerated type, but there's nothing to suggest that enums are sometimes illegal. And that brings us to the heart of the matter: turning alternatives on and off with semantic predicates.

predicates/Enum.g4

```
enumDecl
    :   {java5}? 'enum' name=id '{' id (',' id)* '}'
        {System.out.println("enum "+$name.text);}
    ;
```

Predicate {java5}? evaluates to true or false at runtime, deactivating that alternative when java5 is false.

You'll notice that we're using rule id instead of just token ID like we usually do. That's because the notion of an identifier includes enum when recognizing pre–Java 5. (Our lexer returns enum as a keyword, not an identifier.) To express that choice, we need a rule with a semantic predicate.

predicates/Enum.g4

```
id  :   ID
    |   {!java5}? 'enum'
    ;
```

The {!java5}? predicate allows enum to act as an identifier only when not in Java 5 mode. It literally deactivates the second alternative when java5 is true. Internally, ANTLR parsers view rule id using a graph data structure, sort of like this:

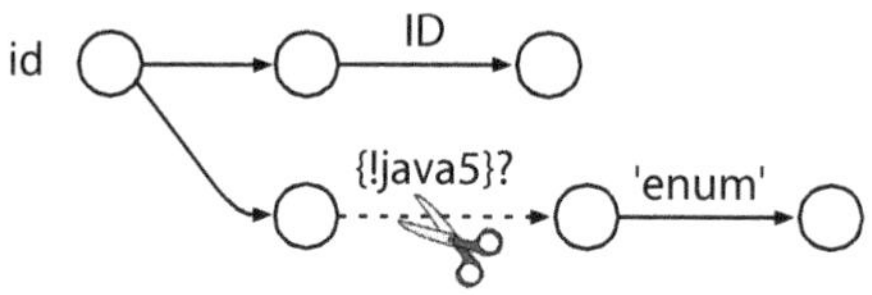

The scissors icon indicates that the parser snips that branch from the graph when !java5 evaluates to false (when java5 is true). Notice that because the predicates are mutually exclusive, enum declarations and enum-as-identifiers are mutually exclusive constructs.

We could use grun to test the grammar, but we need a test rig that can flip between Java dialects. Here are the relevant bits from TestEnum that support a -java5 option for turning on Java 5 mode:

predicates/TestEnum.java
```
int i = 0;
EnumParser.java5 = false; // assume non-Java5 mode by default
if ( args.length>0 && args[i].equals("-java5") ) {
        EnumParser.java5 = true;
        i++;
}
```

Now let's build and compile everything.

```
$ antlr4 -no-listener Enum.g4
$ javac Enum*.java TestEnum.java
```

Let's start with pre–Java 5 mode and make sure it allows enum as an identifier and that it doesn't allow enumerated types.

```
⇒ $ java TestEnum
⇒ enum = 0;
⇒ EOF
❮ enum=0
```

```
⇒ $ java TestEnum
⇒ enum Temp { HOT, COLD }
⇒ EOF
❮ line 1:0 no viable alternative at input 'enum'
```

Java 5 mode, in contrast, shouldn't consider enum to be an identifier, but it should allow enumerated types.

```
⇒ $ java TestEnum -java5
⇒ enum = 0;
⇒ EOF
❮ line 1:0 no viable alternative at input 'enum'

⇒ $ java TestEnum -java5
⇒ enum Temp { HOT, COLD }
⇒ EOF
❮ enum Temp
```

Everything checks out, but let's take a look at predicate placement before moving on. Predicates work by activating or deactivating everything that could be matched after passing through the predicate. That means we don't technically need to put the {java5}? predicate in enumDecl proper. We could drag it out and put it in front of the call to that rule instead.

```
prog:   (   {java5}? enumDecl
        |   stat
        )+
    ;
```

They are functionally equivalent, and their placement in this case is a matter of style. The key is that the parser must encounter a predicate somewhere in the first alternative of the (...)+ subrule before reaching the 'enum' token reference in enumDecl.

And that's how to build a grammar that supports multiple dialects using a runtime Boolean switch. To build a real Java grammar, you could incorporate these predicates into the appropriate rules of a grammar, which we've called enumDecl and id here.

As with embedded actions, semantic predicates are also occasionally useful in the lexer.

11.2 Deactivating Tokens

In this section, we're going to solve the same problem again, but this time using predicates in the lexer instead of the parser. The idea is that predicates in the lexer activate and deactivate *tokens* rather than *phrases* in the language. Our approach will be to deactivate enum as a keyword and match it as a regular identifier in pre–Java 5 mode. In Java 5 mode, we want to separate enum out as its own keyword token. This simplifies the parser considerably because it can match an identifier just by referencing the usual ID token, rather than an id rule.

predicates/Enum2.g4
```
stat:   ID '=' expr ';' {System.out.println($ID.text+"="+$expr.text);} ;

expr:   ID
    |   INT
    ;
```

The lexer sends an ID only when it's appropriate for the current dialect. To pull this off, we need just one predicate in a lexical rule that matches enum.

predicates/Enum2.g4
```
ENUM:   'enum' {java5}? ; // must be before ID
ID  :   [a-zA-Z]+ ;
```

Notice that the predicate appears on the right edge of the lexical rule instead of on the left, like we did for parser alternatives. That's because parsers predict what's coming down the road and need to test the predicates before matching alternatives.

Lexers, on the other hand, don't predict alternatives. They just look for the longest match and make decisions after they've seen the entire token. (We'll learn more about this in the reference chapter, specifically, in Section 15.7, *Semantic Predicates*, on page 288.)

When java5 is false, the predicate deactivates rule ENUM. When it's true, however, both ENUM and ID match character sequence e-n-u-m. Those two rules are ambiguous for that input. ANTLR always resolves lexical ambiguities in favor of the rule specified first, in this case ENUM. If we had reversed the rules, the lexer would always match e-n-u-m as an ID. It wouldn't matter whether ENUM was activated or deactivated.

The beauty of this predicated lexer solution is that we don't need a predicate in the parser for deactivating the enum construct when not in Java 5 mode.

predicates/Enum2.g4
```
// No predicate needed here because 'enum' token undefined if !java5
enumDecl
    :   'enum' name=ID '{' ID (',' ID)* '}'
        {System.out.println("enum "+$name.text);}
    ;
```

Token 'enum', referenced at the start of the alternative, is looking for a specific keyword token. The lexer can present that to the parser only in Java 5 mode, so enumDecl will never match unless java5 is true.

Let's verify now that our lexer-based solution correctly recognizes constructs in the two dialects. In non-Java-5 mode, enum is an identifier.

```
⇒ $ antlr4 -no-listener Enum2.g4
⇒ $ javac Enum2*.java TestEnum2.java
⇒ $ java TestEnum2
⇒ enum = 0;
⇒ EOF
❮ enum=0
```

Because enum is an identifier, not a keyword token, the parser will never attempt to match enumDecl. It has no choice but to treat enum Temp { HOT, COLD } as an assignment, leading to syntax errors.

```
⇒ $ java TestEnum2
⇒ enum Temp { HOT, COLD }
⇒ EOF
❮ line 1:5 missing '=' at 'Temp'
  line 1:15 mismatched input ',' expecting '='
  line 1:22 mismatched input '}' expecting '='
```

In this case, ANTLR's error recovery realizes it doesn't have a valid assignment and scarfs tokens until it finds something that can start an assignment.

In Java 5 mode, an assignment to enum is invalid, but an enumerated type is valid.

```
⇒ $ java TestEnum2 -java5
⇒ enum = 0;
⇒ EOF
❮ line 1:5 mismatched input '=' expecting ID
⇒ $ java TestEnum2 -java5
⇒ enum Temp { HOT, COLD }
⇒ EOF
❮ enum Temp
```

If we wanted to avoid predicates, which can slow down the lexer, we could do away with the ENUM rule altogether and match enum always as an identifier. Then we'd flip the token type appropriately like we did in Section 10.3, *Recognizing Languages Whose Keywords Aren't Fixed*, on page 187.

```
ID  :   [a-zA-Z]+
        {if (java5 && getText().equals("enum")) setType(Enum2Parser.ENUM);}
    ;
```

We would also need a token definition for ENUM.

```
tokens { ENUM }
```

It's a good idea to avoid embedding predicates in the parser when possible for efficiency and clarity reasons. Instead, I recommend choosing one of the lexer-based solutions in this section to support the Java dialects related to enum. Note that predicates slow the lexer down as well, so try to do without them entirely.

That's it for the basic syntax and usage of semantic predicates in the parser and the lexer. Predicates offer a straightforward way to selectively deactivate parts of a grammar, which lets us recognize dialects of the same language using the same grammar. Moreover, we can switch between dialects dynamically by flipping the value of a Boolean expression. Now let's investigate the second major use case: using predicates to resolve ambiguous input phrases in the parser.

11.3 Recognizing Ambiguous Phrases

We've just seen how to strip away parts of a grammar based upon a simple Boolean variable. It wasn't that the grammar matched the same input in multiple ways; we simply wanted to turn off certain language constructs. Now our goal is to force the parser to deactivate all but one interpretation of an ambiguous input phrase. Using our maze analogy, a maze and passphrase are ambiguous when we can follow multiple paths through the maze to the exit using that single passphrase. Predicates are like doors on path forks that we can open and close to direct movement through the maze.

Language Ambiguities Are Bad...Umkay?

Wise language designers deliberately avoid ambiguous constructs because they make it hard to read code. For example, f[0] in Ruby is either a reference to the first element of array f or a function call to f() that returns an array, which we then index. To make things even more fun, f [0] with a space before [0] passes an array with 0 in it to function f() as an argument. This all happens because parentheses are optional in Ruby for function calls. Ruby aficionados currently recommend using parentheses because of these very ambiguities.

Before we begin, let me point out that having more than one way to match an input phrase in a grammar is almost always a grammar bug. In most languages, the syntax alone uniquely dictates how to interpret all valid sentences. (See the sidebar *Language Ambiguities Are Bad...Umkay?*, on page 198.) That means our grammars should match each input stream in just one way. If we find multiple interpretations, we should rewrite the grammar to strip out the invalid interpretation(s).

That said, there are phrases in some languages where syntax alone just isn't enough to identify the meaning. Grammars for these languages will necessarily be ambiguous, but the meaning of syntactically ambiguous phrases will be clear given sufficient context, such as how identifiers are defined (for example, as types or methods). We'll need predicates to properly select an interpretation for each ambiguous phrase by asking context questions. If a predicate successfully resolves a grammar ambiguity for an input phrase, then we say that the phrase is *context-sensitive.*

In this section, we're going to explore some ambiguities in the nooks and crannies of C++. As far as I can tell, C++ is the most difficult programming language to parse accurately and precisely. We'll start with function calls vs. constructor-style type casts and then look at declarations vs. expressions.

Properly Recognizing T(0) in C++

In C++, expression T(0) is either a function call or a constructor-style typecast depending on whether T is a function or type name. The expression is ambiguous because the same phrase syntax applies to both interpretations. To get the right interpretation, the parser needs to deactivate one of the alternatives according to how T is defined in the program. The following grossly simplified C++ expression rule has two predicates that check the ID to see whether it's a function or type name:

predicates/CppExpr.g4

```
/** Distinguish between alts 1, 2 using idealized predicates as demo */
expr:   {«isfunc(ID)»}? ID '(' expr ')' // func call with 1 arg
    |   {«istype(ID)»}? ID '(' expr ')' // ctor-style type cast of expr
    |   INT                             // integer literal
    |   ID                              // identifier
    ;
```

Visually, rule expr looks like the following graph with cut points in front of the first two alternatives:

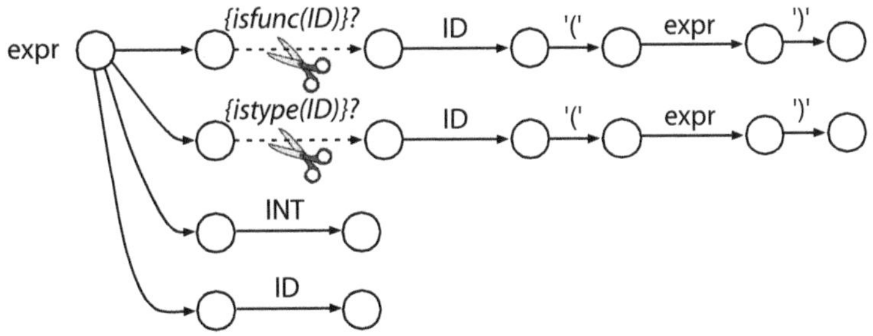

You might be wondering why we simply don't collapse those two alternatives into a single one that handles both cases (function calls and type casts). One reason is that it complicates the job of the parse-tree walker. Instead of two specific methods, one for each case, there is a single enterCallOrTypecast(). Inside that method we'd have to split the two cases manually. That's not the end of the world, though.

The bigger problem is that the ambiguous alternatives are rarely identical like they are here. For example, the function call alternative would also have to handle the case where there are no arguments, such as T(). That would not be a valid typecast, so collapsing the two alternatives wouldn't work in practice. It's also the case that the ambiguous alternatives can be in widely separated rules, which we'll consider in the next example.

Properly Recognizing T(i) in C++

Consider a slight variation of our expression: T(i). To keep things simple, let's assume that there are no constructor-style type casts in our C++ subset. As an expression, then, T(i) must be a function call. Unfortunately, it is also syntactically a valid declaration. It's the same as phrase T i, which defines variable i of type T. The only way to tell the difference is again with context. If T is a type name, then T(i) is a declaration of variable i. Else, it's a function call with i as an argument.

We can demonstrate ambiguous alternatives in separate rules with a small grammar that matches a few bits of C++. Let's say C++ statements can be just declarations or expressions.

predicates/CppStat.g4

```
stat:   decl ';'  {System.out.println("decl "+$decl.text);}
    |   expr ';'  {System.out.println("expr "+$expr.text);}
    ;
```

Syntactically, a declaration can be either T i or T(i).

predicates/CppStat.g4

```
decl:   ID ID             // E.g., "Point p"
    |   ID '(' ID ')'     // E.g., "Point (p)", same as ID ID
    ;
```

And let's say that an expression can be an integer literal, a simple identifier, or a function call with one argument.

predicates/CppStat.g4

```
expr:   INT              // integer literal
    |   ID               // identifier
    |   ID '(' expr ')' // function call
    ;
```

If we build and test the grammar on, say, f(i);, we get an ambiguity warning from the parser (when using the -diagnostics option).

```
⇒ $ antlr4 CppStat.g4
⇒ $ javac CppStat*.java
⇒ $ grun CppStat stat -diagnostics
⇒ f(i);
⇒ EOF
❮ line 1:4 reportAttemptingFullContext d=0, input='f(i);'
  line 1:4 reportAmbiguity d=0: ambigAlts={1, 2}, input='f(i);'
  decl f(i)
```

The parser starts out by notifying us that it detected a problem trying to parse the input with the simple *SLL(*)* parsing strategy. Since that strategy failed, the parser retried with the more powerful *ALL(*)* mechanism. See Section 13.7, *Maximizing Parser Speed*, on page 245. With the full grammar analysis algorithm engaged, the parser again found a problem. At that point, it knew that the input was truly ambiguous. If the parser had not found the problem, it would have printed a reportContextSensitivity message; we'll learn more about that after we add predicates.

That input matches both the second alternative of decl and the third alternative of expr. The parser must choose between them in rule stat. Given two viable alternatives, the parser resolves the ambiguity by choosing the alternative specified first (decl). That's why the parser interprets f(i); as a declaration instead of an expression.

If we had an "oracle" that could tell us whether an identifier was a type name, we could resolve the ambiguity with predicates in front of the ambiguous alternatives.

predicates/PredCppStat.g4

```
decl:   ID ID                           // E.g., "Point p"
    |   {istype()}? ID '(' ID ')'       // E.g., "Point (p)", same as ID ID
    ;

expr:   INT                             // integer literal
    |   ID                              // identifier
    |   {!istype()}? ID '(' expr ')'    // function call
    ;
```

The istype() helper method in the predicates asks the parser for the current token, gets its text, and looks it up in our predefined types table.

predicates/PredCppStat.g4

```
@parser::members {
Set<String> types = new HashSet<String>() {{add("T");}};
boolean istype() { return types.contains(getCurrentToken().getText()); }
}
```

When we test this predicated version of our grammar, input `f(i);` is interpreted properly as a function call expression, not a declaration. Input `T(i);` is unambiguously interpreted as a declaration.

```
⇒ $ antlr4 PredCppStat.g4
⇒ $ javac PredCppStat*.java
⇒ $ grun PredCppStat stat -diagnostics
⇒ f(i);
⇒ EOF
❮ expr f(i)
⇒ $ grun PredCppStat stat -diagnostics
⇒ T(i);
⇒ EOF
❮ decl T(i)
```

The following parse trees (created using the `grun -ps file.ps` option) illustrate clearly that the parser properly interprets the input phrases:

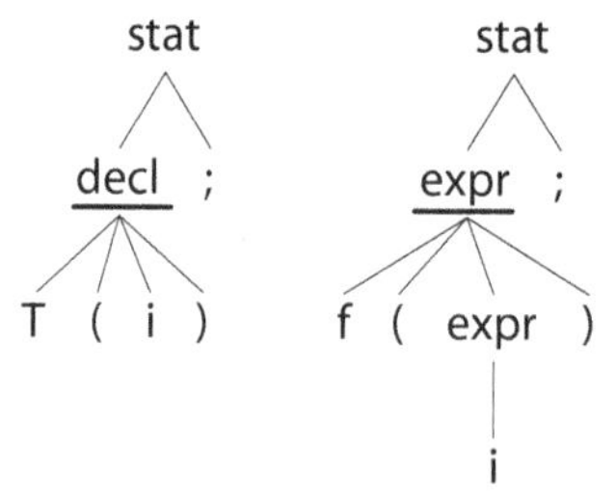

The key nodes in the parse tree are the underlined parents of `T` and `f`. Those internal nodes tell us what kind of thing the parser matched. Remember that the idea behind recognition is that we can distinguish one phrase from the other and can identify the constituent components. We could match any possible input file with grammar fragment `.+` (match one or more of any symbol), but it wouldn't tell us anything about the input. Getting the correct structure from the input is crucial to building a language application.

The ambiguities in these C++ examples disappear because the predicates cut out the improper interpretation. Unfortunately, there are some ambiguities for which no predicate exists to resolve them. Let's tackle one more C++ example to see how this can happen.

Properly Recognizing T(i)[5] in C++

C++ is exciting because some phrases have two valid meanings. Consider the C++ phrase `T(i)[5]`. Syntactically this looks like both a declaration and an expression *even if we know that `T` is a type name*. That means we can't test identifier `T` and switch interpretations because there are two interpretations when `T` is a type name.

The declaration interpretation is as an array of five `T` elements: `T i[5]`. The expression interpretation is a typecast of `i` to `T` and then an index operation on the resulting array.

The C++ language specification document resolves this ambiguity by always choosing declarations over expressions. The language specification unambiguously tells us humans how to interpret `T(i)[5]`, but it's impossible to build a conventional grammar that is unambiguous even if we add semantic predicates.

Fortunately, the parser resolves this ambiguity automatically so that it behaves naturally. Parsers resolve ambiguities by choosing the alternative specified first. So, we just have to make sure we put the `decl` alternative before the `expr` alternative in `stat`.

There's one final complication to consider when parsing C++.

Resolving Forward References

To compute our `types` table from the previous section or some other table to distinguish functions from type names, a real C++ parser would have to track names as it encountered them during the parse. Tracking symbols in C++ is a bit tricky but conceptually not a problem. We learned how to track name-value pairs for our calculator in the previous chapter. The problem is that C++ sometimes allows forward references to symbols like method and variable names. That means we might not know that `T` is a function name until after the parser has seen expression `T(i)`. Gulp.

This should give you some idea of why C++ is so hard to parse. The only solution is to make multiple passes over the input or over an internal representation of the input such as a parse tree.

Using ANTLR, the simplest approach would probably be to tokenize the input, scan it quickly to find and record all of the symbol definitions, and then parse those tokens again "with feeling" to get the proper parse tree.

While most languages don't have such diabolical ambiguity-related issues, just about every language is ambiguous simply because it contains arithmetic expressions. For example, in Section 5.4, *Dealing with Precedence, Left Recursion, and Associativity*, on page 71, we saw that `1+2*3` is ambiguous because we can interpret it as `(1+2)*3` or `1+(2*3)`.

The behavior of semantic predicates is more or less straightforward if we think of them as simple Boolean expressions that turn alternatives on and off. Unfortunately, things can get fairly complicated in grammars with multiple predicates and embedded actions. The reference chapter goes over the details of when and how ANTLR uses predicates. If you don't plan on using lots of predicates mixed with actions in your grammar, you can probably skip Section 15.7, *Semantic Predicates*, on page 288. Later these details might help explain some perplexing grammar behavior.

Now that we know how to customize generated parsers using actions and semantic predicates, we have some fearsome skills. In the next chapter, we're going to solve some very difficult recognition problems using what we've learned so far in Part III.

CHAPTER 12

Wielding Lexical Black Magic

In this part of the book, we've learned some advanced skills. We know how to execute arbitrary code while parsing, and we can alter syntax recognition with semantic predicates. Now it's time to put those skills to work solving some challenging language recognition problems but in the lexer this time, not the parser.

In my experience, if a language problem is hard to solve, most of the head-scratching occurs in the lexer (well, with the exception of C++, which is hard all over). That's counterintuitive because the lexer rules we've seen so far have been pretty simple, such as identifiers, integers, and arithmetic expression operators. But, consider the harmless-looking two-character Java sequence: `>>`. A Java lexer could match it either as the right shift operator or as two `>` operators, which the parser could use to close a nested generic type like `List<List<String>>`.

The fundamental problem is that the lexer does the tokenizing, but sometimes only the parser has the context information needed to make tokenizing decisions. We'll explore this issue in Section 12.2, *Context-Sensitive Lexical Problems*, on page 210. During that discussion, we'll also look at the "keywords can be identifiers" problem and build a lexer to deal with Python's context-sensitive newline handling.

The next problem we'll look at involves *island languages* whose sentences have islands of interesting bits surrounded by a sea of stuff we don't care about. Examples include XML and template languages like StringTemplate. To parse these, we need *island grammars* and *lexical modes*, which we'll explore in Section 12.3, *Islands in the Stream*, on page 221.

Finally, we'll build an ANTLR XML parser and lexer from the XML specification. It's a great example of how to deal with input streams containing different contexts (regions), how to draw a line between the parser and lexer, and how to accept non-ASCII input characters.

To get warmed up, let's learn how to ignore but not throw out special input regions such as comments and whitespace. The technique can be used to solve lots of language translation problems, and we'll demonstrate the most common use case here.

12.1 Broadcasting Tokens on Different Channels

Most programming languages ignore whitespace and comments in between tokens, which means they can appear anywhere. That presents a problem for a parser since it has to constantly check for optional whitespace and comment tokens. The common solution is to simply have the lexer match those tokens but throw them out, which is what we've done so far in this book. For example, our Cymbol grammar from Section 6.4, *Parsing Cymbol*, on page 100 threw out whitespace and comments using the skip lexer command.

examples/Cymbol.g4
```
WS  :   [ \t\n\r]+ -> skip ;

SL_COMMENT
    :   '//' .*? '\n' -> skip
    ;
```

That works great for many applications, such as compilers, because the comments don't affect code generation. If, on the other hand, we're trying to build a translator to convert legacy code into a modern language, we really should keep the comments around because they're part of the program. This presents a conundrum: we want to keep the comments and whitespace, but we don't want to burden the parser with constant checks for them in between tokens.

Filling Token Channels

ANTLR's solution is to send the actual language tokens like identifiers to the parser on one *channel* and everything else on a different channel. Channels are like different radio frequencies. The parser tunes to exactly one channel and ignores tokens on the other channels. Lexer rules are responsible for putting tokens on different channels, and class CommonTokenStream is responsible for presenting only one channel to the parser. CommonTokenStream does this while preserving the original relative token order so we can request the comments before or after a particular language token. The following image represents CommonTokenStream's view of the tokens emitted by a C lexer that puts comments and whitespace on a hidden channel:

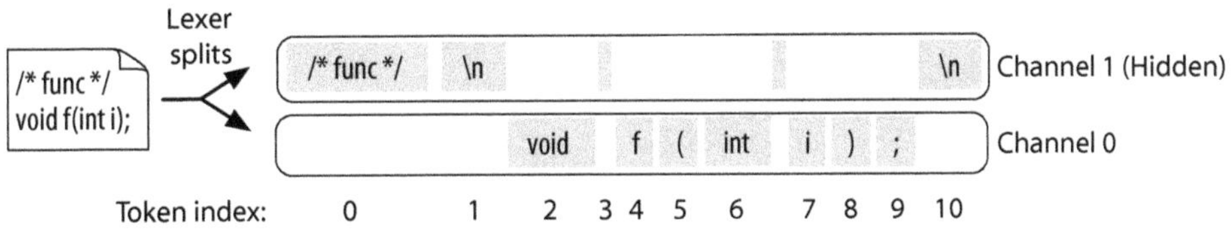

We can just as easily isolate the comments on one channel and the whitespace on another, leaving the real tokens on the default channel 0.

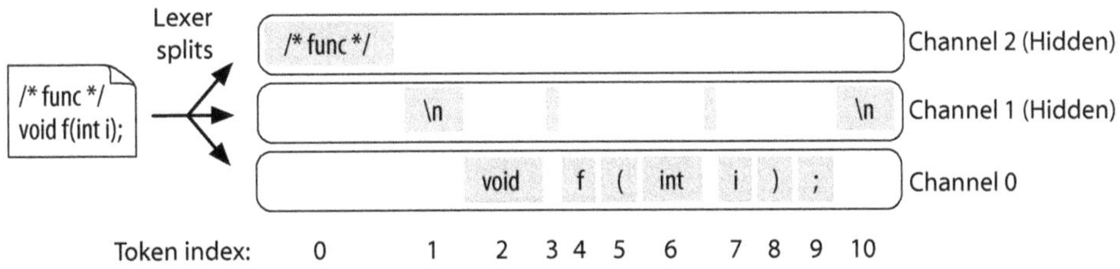

That way, we can ask for the comments and whitespace separately.

To transmit tokens on a different channel, we use lexer command channel(...) in the appropriate lexer rule. Let's demonstrate this technique by altering our Cymbol grammar to put comments on hidden channel 2 and whitespace on hidden channel 1, like the last image.

lexmagic/Cymbol.g4
```
WS  :   [ \t\n\r]+ -> channel(WHITESPACE) ;  // channel(1)

SL_COMMENT
    :   '//' .*? '\n' -> channel(COMMENTS)    // channel(2)
    ;
```

Constants WHITESPACE and COMMENTS come from a declaration in our grammar.

lexmagic/Cymbol.g4
```
@lexer::members {
    public static final int WHITESPACE = 1;
    public static final int COMMENTS = 2;
}
```

ANTLR translates channel(HIDDEN) to Java as _channel = HIDDEN, which sets class Lexer's _channel field to constant HIDDEN. We can use any valid Java qualified identifier as an argument to command channel().

Testing the grammar with grun shows that the comments appear on channel 2, whitespace appears on channel 1, and the other tokens appear on the default channel.

```
⇒ $ antlr4 Cymbol.g4
⇒ $ javac Cymbol*.java
⇒ $ grun Cymbol file -tokens -tree
⇒ int i = 3; // testing
⇒ EOF
❮ [@0,0:2='int',<10>,1:0]
  [@1,3:3=' ',<24>,channel=1,1:3]                 <-- HIDDEN channel 1
  [@2,4:4='i',<22>,1:4]
  [@3,5:5=' ',<24>,channel=1,1:5]                 <-- HIDDEN channel 1
  [@4,6:6='=',<11>,1:6]
  [@5,7:7=' ',<24>,channel=1,1:7]                 <-- HIDDEN channel 1
  [@6,8:8='3',<23>,1:8]
  [@7,9:9=';',<13>,1:9]
  [@8,10:10=' ',<24>,channel=1,1:10]              <-- HIDDEN channel 1
  [@9,11:21='// testing\n',<25>,channel=2,1:11]   <-- HIDDEN channel 2
  [@10,22:21='<EOF>',<-1>,2:22]
  (file (varDecl (type int) i = (expr 3) ;))      <-- parse tree
```

The parse tree also looks right, which means that the parser correctly interpreted the input. The lack of syntax error indicates that the parser didn't plow into a comment token. Now let's figure out how to access hidden comments from a language application.

Accessing Hidden Channels

To illustrate how to access the hidden channels from a language application, let's build a parse-tree listener that shifts comments following declarations to precede the declarations, tweaking them to use /*...*/-style comments. For example, given the following input:

lexmagic/t.cym
```
int n = 0; // define a counter
int i = 9;
```

we want to generate the following output:

```
/* define a counter */
int n = 0;
int i = 9;
```

Our basic strategy will be to rewrite the token stream using a TokenStreamRewriter, as we did in *Rewriting the Input Stream*, on page 54. Upon seeing a variable declaration, our application will grab the comment, if any, to the right of the semicolon and insert it before the first token of the declaration. Here's a Cymbol parse-tree listener called CommentShifter that sits inside a test rig class called ShiftVarComments:

lexmagic/ShiftVarComments.java

```
1  public static class CommentShifter extends CymbolBaseListener {
2      BufferedTokenStream tokens;
3      TokenStreamRewriter rewriter;
4              /** Create TokenStreamRewriter attached to token stream
5               *  sitting between the Cymbol lexer and parser.
6               */
7      public CommentShifter(BufferedTokenStream tokens) {
8          this.tokens = tokens;
9          rewriter = new TokenStreamRewriter(tokens);
10     }
11
12     @Override
13     public void exitVarDecl(CymbolParser.VarDeclContext ctx) {
14         Token semi = ctx.getStop();
15         int i = semi.getTokenIndex();
16         List<Token> cmtChannel =
17             tokens.getHiddenTokensToRight(i, CymbolLexer.COMMENTS);
18         if ( cmtChannel!=null ) {
19             Token cmt = cmtChannel.get(0);
20             if ( cmt!=null ) {
21                 String txt = cmt.getText().substring(2);
22                 String newCmt = "/* " + txt.trim() + " */\n";
23                 rewriter.insertBefore(ctx.start, newCmt);
24                 rewriter.replace(cmt, "\n");
25             }
26         }
27     }
28 }
```

All of the work happens in exitVarDecl(). First we get the token index of the declaration semicolon (line 14) because we're looking for comments after that token. Line 17 asks the token stream if there are any hidden tokens on channel COMMENTS to the right of the semicolon. For simplicity, the code assumes there is only one, so line 19 grabs the first comment from the list. Then we derive the new style comment from the old comment and inject it using TokenStreamRewriter before the start of the variable declaration (line 23). Finally, we replace the existing following comment with a newline (line 24), effectively erasing it.

The test rig itself is the same old story, but at the end, we ask the TokenStreamRewriter class to give us the rewritten input with getText().

lexmagic/ShiftVarComments.java

```
CymbolLexer lexer = new CymbolLexer(input);
CommonTokenStream tokens = new CommonTokenStream(lexer);
CymbolParser parser = new CymbolParser(tokens);
RuleContext tree = parser.file();
```

```
ParseTreeWalker walker = new ParseTreeWalker();
CommentShifter shifter = new CommentShifter(tokens);
walker.walk(shifter, tree);
System.out.print(shifter.rewriter.getText());
```

Here's the build and test sequence:

```
$ antlr4 Cymbol.g4
$ javac Cymbol*.java ShiftVarComments.java
$ java ShiftVarComments t.cym
/* define a counter */
int n = 0;
int i = 9;
```

Note that if we had thrown out whitespace, rather than sending it on a hidden channel, that output would be all bunched together like `intn=0;`.

Token channels solve a tricky language translation problem by categorizing input tokens. Now, we're going to focus on problems related to the construction of the tokens themselves.

12.2 Context-Sensitive Lexical Problems

Consider the phrase "Brown leaves in the fall." It's ambiguous because there are two interpretations. If we're talking about trees, the phrase refers to nature's photosynthesis engine. If, on the other hand, we're discussing a certain Ms. Jane Brown, the context totally changes the function of those words. "Leaves" shifts from a noun to a verb.

This situation resembles the problems we solved in Section 11.3, *Recognizing Ambiguous Phrases*, on page 198 where context-sensitive C++ phrases like `T(0)` could be function calls or type casts depending on how `T` was defined elsewhere in the program. Such syntactic ambiguities arose because our C++ lexer sent vague generic `ID` tokens to the parser. We needed semantic predicates in the parser rules to choose between alternative interpretations.

To get rid of the predicates in the parser rules, we could have the lexer send more precise tokens to the parser such as `FUNCTION_NAME` vs. `TYPE_NAME`, depending on context. (For input "Brown leaves," we'd have the lexer send token sequence `ADJECTIVE NOUN` vs. `PROPER_NAME VERB`.) Unfortunately, that just shifts the context-sensitivity problem to the lexer, and the lexer has nowhere near as much context information as the parser. That's why we predicated parser rules in the previous chapter instead of trying to use lexer context to send more precise tokens to the parser.

Hack Alert: Parser Feedback

A common practice that's been around forever involves sending feedback from the parser to the lexer so that the lexer can send precise tokens to the parser. The parser can then be simpler because of the reduction in predicates. Unfortunately, this is not possible with ANTLR grammars because ANTLR-generated parsers often look very far ahead in the token stream to make parsing decisions. That means the lexer could be asked to tokenize input characters long before the parser has had a chance to execute actions that provide context information to the lexer.

We can't always escape context-sensitivity issues related to tokenizing input characters. In this section, we're going to look at three lexical problems that fit into the context-sensitivity bucket.

- *The same token character sequence can mean different things to the parser.* We'll tackle the well-known "keywords can also be identifiers" problem.
- *The same character sequence can be one token or multiple.* We'll see how to treat Java character sequence >> either as two close-type-parameter tokens or as a single right shift operator token.
- *The same token must sometimes be ignored and sometimes be recognized by the parser.* We'll learn how to distinguish between Python's physical and logical input lines. The solution requires both lexical actions and semantic predicates, techniques we learned in the previous two chapters.

Treating Keywords As Identifiers

Lots of languages, both old and new, allow keywords as identifiers, depending on the context. In Fortran, we could say things like `end = goto + if/while`. C# supports SQL queries with its Language-Integrated Query (LINQ) feature. Queries begin with keyword `from`, but we can also use `from` as a variable: `x = from + where;`. That's unambiguously an expression, not a query syntactically, so the lexer should treat `from` as an identifier, not a keyword. The problem is that the lexer doesn't parse the input. It doesn't know whether to send, say, `KEYWORD_FROM` or `ID` to the parser.

There are two approaches to allowing keywords to act as identifiers in some syntactic contexts. The first approach has the lexer pass all keywords to the parser as keyword token types, and then we create a parser `id` rule that matches `ID` and any of the keywords. The second approach has the lexer pass keywords as identifiers, and then we use predicates to test identifier names in the parser like this:

When in Paris...

I worked in France in the late 1980s and quickly found a problem when calling people on the phone. When the receiving end asked who was calling, I'd reply *Monsieur Parr*, but Parr sounds just like *part*, the third-person singular of the verb "to leave." It sounds like I'm saying that I'm going to hang up. Hilarious.

Here's a fun tongue twister in French where each word requires heavy context to decipher: "Si six cent scies scient six cent saucisses, six cent six scies scieront six cent six saucissons." The written form is repetitive but clear. When spoken, however, the pronunciation in English is something like this: "See see saw, see see see saw, sawcease, see saw see see seeron see saw see sawcease." The translation is "If six hundred saws saw six hundred sausages, six hundred and six saws will saw six hundred six sausages." Don't make fun of the French for the fact that *si*, *six*, *scies*, and *scient* all sound exactly the same. English has words that are written the same but pronounced differently, like read (present tense) and read (past tense)!

```
keyIF : {_input.LT(1).getText().equals("if")}? ID ;
```

That's pretty ugly, and likely slow, so we'll stick with the first approach. (For completeness, I've left a small but working predicated keyword example in PredKeyword.g4.)

To illustrate the recommended approach, here's a simple grammar that matches nutty statements like `if if then call call;`:

lexmagic/IDKeyword.g4

```
grammar IDKeyword;

prog: stat+ ;

stat: 'if' expr 'then' stat
    | 'call' id ';'
    | ';'
    ;

expr: id ;

id  :   'if' | 'call' | 'then' | ID ;

ID : [a-z]+ ;
WS : [ \r\n]+ -> skip ;
```

In a nutshell, the approach replaces all references to token `ID` with references to rule `id`. If you're faced with a language that allows different sets of keywords to be identifiers in different contexts, you'll need more than one `id` rule (one per context).

Here's the build and test sequence for grammar IDKeyword:

```
⇒ $ antlr4 IDKeyword.g4
⇒ $ javac IDKeyword*.java
⇒ $ grun IDKeyword prog
⇒ if if then call call;
⇒ EOF
```

The parse tree shows that the grammar treats the second if and second call symbols as identifiers.

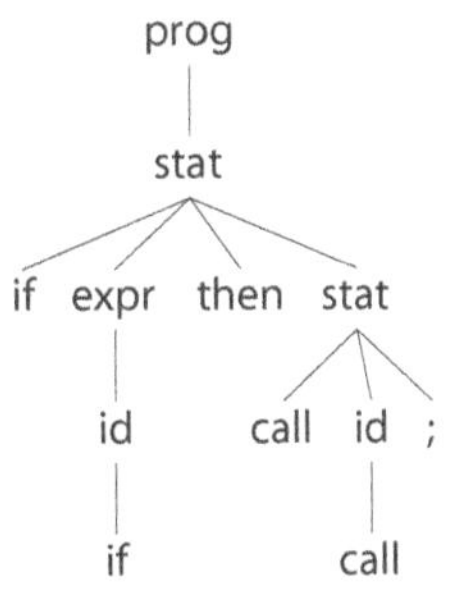

In this problem, the lexer has to decide whether to return keyword or identifier tokens, but it doesn't have to worry about which characters constitute the tokens. Now we're going to work on a problem where the lexer doesn't know how much input to consume for each token.

Avoiding the Maximal Munch Ambiguity

There is a general assumption made by lexer-generator tools that lexers should match the longest possible token at each input position. That assumption usually gives lexers the most natural behavior. For example, given C input +=, a C lexer should match the single token +=, not two separate tokens, as in + and =. Unfortunately, there are a few cases we need to handle differently.

In C++, we can't close nested parameterized types with a double angle bracket like this: A<B<C>>. We have to use a space in between the final angle brackets, A<B<C> >, so the lexer doesn't confuse the double angle brackets with the right shift operator, >>.[1] It was considered a hard enough problem that the designers of C++ altered the language to overcome a nasty lexical implementation problem.

A number of suitable solutions have since popped up, but the simplest is to never have the lexer match the >> character sequence as a right shift operator. Instead, the lexer sends two > tokens to the parser, which can use context

1. http://www.open-std.org/jtc1/sc22/wg21/docs/papers/2005/n1757.html

to pack the tokens together appropriately. For example, a C++ parser expression rule would match two right angle brackets in a row instead of a single token. If you look back at the Java of grammar from Section 4.3, *Building a Translator with a Listener*, on page 44, you'll see an example implementation of this approach. Here are two `expr` rule alternatives that combine single-character tokens into multicharacter operators:

tour/Java.g4

```
|   expression ('<' '<' | '>' '>' '>' | '>' '>') expression
|   expression ('<' '=' | '>' '=' | '>' | '<') expression
```

Let's look at the tokens passed by the lexer to the parser for the shift operator.

```
$ antlr4 Java.g4
$ javac Java*.java
$ grun Java tokens -tokens
i = 1 >> 5;
EOF
[@0,0:0='i',<98>,1:0]
[@1,1:1=' ',<100>,channel=1,1:1]
[@2,2:2='=',<25>,1:2]
[@3,3:3=' ',<100>,channel=1,1:3]
[@4,4:4='1',<91>,1:4]
[@5,5:5=' ',<100>,channel=1,1:5]
[@6,6:6='>',<81>,1:6]            <-- two '>' tokens not one '>>'
[@7,7:7='>',<81>,1:7]
[@8,8:8=' ',<100>,channel=1,1:8]
[@9,9:9='5',<91>,1:9]
[@10,10:10=';',<77>,1:10]
[@11,11:11='\n',<100>,channel=1,1:11]
[@12,12:11='<EOF>',<-1>,2:12]
```

And here's what the token stream looks like for a nested generic type reference:

```
$ grun Java tokens -tokens
List<List<String>> x;
EOF
[@0,0:3='List',<98>,1:0]
[@1,4:4='<',<5>,1:4]
[@2,5:8='List',<98>,1:5]
[@3,9:9='<',<5>,1:9]
[@4,10:15='String',<98>,1:10]
[@5,16:16='>',<81>,1:16]
[@6,17:17='>',<81>,1:17]
[@7,18:18=' ',<100>,channel=1,1:18]
[@8,19:19='x',<98>,1:19]
[@9,20:20=';',<77>,1:20]
[@10,21:21='\n',<100>,channel=1,1:21]
[@11,22:21='<EOF>',<-1>,2:22]
```

Now let's generate the parse trees for those phrases because they make it clear how the grammar uses the > tokens.

```
⇒ $ grun Java statement -gui
⇒ i = 1 >> 5;
⇒ EOF
⇒ $ grun Java localVariableDeclarationStatement -gui
⇒ List<List<String>> x;
⇒ EOF
```

Here are the parse trees side by side, rooted at rules statement and localVariableDeclarationStatement with the angle brackets highlighted:

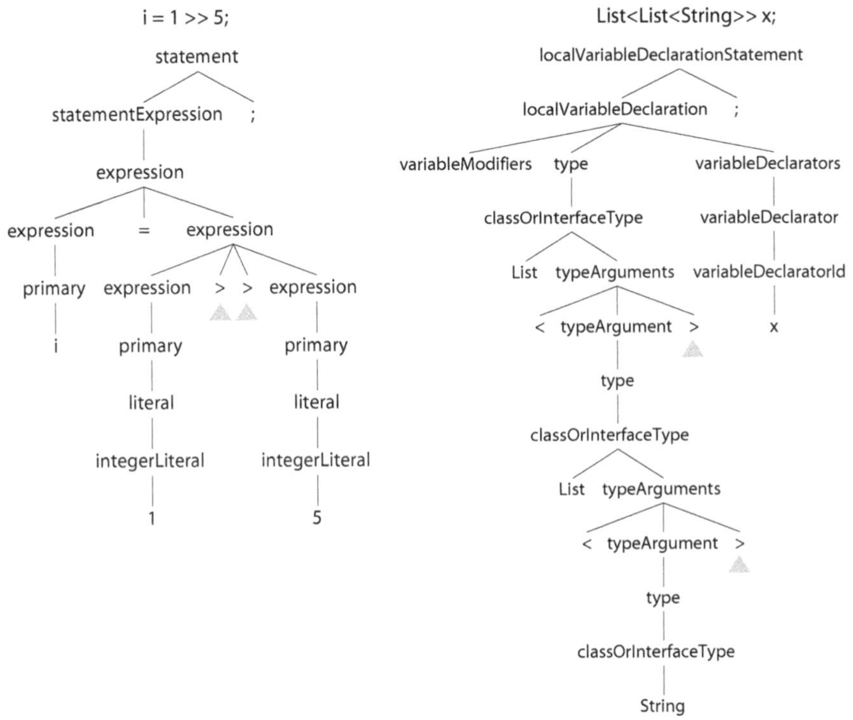

The only problem with splitting the two right angle brackets of the shift operator is that the parser will also accept angle brackets separated by a space character, > >. To address this, either we can add semantic predicates to the grammar or we can check the parse tree afterward using a listener or visitor to ensure that the > token column numbers are adjacent for shift operators. It'd be inefficient to use predicates during the parse, so it's better to check the right shift operators after the parse. Most language applications need to walk the parse tree anyway. (Predicates in an expression rule would also break ANTLR's left-recursive rule pattern that it knows how to convert to a non-left-recursive version. See Chapter 14, *Removing Direct Left Recursion*, on page 249.)

At this point, we've seen how to put tokens on different channels and how to split context-sensitive tokens into their smallest valid token components. Now we're going to figure out how to treat the same character sequence as two different token types, depending on the context.

Fun with Python Newlines

Python's newline handling is very natural for the programmer. Rather than using a semicolon, newlines terminate statements. Most of us put one statement per line anyway, so typing the semicolon constantly is a nuisance. At the same time, we don't want to put really long expressions on the same physical line, so Python ignores newlines in certain contexts. For example, Python lets us split method calls over multiple lines like this:

```
f(1,
2,
3)
```

To figure out when to ignore newlines, let's put together all of the bits of documentation concerning newlines from the Python reference manual.[2] The most important rule is as follows:

> Expressions in parentheses, square brackets, or curly braces can be split over more than one physical line [...].

So, if we try to split expression 1+2 after the + with a newline, Python emits an error. We can, however, split (1+2) across lines. The manual also says that "Implicitly continued lines can carry comments" and "Blank continuation lines are allowed," like this:

```
f(1,  # first arg

2,    # second arg
      # blank line with a comment
3)    # third arg
```

We can also explicitly join physical lines into one logical line using a backslash.

> Two or more physical lines may be joined into logical lines using backslash characters (\), as follows: when a physical line ends in a backslash that is not part of a string literal or comment, it is joined with the following, forming a single logical line, deleting the backslash and the following end-of-line character.

That means we can split lines even outside of grouping symbols like this:

```
1+\
2
```

2. http://docs.python.org/reference/lexical_analysis.html

The manual does not explicitly say so, but the "line ends in a backslash" clause implies that there can't be a comment between the \ and the newline character.

The upshot is that either the parser or the lexer needs to toss out some newlines but not others. As we saw earlier with token channels, having the parser check all the time for optional whitespace isn't a good solution. That means that a Python lexer needs to handle the optional newlines. This then is another case of syntactic context dictating lexer behavior.

With all of these rules in mind, let's build a grammar for a trivial version of Python that matches assignments and simple expressions. We'll ignore strings in order to focus solely on proper comments and newline handling. Here are the syntax rules:

lexmagic/SimplePy.g4

```
file:   stat+ EOF ;

stat:   assign NEWLINE
    |   expr NEWLINE
    |   NEWLINE          // ignore blank lines
    ;

assign: ID '=' expr ;

expr:   expr '+' expr
    |   '(' expr ')'
    |   call
    |   list
    |   ID
    |   INT
    ;

call:   ID '(' ( expr (',' expr)* )? ')' ;

list:   '[' expr (',' expr)* ']' ;
```

To build the lexer, let's get the familiar rules out of the way first. The INT rule for integers is the usual one, and, according to the reference, identifiers look like this:

```
identifier ::=  (letter|"_") (letter | digit | "_")*
letter     ::=  lowercase | uppercase
```

In ANTLR notation, that's as follows:

lexmagic/SimplePy.g4

```
ID  :   [a-zA-Z_] [a-zA-Z_0-9]* ;
```

Then, we need the usual whitespace rule and a rule to match newlines, which sends NEWLINE tokens to the parser.

lexmagic/SimplePy.g4

```
/** A logical newline that ends a statement */
NEWLINE
    :   '\r'? '\n'
    ;

/** Warning: doesn't handle INDENT/DEDENT Python rules */
WS  :   [ \t]+ -> skip
    ;
```

To handle Python's line comments, we need a rule that strips out the comment part but doesn't touch the newline.

lexmagic/SimplePy.g4

```
/** Match comments. Don't match \n here; we'll send NEWLINE to the parser. */
COMMENT
    :    '#' ~[\r\n]* -> skip
    ;
```

We want NEWLINE to handle all newlines so that the following:

```
i = 3 # assignment
```

looks like an assignment followed by NEWLINE.

Now it's time to handle the special newline stuff. Let's start with explicit line joining. We add a rule to match \ immediately followed by a newline, tossing it out.

lexmagic/SimplePy.g4

```
/** Ignore backslash newline sequences. This disallows comments
 *  after the backslash because newline must occur next.
 */
LINE_ESCAPE
    :   '\\' '\r'? '\n' -> skip
    ;
```

That means the parser won't see either the \ or the newline character(s).

Now we have to make the lexer ignore newlines inside grouping symbols like parentheses and brackets. That means we need a lexer rule called IGNORE_NEWLINE that matches newlines like NEWLINE but skips the token if it's within grouping symbols. Because those two rules match the same character sequence, they're ambiguous, and we need a semantic predicate to differentiate them. If we imagine for the moment that there's a magic nesting variable that is greater than zero when the lexer has seen an open grouping symbol but not the closing symbol, we can write IGNORE_NEWLINE like this:

lexmagic/SimplePy.g4

```
/** Nested newline within a (..) or [..] are ignored. */
IGNORE_NEWLINE
    :   '\r'? '\n' {nesting>0}? -> skip
    ;
```

That rule must appear before rule NEWLINE so that when the predicate is true, the lexer resolves the ambiguity by choosing rule IGNORE_NEWLINE. We could also put a {nesting==0}? predicate in NEWLINE to resolve the order dependency.

Now let's wiggle this variable appropriately as we see opening and closing parentheses and brackets. (Our syntax does not allow curly braces.) First, let's define the magic nesting variable.

lexmagic/SimplePy.g4

```
@lexer::members {
    int nesting = 0;
}
```

Then, we need to execute actions that bump nesting up and down as we see the grouping symbols. The following rules do the trick:

lexmagic/SimplePy.g4

```
LPAREN    : '(' {nesting++;} ;

RPAREN    : ')' {nesting--;} ;

LBRACK    : '[' {nesting++;} ;

RBRACK    : ']' {nesting--;} ;
```

To be strictly correct, we should use a different variable for parentheses and for brackets so that we can make sure they balance. But we don't really have to worry about imbalances like [1,2) because the parser will detect an error. Any inexact behavior with ignored newlines is not important in the presence of such a syntax error.

To test our SimplePy grammar, the following test file exercises the key elements of Python newline and comment processing: blanks are ignored, newlines are ignored within grouping symbols, backslashes hide the next newline, and comments don't affect newline processing inside grouping symbols.

lexmagic/f.py

```
# a test
f(1, # first arg

  2, # second arg
     # blank line with a comment
  3) # third arg
```

```
g() # on end

1+\
2+\
3
```

Here's the build and test sequence showing the token stream sent to the parser with highlighted NEWLINE tokens:

```
$ antlr4 SimplePy.g4
$ javac SimplePy*.java
$ grun SimplePy file -tokens f.py
[@0,8:8='\n',<11>,1:8]
[@1,9:9='f',<4>,2:0]
[@2,10:10='(',<6>,2:1]
[@3,11:11='1',<5>,2:2]
[@4,12:12=',',<1>,2:3]
[@5,29:29='2',<5>,4:2]
[@6,30:30=',',<1>,4:3]
[@7,80:80='3',<5>,6:2]
[@8,81:81=')',<7>,6:3]
[@9,94:94='\n',<11>,6:16]
[@10,95:95='\n',<11>,7:0]
[@11,96:96='g',<4>,8:0]
[@12,97:97='(',<6>,8:1]
[@13,98:98=')',<7>,8:2]
[@14,108:108='\n',<11>,8:12]
[@15,109:109='\n',<11>,9:0]
[@16,110:110='1',<5>,10:0]
[@17,111:111='+',<2>,10:1]
[@18,114:114='2',<5>,11:0]
[@19,115:115='+',<2>,11:1]
[@20,118:118='3',<5>,12:0]
[@21,119:119='\n',<11>,12:1]
[@22,120:119='<EOF>',<-1>,13:2]
```

The key thing to notice is that there are six NEWLINE tokens in the stream but twelve newlines in file f.py. Our lexer successfully chucks out six newlines. The parse tree with highlighted newline tokens looks like Figure 11, *Parse tree with highlighted newline tokens*, on page 221.

The first newline is a blank line and matched as an empty statement (rule stat) by the parser. The third and fifth newlines are also empty statements. The three other newlines terminate expression statements. Running f.py into a Python interpreter (with suitable f() and g() definitions) confirms that f.py is valid Python.

We've just worked through three kinds of context-sensitivity problems associated with tokens. The contexts we considered were defined by the syntax, not

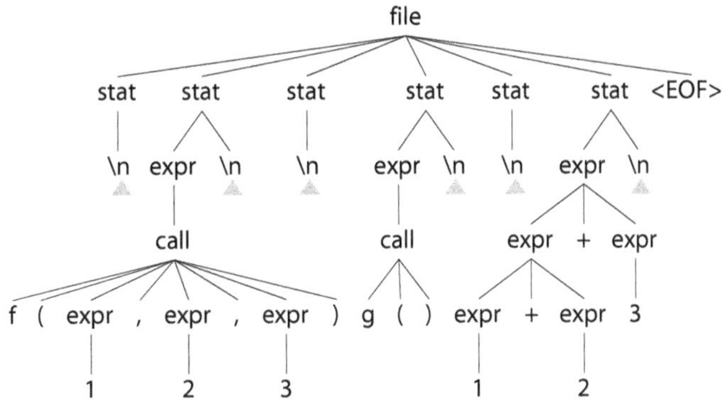

Figure 11—Parse tree with highlighted newline tokens

a region of the input file. Next, we're going to look at input files that have isolated regions of interest surrounded by regions we don't care about.

12.3 Islands in the Stream

The input files we've discussed so far all contain a single language. For example, DOT, CSV, Python, and Java files contain nothing but text conforming to those languages. But, there are file formats that contain random text surrounding structured regions or *islands*. We call such formats *island languages* and describe them with *island grammars*. Examples include template engine languages such as StringTemplate and the LaTeX document preparation language, but XML is the quintessential island language. XML files contain structured tags and & entities surrounded by a sea of stuff we don't care about. (Because there is some structure between the tags themselves, we might call XML an *archipelago language*.)

Classifying something as an island language often depends on our perspective. If we're building a C preprocessor, the preprocessor commands form an island language where the C code is the sea. On the other hand, if we're building a C parser suitable for an IDE, the parser must ignore the sea of preprocessor commands.

Our goal in this section is to learn how to ignore the sea and tokenize the islands so the parser can verify syntax within those islands. We'll need both of those techniques to build a real XML parser in the next section. Let's start by learning how to distinguish XML islands from the sea.

Separating XML Islands from a Sea of Text

To separate XML tags from text, our first thought might be to build an input character stream filter that strips everything between tags. This might make it easy for the lexer to identify the islands, but the filter would throw out all of the text data, which is not what we want. For example, given input <name>John</name>, we don't want to throw out John.

Instead, let's build a baby XML grammar that lumps the text inside of tags together as one token and the text outside of tags as another token. Since we're focusing on the lexer here, we'll use a single syntactic rule that matches a bunch of tags, & entities, CDATA sections, and text (the sea).

lexmagic/Tags.g4

```
grammar Tags;
file : (TAG|ENTITY|TEXT|CDATA)* ;
```

Rule file makes no attempt to ensure the document is well formed—it just indicates the kinds of tokens found in an XML file.

To split up an XML file with lexer rules, we can just give rules for the island and then a catchall rule called TEXT at the end to match everything else.

lexmagic/Tags.g4

```
COMMENT : '<!--' .*? '-->' -> skip ;
CDATA : '<![CDATA[' .*? ']]>' ;
TAG : '<' .*? '>' ; // must come after other tag-like structures
ENTITY : '&' .*? ';' ;
TEXT : ~[<&]+ ;     // any sequence of chars except < and & chars
```

Those rules make heavy use of the nongreedy .*? operator (see *Matching String Literals*, on page 77) that scans until it sees what follows that operation in the rule.

Rule TEXT matches one or more characters, as long as the character isn't the start of a tag or entity. It's tempting to put .+ instead of ~[<&]+, but that would consume until the end of the input once it got into the loop. There's no string to match following .+ in TEXT that would tell the loop when to stop.

An important but subtle ambiguity-resolving mechanism is in play here. In Section 2.3, *You Can't Put Too Much Water into a Nuclear Reactor*, on page 14, we learned that ANTLR lexers resolve ambiguities in favor of the rule specified first in the grammar file. For example, rule TAG matches anything in angle brackets, which includes comments and CDATA sections. Because we specified COMMENT and CDATA first, rule TAG matches only those tags that failed to match the other tag rules.

As a side note, XML technically doesn't allow comments that end with ---> or comments that contain --. Using what we learned in Section 9.4, *Error Alternatives*, on page 172, we could add lexical rules to look for bad comments and give specific and informative error messages.

```
BAD_COMMENT1:   '<!--' .*? '--->'
                {System.err.println("Can't have ---> end comment");} -> skip ;
BAD_COMMENT2:   '<!--' ('--'|.)*? '-->'
                {System.err.println("Can't have -- in comment");}    -> skip ;
```

I've left them out of grammar Tags for simplicity.

Now let's see what our baby XML grammar does with the following input:

lexmagic/XML-inputs/cat.xml

```
<?xml version="1.0" encoding="UTF-8"?>
<?do not care?>
<CATALOG>
<PLANT id="45">Orchid</PLANT>
</CATALOG>
```

Here's the build and test sequence, using grun to print out the tokens:

```
$ antlr4 Tags.g4
$ javac Tags*.java
$ grun Tags file -tokens XML-inputs/cat.xml
[@0,0:37='<?xml version="1.0" encoding="UTF-8"?>',<3>,1:0]
[@1,38:38='\n',<5>,1:38]
[@2,39:53='<?do not care?>',<3>,2:0]
[@3,54:54='\n',<5>,2:15]
[@4,55:63='<CATALOG>',<3>,3:0]
[@5,64:64='\n',<5>,3:9]
[@6,65:79='<PLANT id="45">',<3>,4:0]
[@7,80:85='Orchid',<5>,4:15]
[@8,86:93='</PLANT>',<3>,4:21]
[@9,94:94='\n',<5>,4:29]
[@10,95:104='</CATALOG>',<3>,5:0]
[@11,105:105='\n',<5>,5:10]
[@12,106:105='<EOF>',<-1>,6:11]
```

This baby XML grammar properly reads in XML files and matches a sequence of the various islands and text. What it doesn't do is pull apart the tags and pass the pieces to a parser so it can check the syntax.

Issuing Context-Sensitive Tokens with Lexical Modes

The text inside and outside of tags conform to different languages. For example, id="45" is just a lump of text outside of a tag, but it's three tokens inside of a tag. In a sense, we want an XML lexer to match different sets of rules depending on the context. ANTLR provides *lexical modes* that let lexers switch between contexts (modes). In this section, we'll learn to use lexical modes by improving the baby XML grammar from the previous section so that it passes tag components to the parser.

Lexical modes allow us to split a single lexer grammar into multiple sublexers. The lexer can return only those tokens matched by entering a rule in the current mode. One of the most important requirements for mode switching is that the language have clear lexical sentinels that can trigger switching back and forth, such as left and right angle brackets. To be clear, modes rely on the fact that the lexer doesn't need syntactic context to distinguish between different regions in the input.

To keep things simple, let's build a grammar for an XML subset where tags contain an identifier but no attributes. We'll use the default mode to match the sea outside of tags and another mode to match the inside of tags. When the lexer matches < in default mode, it should switch to island mode (inside tag mode) and return a tag start token to the parser. When the inside mode sees >, it should switch back to default mode and return a tag stop token. The inside mode also needs rules to match identifiers and /. The following lexer encodes that strategy:

lexmagic/ModeTagsLexer.g4

```
lexer grammar ModeTagsLexer;

// Default mode rules (the SEA)
OPEN  : '<'     -> mode(ISLAND) ;       // switch to ISLAND mode
TEXT  : ~'<'+ ;                         // clump all text together

mode ISLAND;
CLOSE : '>'     -> mode(DEFAULT_MODE) ; // back to SEA mode
SLASH : '/' ;
ID    : [a-zA-Z]+ ;                     // match/send ID in tag to parser
```

Rules OPEN and TEXT are in the default mode. OPEN matches a single < and uses lexer command mode(ISLAND) to switch modes. Upon the next token request from the parser, the lexer will consider only those rules in ISLAND mode. TEXT matches any sequence of characters that doesn't start a tag. Because none of the lexical rules in this grammar uses lexical command skip, all of them return a token to the parser when they match.

In ISLAND mode, the lexer matches closing >, /, and ID tokens. When the lexer sees >, it will execute the lexer command to switch back to the default mode, identified by constant DEFAULT_MODE in class Lexer. This is how the lexer ping-pongs back and forth between modes.

The parser for our slightly augmented XML subset matches tags and text chunks as in grammar Tags, but now we're using rule tag to match the individual tag elements instead of a single lumped token.

lexmagic/ModeTagsParser.g4
```
parser grammar ModeTagsParser;

options { tokenVocab=ModeTagsLexer; } // use tokens from ModeTagsLexer.g4

file: (tag | TEXT)* ;

tag : '<' ID '>'
    | '<' '/' ID '>'
    ;
```

The only unfamiliar syntax in the parser is the tokenVocab option. When we have the parser and lexer in separate files, we need to make sure that the token types and token names from the two files are synchronized. For example, lexer token OPEN must have the same token type in the parser as it does in the lexer.

Let's build the grammar and try it on some simple XML input.

```
⇒ $ antlr4 ModeTagsLexer.g4   # must be done first to get ModeTagsLexer.tokens
⇒ $ antlr4 ModeTagsParser.g4
⇒ $ javac ModeTags*.java
⇒ $ grun ModeTags file -tokens
⇒ Hello <name>John</name>
⇒ EOF
❮ [@0,0:5='Hello ',<2>,1:0]
  [@1,6:6='<',<1>,1:6]
  [@2,7:10='name',<5>,1:7]
  [@3,11:11='>',<3>,1:11]
  [@4,12:15='John',<2>,1:12]
  [@5,16:16='<',<1>,1:16]
  [@6,17:17='/',<4>,1:17]
  [@7,18:21='name',<5>,1:18]
  [@8,22:22='>',<3>,1:22]
  [@9,23:23='\n',<2>,1:23]
  [@10,24:23='<EOF>',<-1>,2:24]
```

The lexer sends <name> to the parser as the three tokens at indexes 1, 2, and 3. Also notice that Hello, which lives in the sea, would match rule ID but only in ISLAND mode. Since the lexer starts out in default mode, Hello matches as token TEXT. You can see the difference in the token types between tokens at index 0 and 2 where name matches as token ID (token type 5).

Another reason that we want to match tag syntax in the parser instead of the lexer is that the parser has much more flexibility to execute actions. Furthermore, the parser automatically builds a parse tree for us.

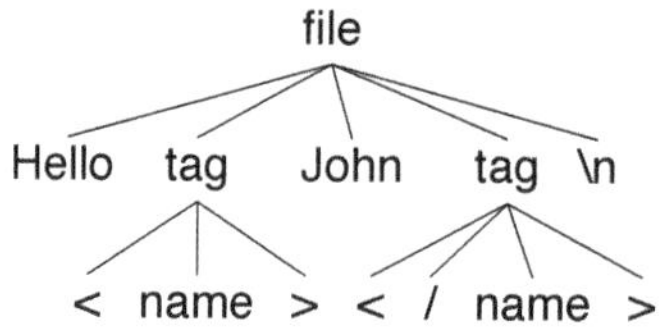

To use our grammar for an application, we could either use the usual listener or visitor mechanism or add actions to the grammar. For example, to implement an XML SAX event mechanism, we could shut off the automatic tree construction and embed grammar actions to trigger SAX method calls.

Now that we know how to separate the XML islands from the sea and how to send tag components to a parser, let's build a real XML parser.

12.4 Parsing and Lexing XML

Because XML is a well-defined language, it's a good idea to start our XML project by reviewing the W3C XML language definition.[3] Unfortunately, the XML specification (henceforth *the spec*) is huge, and it's very easy to get lost in all of the details. To make our lives easier, let's get rid of stuff we don't need in order to parse XML files: `<!DOCTYPE..>` document type definitions (DTDs), `<!ENTITY..>` entity declarations, and `<!NOTATION..>` notation declarations. Besides, handling those tags wouldn't teach us anything beyond what we need to handle the other constructs.

We're going to start out by building the syntactic rules for XML. The good news is that we can reuse the informal grammar rules from the spec almost verbatim by changing them to ANTLR notation.

XML Spec to ANTLR Parser Grammar

Using our experience with XML, we could probably come up with a reasonably complete and accurate XML grammar. To make sure we don't forget anything, however, let's filter and condense the spec to its key grammatical rules.

```
document     ::=  prolog element Misc*
prolog       ::=  XMLDecl? Misc*
content      ::=  CharData?
                  ((element | Reference | CDSect | PI | Comment) CharData?)*
element      ::=  EmptyElemTag
              |   STag content ETag
```

3. http://www.w3.org/TR/REC-xml/

```
EmptyElemTag ::=  '<' Name (S Attribute)* S? '/>'
STag         ::=  '<' Name (S Attribute)* S? '>'
ETag         ::=  '</' Name S? '>'
XMLDecl      ::=  '<?xml' VersionInfo EncodingDecl? SDDecl? S? '?>'
Attribute    ::=  Name Eq AttValue
Reference    ::=  EntityRef | CharRef
Misc         ::=  Comment | PI | S
```

There are lots of other rules we'll need, but they'll go into our lexer. This is a good example of where to draw the line, per our discussion in Section 5.6, *Drawing the Line Between Lexer and Parser*, on page 81. The key criterion to follow is whether we need to see inside the element's structure. For example, we don't care about the inside of comments or processing instructions (PI), so we can have the lexer match them as lumps.

Let's compare these informal spec rules with the following complete ANTLR parser grammar. Relative to the grammars we've built for languages like JSON and Cymbol, the XML parser rules are pretty simple.

lexmagic/XMLParser.g4
```
parser grammar XMLParser;
options { tokenVocab=XMLLexer; }

document    :   prolog? misc* element misc*;

prolog      :   XMLDeclOpen attribute* SPECIAL_CLOSE ;

content     :   chardata?
                ((element | reference | CDATA | PI | COMMENT) chardata?)* ;

element     :   '<' Name attribute* '>' content '<' '/' Name '>'
            |   '<' Name attribute* '/>'
            ;

reference   :   EntityRef | CharRef ;

attribute   :   Name '=' STRING ; // Our STRING is AttValue in spec
/** ``All text that is not markup constitutes the character data of
 *  the document.''
 */
chardata    :   TEXT | SEA_WS ;

misc        :   COMMENT | PI | SEA_WS ;
```

There are a number of important differences between the spec's rules and ours. First, the spec rule XMLDecl can match three specific attributes (version, encoding, and standalone), whereas ours matches any set of attributes inside <?xml ...?>. Later, a semantic phase would have to check that the attribute names were correct.

Alternatively, we could put predicates inside the grammar, but it makes the grammar hard to read and would slow down the generated parser.

```
prolog       : XMLDecl versionInfo encodingDecl? standalone? SPECIAL_CLOSE ;
versionInfo  : {_input.LT(1).getText().equals("version")}? Name '=' STRING ;
encodingDecl : {_input.LT(1).getText().equals("encoding")}? Name '=' STRING ;
standalone   : {_input.LT(1).getText().equals("standalone")}? Name '=' STRING ;
```

The next difference is that our lexer will match and discard whitespace inside of tags between the attributes, so we don't need to check for whitespace inside of our element rule. (element is an expanded version of rule tag from the previous section.) Our lexer also differentiates between whitespace (SEA_WS) and non-whitespace text (TEXT) outside of tags but returns both to the parser as tokens. (The previous two sections lumped all text outside of tags into a single TEXT token.) That's because the spec allows whitespace but not text in certain locations such as before the root element. Therefore, chardata is a parser rule, not a token in our grammar.

The XML parser is not too bad, but we're going to earn hazardous-duty pay building the lexer.

Tokenizing XML

Let's start our XML lexer by extracting the relevant rules from the spec to see what we're dealing with.

```
Comment    ::=  '<!--' ((Char - '-') | ('-' (Char - '-')))* '-->'
CDSect     ::=  '<![CDATA[' CData ']]>'
CData      ::=  (Char* - (Char* ']]>' Char*)) // anything but ']]>'
PI         ::=  '<?' PITarget (S (Char* - (Char* '?>' Char*)))? '?>'
/** Any name except 'xml' */
PITarget  ::=  Name - (('X' | 'x') ('M' | 'm') ('L' | 'l'))
/** Spec: ``CharData is any string of characters which does not contain the
 *  start-delimiter of any markup and does not include the
 *  CDATA-section-close delimiter, "]]>".''
 */
CharData  ::=  [^<&]* - ([^<&]* ']]>' [^<&]*)
EntityRef ::=  '&' Name ';'
CharRef   ::=  '&#' [0-9]+ ';'
          |    '&#x' [0-9a-fA-F]+ ';'
Name      ::=  NameStartChar (NameChar)*
NameChar  ::=  NameStartChar | "-" | "." | [0-9] | #xB7
          |    [#x0300-#x036F] | [#x203F-#x2040]
NameStartChar
          ::=  ":" | [A-Z] | "_" | [a-z] | [#xC0-#xD6] | [#xD8-#xF6]
          |    [#xF8-#x2FF] | [#x370-#x37D] | [#x37F-#x1FFF]
          |    [#x200C-#x200D] | [#x2070-#x218F] | [#x2C00-#x2FEF]
          |    [#x3001-#xD7FF] | [#xF900-#xFDCF] | [#xFDF0-#xFFFD]
          |    [#x10000-#xEFFFF]
```

```
AttValue   ::=   '"' ([^<&"] | Reference)* '"'
           |     "'" ([^<&'] | Reference)* "'"
S          ::=   (#x20 | #x9 | #xD | #xA)+
```

Blech! That looks kind of complicated, but we'll break it down into three different modes and build them one by one. We'll need modes to handle outside tags, inside tags, and inside of the special <?...?> tags, very much like we did in *Issuing Context-Sensitive Tokens with Lexical Modes*, on page 223.

When you compare the spec rules to our ANTLR lexer rules, you'll see that we can reuse most of the same rule names. The specs notation is quite different from ANTLR's, but we can reuse the spirit of most rule right sides. Let's start with the default mode that matches the sea outside of tags. Here's that piece of our lexer grammar:

lexmagic/XMLLexer.g4

```
lexer grammar XMLLexer;

// Default "mode": Everything OUTSIDE of a tag
COMMENT     :   '<!--' .*? '-->' ;
CDATA       :   '<![CDATA[' .*? ']]>' ;
/** Scarf all DTD stuff, Entity Declarations like <!ENTITY ...>,
 *  and Notation Declarations <!NOTATION ...>
 */
DTD         :   '<!' .*? '>'            -> skip ;
EntityRef   :   '&' Name ';' ;
CharRef     :   '&#' DIGIT+ ';'
            |   '&#x' HEXDIGIT+ ';'
            ;
SEA_WS      :   (' '|'\t'|'\r'? '\n') ;

OPEN        :   '<'                     -> pushMode(INSIDE) ;
XMLDeclOpen :   '<?xml' S               -> pushMode(INSIDE) ;
SPECIAL_OPEN:   '<?' Name               -> more, pushMode(PROC_INSTR) ;

TEXT        :   ~[<&]+ ;        // match any 16 bit char other than < and &
```

The lexer grammar starts by dealing with all of the lexical structures that we can treat as complete tokens. First, we give rules for COMMENT and CDATA tokens. Next, we match and discard anything related to document, entity, and notation declarations of the following form: <!...>. We don't care about that stuff for this project. We then need rules to match the various entities and the whitespace token. Jumping ahead for a second, rule TEXT matches anything else in the input until the start of a tag or entity reference. This is sort of the "else clause."

And now for the fun stuff. When the lexer sees the start of the tag, it needs to switch contexts so that the next lexer token match will find a token that's valid within a tag. That's what rule OPEN does. Unlike the ModeTagsLexer grammar that used just the mode command, we're using pushMode (and popMode in a moment). By pushing the mode, the lexer can pop the mode to return to the "invoking" mode. This is useful for nested mode switches, though we're not doing that here.

The next two rules distinguish between the special <?xml...?> tag and the regular <?...?> processing instruction. Because we want the parser prolog rule to match the attributes inside the <?xml...?> tag, we need the lexer to return an XMLDeclOpen token and then switch to the INSIDE tag mode, which will match the attribute tokens. Rule SPECIAL_OPEN matches the start of any other <?...?> tag and then switches to the PROC_INSTR mode (which we'll see shortly). It also uses an unfamiliar lexer command called more that instructs the lexer to look for another token and keep the text of the just-matched token.

Once inside mode PROC_INSTR, we want the lexer to keep consuming and piling up characters via rule IGNORE until it sees the end of the processing instruction, ?>.

lexmagic/XMLLexer.g4
```
mode PROC_INSTR;
PI          :   '?>'                    -> popMode ; // close <?...?>
IGNORE      :   .                       -> more ;
```

This is all a fancy way to match '<?' .*? '?>' for every processing instruction except for the <?xml...?> tag. The SPECIAL_OPEN rule matches <?xml also, but the lexer gives precedence to rule XMLDeclOpen since it's listed first per our discussion in Section 2.3, *You Can't Put Too Much Water into a Nuclear Reactor*, on page 14. Unfortunately, we can't just have a simple rule like '<?' .*? '?>' and do away with the PROC_INSTR mode. Since '<?' .*? '?>' matches a longer character sequence than '<?xml' S, the lexer would never match XMLDeclOpen. This is similar to the situation in *Avoiding the Maximal Munch Ambiguity*, on page 213, where the lexer favored one >> token over two > tokens.

Notice that SPECIAL_OPEN references rule Name, which doesn't appear in either mode we've looked at. It appears in the INSIDE mode we'll look at next. Modes just tell the lexer which set of rules it should consider matching when asked for a token. It's OK for one rule to call another in a different mode as a helper. But, keep in mind that the lexer can return token types to the parser only from those defined within the current lexer mode.

Our final mode is the INSIDE mode, which recognizes all of the elements within tags like this:

```
title id="chap2", center="true"
```

The lexical structure within tags reinforces the idea from Section 5.3, *Recognizing Common Language Patterns with ANTLR Grammars*, on page 63, that many languages look the same from a lexical perspective. For example, a lexer for C would have no problem tokenizing that tag content.

Here's our (final) mode that handles the structures within tags:

lexmagic/XMLLexer.g4

```
mode INSIDE;

CLOSE        :   '>'                    -> popMode ;
SPECIAL_CLOSE:   '?>'                   -> popMode ; // close <?xml...?>
SLASH_CLOSE  :   '/>'                   -> popMode ;
SLASH        :   '/' ;
EQUALS       :   '=' ;
STRING       :   '"' ~[<"]* '"'
             |   '\'' ~[<']* '\''
             ;
Name         :   NameStartChar NameChar* ;
S            :   [ \t\r\n]              -> skip ;

fragment
HEXDIGIT     :   [a-fA-F0-9] ;

fragment
DIGIT        :   [0-9] ;

fragment
NameChar     :   NameStartChar
             |   '-' | '.' | DIGIT
             |   '\u00B7'
             |   '\u0300'..'\u036F'
             |   '\u203F'..'\u2040'
             ;

fragment
NameStartChar
             :   [:a-zA-Z]
             |   '\u2070'..'\u218F'
             |   '\u2C00'..'\u2FEF'
             |   '\u3001'..'\uD7FF'
             |   '\uF900'..'\uFDCF'
             |   '\uFDF0'..'\uFFFD'
             ;
```

The first three rules match the end tag sequences. Here is where the popMode lexical command comes in handy. We don't have to specify the mode to switch to; the rules can just say "pop." The previous mode is on a mode stack.

Rule STRING matches rule AttValue from the spec and differs only in that STRING does not specifically match entities inside strings. We don't care about the inside of strings, so there's no point in carefully matching those characters.

We just have to make sure that we don't allow < or quotes inside of strings, per the spec.

Now that we have a parser and lexer grammar, let's build and test them.

Testing Our XML Grammar

As usual, we need to run ANTLR on the two grammars, being careful to process the lexer first because the parser depends on the token types generated by ANTLR for XMLLexer.g4.

```
$ antlr4 XMLLexer.g4
$ antlr4 XMLParser.g4
$ javac XML*.java
```

Here's a sample XML input file:

lexmagic/XML-inputs/entity.xml

```
<!-- a comment
-->
<root><!-- comment --><message>if salary &lt; 1000</message>
&apos; <a>hi</a>  <foo/>
</root>
```

Let's use grun to generate a parse tree.

```
$ grun XML document -gui XML-inputs/entity.xml
```

The parse tree indicates that our parser correctly handles comments, entities, tags, and text.

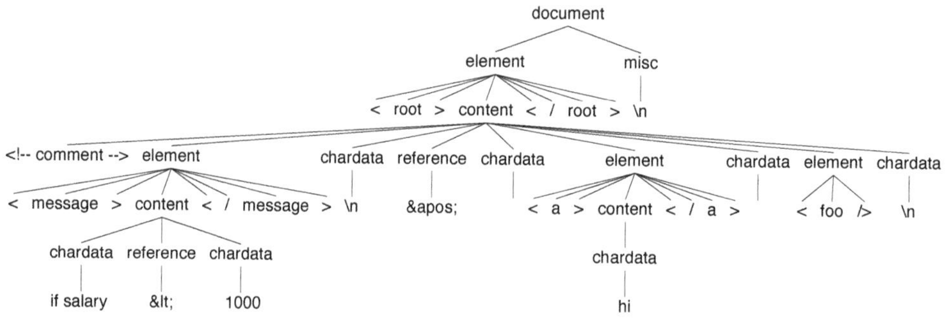

Now, let's check to make sure that our parser correctly handles <?xml...?> vs. other processing instruction tags. Here's a sample input file:

lexmagic/XML-inputs/cat.xml

```
<?xml version="1.0" encoding="UTF-8"?>
<?do not care?>
<CATALOG>
<PLANT id="45">Orchid</PLANT>
</CATALOG>
```

We can generate a parse tree with this:

```
$ grun XML document -ps /tmp/t.ps XML-inputs/cat.xml
```

The following tree shows that the XML declaration tag is properly sent in pieces to the parser, whereas <?do not care?> comes as one PI chunk.

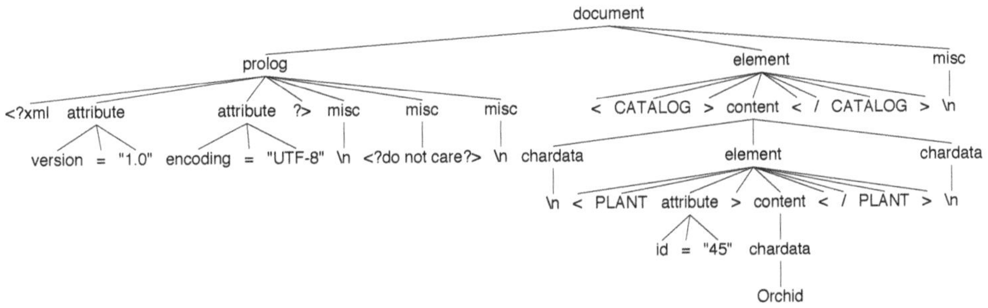

Most of the lexer rules in mode INSIDE deal with properly matching tag names, using all of the valid Unicode code points. That allows us to recognize, for example, XML files with Japanese tag names.[4] Running sample file weekly-euc-jp.xml into our parser requires the proper Japanese encoding option for grun.

```
$ grun XML document -gui -encoding euc-jp XML-inputs/weekly-euc-jp.xml
```

Figure 12, *A window into a dialog box*, on page 234 shows a window into the much larger dialog box.

This XML grammar is a great example of how complexity often resides in the lexer. Parsers can often be big, but they're usually not that difficult. When a language is hard to recognize, it's usually because it's hard to group the characters into tokens. This is either because the lexer really needs syntactic context to make decisions or because there are different regions in the file with different lexical rules.

This chapter is big, and we went through a lot of material, but it will serve as a good resource when you run into challenging recognition problems. We started out learning how to send different tokens on different channels so that we can ignore but not throw out key tokens such as comments and whitespace. Next, we looked at how to solve some context-sensitive lexical problems such as the pesky keywords-as-identifiers problem. Then, we learned how to tokenize multiple regions of the input differently using lexical modes, separating the islands from the sea. In our grand finale, we used lexical modes to build a precise XML lexer.

4. http://people.apache.org/~edwingo/jaxp-ri-1.2.0-fcs/samples/data/weekly-euc-jp.xml

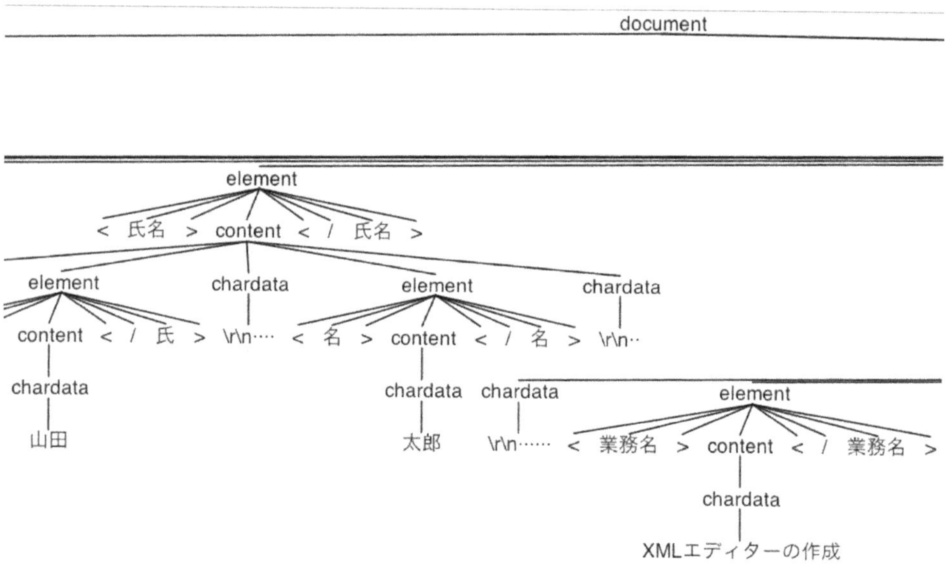

Figure 12—A window into a dialog box

At this point, we've learned a great deal about how to use ANTLR. The next part of the book is a reference section that fills in a lot of details we avoided for clarity earlier in the book.

Part IV

ANTLR Reference

The first three parts of this book were a guide to using ANTLR, whereas this final part is primarily reference material. We'll start by summarizing the runtime API and looking at how ANTLR handles left-recursive rules. And, finally, we'll see the giant reference chapter.

CHAPTER 13

Exploring the Runtime API

This chapter gives an overview of the ANTLR runtime API and is meant to kick-start your exploration of the runtime library. It describes the programmer-facing classes but does not reproduce the details from the Javadoc.[1] Please see the comments on the classes and individual methods for detailed information on their usage.

13.1 Library Package Overview

ANTLR's runtime consists of six packages, with most of the application-facing classes in the main org.antlr.v4.runtime package. By far the most common classes are the ones used to launch a parser on some input. Here is the typical code snippet for a grammar file called X.g and a parse-tree listener called MyListener that implements XListener:

```
XLexer lexer = new XLexer(input);
CommonTokenStream tokens = new CommonTokenStream(lexer);
XParser parser = new XParser(tokens);
ParseTree tree = parser.XstartRule();

ParseTreeWalker walker = new ParseTreeWalker();
MyListener listener = new MyListener(parser);
walker.walk(listener, tree);
```

We first encountered this in Section 3.3, *Integrating a Generated Parser into a Java Program*, on page 28.

Here is a summary of the packages:

org.antlr.v4.runtime This package contains the most commonly used classes and interfaces, such as the hierarchies for input streams, character and token buffers, error handling, token construction, lexing, and parsing.

1. http://www.antlr.org/api

org.antlr.v4.runtime.atn This is used internally for ANTLR's Adaptive *LL(*)* lexing and parsing strategy. The *atn* term means *augmented transition network*[2] and is a state machine that can represent a grammar where edges represent grammar elements. ANTLR walks the ATN during lexing and parsing to make predictions based upon lookahead symbols.

org.antlr.v4.runtime.dfa Using the ATN to make predictions is expensive, so the runtime caches prediction results in *deterministic finite automata* (DFA).[3] This package holds all of the DFA implementation classes.

org.antlr.v4.runtime.misc This package holds miscellaneous data structures but also the commonly used TestRig class that we've used throughout this book via command-line alias grun.

org.antlr.v4.runtime.tree ANTLR-generated parsers build parse trees by default, and this package holds all of the classes and interfaces needed to implement them. It also contains the basic parse-tree listener, walker, and visitor mechanisms.

org.antlr.v4.runtime.tree.gui ANTLR ships with a basic parse tree viewer accessible via tree method inspect(). You can also save trees in PostScript form via save(). TestRig's -gui option launches this viewer.

The remaining sections describe the runtime API grouped by functionality.

13.2 Recognizers

ANTLR generates lexers and parsers that are subclasses of Lexer and Parser. Superclass Recognizer abstracts the notion of recognizing structure within a sequence of characters or tokens. Recognizers feed off of IntStreams, which we'll look at later. Here is the inheritance and interface implementation relationships (interfaces are in italics).

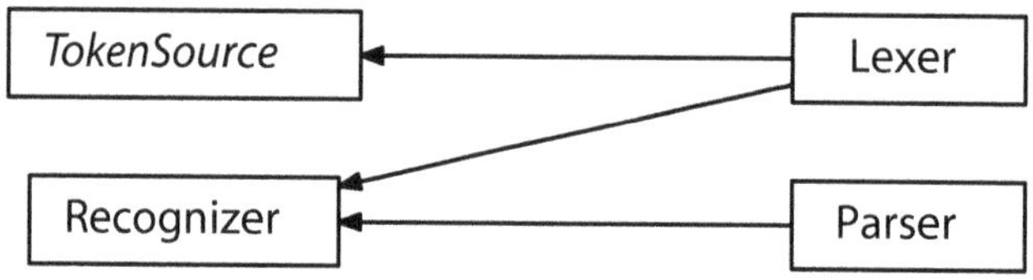

Lexer implements interface TokenSource, which specifies the core lexer functionality: nextToken(), getLine(), and getCharPositionInLine(). Rolling our own lexer to use with an ANTLR parser grammar is not too much work. Let's build a lexer that tokenizes simple identifiers and integers like the following input file:

---

2. http://en.wikipedia.org/wiki/Augmented_transition_network
3. http://en.wikipedia.org/wiki/Deterministic_finite_automaton

api/Simple-input

```
a 343x
abc 9 ;
```

Here's the core of a handbuilt lexer:

api/SimpleLexer.java

```
@Override
public Token nextToken() {
    while (true) {
        if ( c==(char)CharStream.EOF ) return createToken(Token.EOF);
        while ( Character.isWhitespace(c) ) consume(); // toss out whitespace
        startCharIndex = input.index();
        startLine = getLine();
        startCharPositionInLine = getCharPositionInLine();
        if ( c==';' ) {
            consume();
            return createToken(SEMI);
        }
        else if ( c>='0' && c<='9' ) {
            while ( c>='0' && c<='9' ) consume();
            return createToken(INT);
        }
        else if ( c>='a' && c<='z' ) { // VERY simple ID
            while ( c>='a' && c<='z' ) consume();
            return createToken(ID);
        }
        // error; consume and try again
        consume();
    }
}

protected Token createToken(int ttype) {
    String text = null; // we use start..stop indexes in input
            Pair<TokenSource, CharStream> source =
                    new Pair<TokenSource, CharStream>(this, input);
    return factory.create(source, ttype, text, Token.DEFAULT_CHANNEL,
                          startCharIndex, input.index()-1,
                          startLine, startCharPositionInLine);
}

protected void consume() {
    if ( c=='\n' ) {
        line++;  // \r comes back as a char, but \n means line++
        charPositionInLine = 0;
    }
    if ( c!=(char)CharStream.EOF ) input.consume();
    c = (char)input.LA(1);
    charPositionInLine++;
}
```

With a handbuilt lexer, we need a way to share the same token names in the ANTLR parser grammar. For parser code generation, we also need to inform ANTLR of the token type integer values established in the lexer source. This is the role of the .tokens file.

api/SimpleLexer.tokens
```
ID=1
INT=2
SEMI=3
```

Here's a simple grammar that feeds off of those token definitions:

api/SimpleParser.g4
```
parser grammar SimpleParser;
options {
  // get token types from SimpleLexer.tokens; don't name it
  // SimpleParser.tokens as ANTLR will overwrite!
  tokenVocab=SimpleLexer;
}

s : ( ID | INT )* SEMI ;
```

And here's the build and test sequence:

```
$ antlr4 SimpleParser.g4
$ javac Simple*.java TestSimple.java
$ java TestSimple Simple-input
(s a 343 x abc 9 ;)
```

13.3 Input Streams of Characters and Tokens

At the most abstract level, both lexers and parsers check the syntax of integer streams. Lexers process characters (short integers), and parsers process token types (integers). That is why the root of the ANTLR input stream class hierarchy is called IntStream.

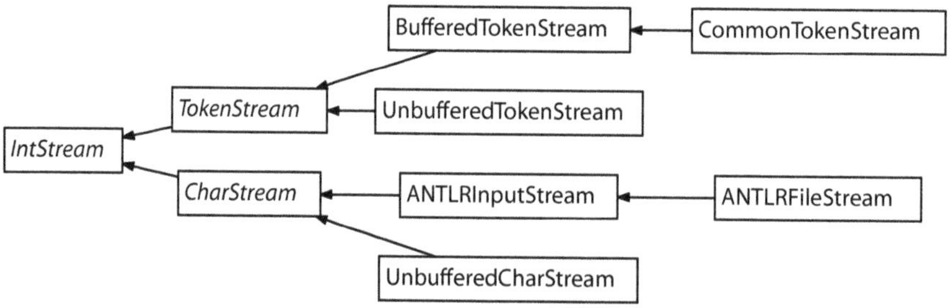

Interface IntStream defines most of the key operations for a stream, including methods to consume symbols and fetch lookahead symbols, namely, consume() and LA(). Because ANTLR recognizers need to scan ahead and rewind the input, IntStream defines the mark() and seek() methods.

The CharStream and TokenStream subinterfaces add methods to extract text from the streams. The classes implementing those interfaces typically read all of the input in one go and buffer it. That's because it is easier to build those classes, it provides ready access to the input, and it suits the common case. If your input is too big to buffer or is infinite (for example, via a socket), you can use UnbufferedCharStream and UnbufferedTokenStream.

The usual code sequence to perform a parse is to create an input stream, attach a lexer to it, create a token stream attached to the lexer, and then create a parser attached to the token stream.

```
ANTLRInputStream input = new ANTLRFileStream("an-input-file");
//ANTLRInputStream input = new ANTLRInputStream(System.in); // or read stdin
SimpleLexer lexer = new SimpleLexer(input);
CommonTokenStream tokens = new CommonTokenStream(lexer);
SimpleParser parser = new SimpleParser(tokens);
ParseTree t = parser.s();
```

13.4 Tokens and Token Factories

Lexers break up character streams into Token objects, and parsers apply grammatical structure to the stream of tokens. Generally, we think of tokens as immutable after construction in the lexer, but sometimes we need to alter token fields after we've created them. For example, the token streams like to set the token index of the tokens as they go by. To support this, ANTLR uses interface WritableToken, which is a kind of Token with "setter" methods. Finally, we have CommonToken that implements a full-featured token.

We usually don't need to define our own kind of tokens, but it's a useful capability. Here's a sample specialized Token implementation that adds a field to every token object:

api/MyToken.java
```
import org.antlr.v4.runtime.CharStream;
import org.antlr.v4.runtime.CommonToken;
import org.antlr.v4.runtime.TokenSource;
import org.antlr.v4.runtime.misc.Pair;

/** A Token that tracks the TokenSource name in each token. */
public class MyToken extends CommonToken {
    public String srcName;

    public MyToken(int type, String text) {
        super(type, text);
    }
```

```
    public MyToken(Pair<TokenSource, CharStream> source, int type,
                   int channel, int start, int stop)
    {
        super(source, type, channel, start, stop);
    }

    @Override
    public String toString() {
        String t = super.toString();
        return srcName +":"+t;
    }
}
```

To get the lexer to create these special tokens, we need to create a factory and pass it to the lexer. We also tell the parser so that its error handler can conjure up the right kind of tokens if necessary.

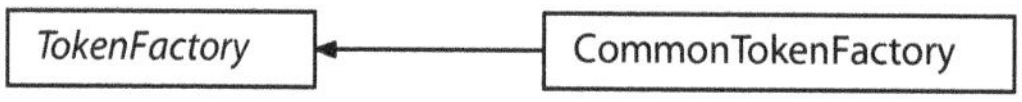

Here's a token factory that creates `MyToken` objects:

api/MyTokenFactory.java

```
import org.antlr.v4.runtime.CharStream;
import org.antlr.v4.runtime.TokenFactory;
import org.antlr.v4.runtime.TokenSource;
import org.antlr.v4.runtime.misc.Interval;
import org.antlr.v4.runtime.misc.Pair;

/** A TokenFactory that creates MyToken objects */
public class MyTokenFactory implements TokenFactory<MyToken> {
    CharStream input;

    public MyTokenFactory(CharStream input) { this.input = input; }
    @Override
    public MyToken create(int type, String text) {
        return new MyToken(type, text);
    }
    @Override
    public MyToken create(Pair<TokenSource, CharStream> source, int type,
                          String text,
                          int channel, int start, int stop, int line,
                          int charPositionInLine)
    {
        MyToken t = new MyToken(source, type, channel, start, stop);
        t.setLine(line);
        t.setCharPositionInLine(charPositionInLine);
        t.srcName = input.getSourceName();
        return t;
    }
}
```

And here's some sample code that notifies the lexer and parser of the factory:

api/TestSimpleMyToken.java

```
ANTLRInputStream input = new ANTLRFileStream(args[0]);
SimpleLexer lexer = new SimpleLexer(input);
MyTokenFactory factory = new MyTokenFactory(input);
lexer.setTokenFactory(factory);
CommonTokenStream tokens = new CommonTokenStream(lexer);

// now, print all tokens
tokens.fill();
List<Token> alltokens = tokens.getTokens();
for (Token t : alltokens) System.out.println(t.toString());

// now parse
SimpleParser parser = new SimpleParser(tokens);
parser.setTokenFactory(factory);
ParseTree t = parser.s();
System.out.println(t.toStringTree(parser));
```

It reuses the SimpleParser.g4 grammar from before. Here's the build and test sequence:

```
$ antlr4 SimpleParser.g4
$ javac Simple*.java MyToken*.java TestSimpleMyToken.java
$ java TestSimpleMyToken Simple-input
Simple-input:[@0,0:0='a',<1>,1:0]
Simple-input:[@1,2:4='343',<2>,1:2]
Simple-input:[@2,5:5='x',<1>,1:5]
Simple-input:[@3,7:9='abc',<1>,2:1]
Simple-input:[@4,11:11='9',<2>,2:5]
Simple-input:[@5,13:13=';',<3>,2:7]
Simple-input:[@6,15:14='<EOF>',<-1>,3:1]
(s a 343 x abc 9 ;)
```

The toString() method in MyToken adds the Simple-input: prefix to the normal token string representation.

13.5 Parse Trees

Interface Tree defines the basic notion of a tree that has a payload and children. A SyntaxTree is a tree that knows how to associate tree nodes with tokens in a TokenStream. Getting more specific, interface ParseTree represents a node in a parse tree. It knows how to return the text associated with all leaf nodes below it in the tree. We saw sample parse trees in Section 2.4, *Building Language Applications Using Parse Trees*, on page 16, and how the nodes correspond to the types in this class hierarchy. ParseTree also provides the usual visitor pattern double-dispatch accept() method for ParseTreeVisitor, which we looked at in Section 2.5, *Parse-Tree Listeners and Visitors*, on page 18.

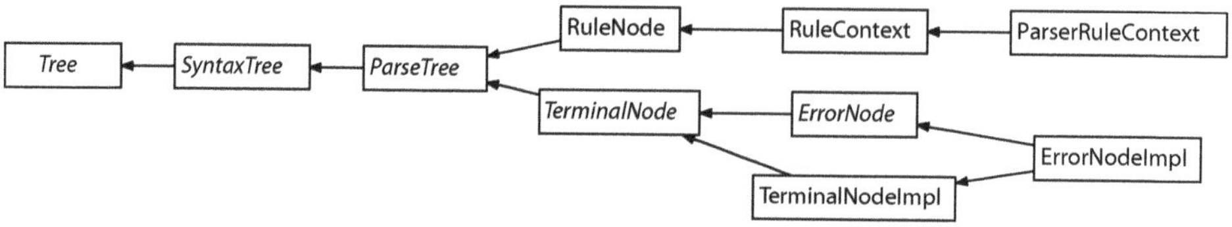

Classes RuleNode and TerminalNode correspond to subtree roots and leaf nodes. ANTLR creates ErrorNodeImpl nodes during single-token-insertion recovery (see *Recovering from Mismatched Tokens*, on page 164).

A RuleContext is a record of a single rule invocation and knows which context invoked it, if any, by walking up the getParent() chain. ParserRuleContext has a field to track parse-tree children, if the parser is creating trees. These are primarily implementation classes so you can focus on the specialized subclasses that ANTLR generates for each rule in your grammar.

13.6 Error Listeners and Strategies

There are two key interfaces associated with ANTLR's syntax error mechanism: ANTLRErrorListener and ANTLRErrorStrategy. We learned about the former in Section 9.2, *Altering and Redirecting ANTLR Error Messages*, on page 155, and the latter in Section 9.5, *Altering ANTLR's Error Handling Strategy*, on page 173. Listeners let us alter error messages and where they go. Strategy implementations alter how parsers react to errors.

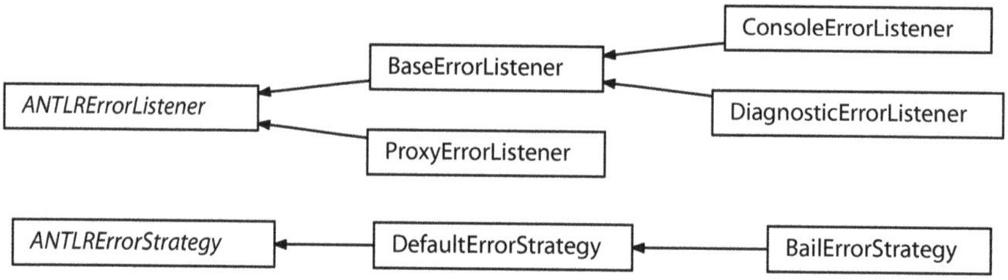

ANTLR throws specific RecognitionExceptions according to the error. Note that they are unchecked runtime exceptions, so you don't have to specify throws clauses all the time in your methods.

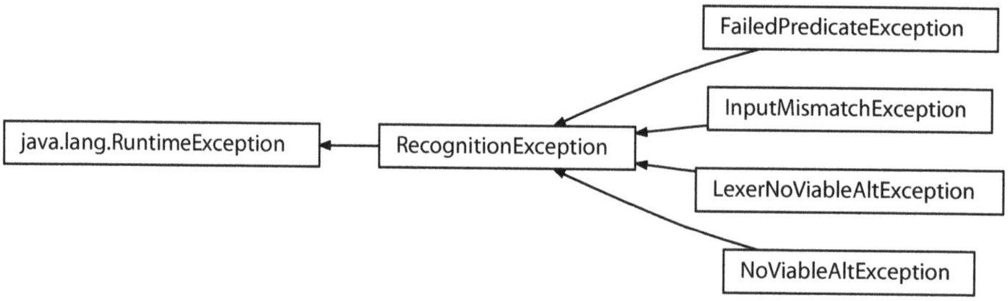

13.7 Maximizing Parser Speed

ANTLR v4's adaptive parsing strategy is more powerful than v3's, but it comes at the cost of a little bit of speed. If you need the most speed and the smallest memory footprint possible, you can do a two-step parsing strategy. The first step uses a slightly weaker parsing strategy, *SLL(*)*, that almost always works. (It's very similar to v3's strategy, except it doesn't need to backtrack.) If the first parsing step fails, you have to try the full *LL(*)* parse. After failing the first step, we don't know whether it's a true syntax error or whether it's because the *SLL(*)* strategy wasn't strong enough. Input that passes the *SLL(*)* step is guaranteed to pass the full *LL(*)*, so there's no point in trying out that more expensive strategy.

```
// try with simpler/faster SLL(*)
parser.getInterpreter().setPredictionMode(PredictionMode.SLL);
// we don't want error messages or recovery during first try
parser.removeErrorListeners();
parser.setErrorHandler(new BailErrorStrategy());
try {
    parser.startRule();
    // if we get here, there was no syntax error and SLL(*) was enough;
    // there is no need to try full LL(*)
}
catch (ParseCancellationException ex) { // thrown by BailErrorStrategy
    tokens.reset(); // rewind input stream
    parser.reset();
    // back to standard listeners/handlers
    parser.addErrorListener(ConsoleErrorListener.INSTANCE);
    parser.setErrorHandler(new DefaultErrorStrategy());
    // full now with full LL(*)
    parser.getInterpreter().setPredictionMode(PredictionMode.LL);
    parser.startRule();
}
```

Input that fails the second step is truly syntactically invalid.

13.8 Unbuffered Character and Token Streams

Because ANTLR recognizers buffer up the entire input character stream and all input tokens by default, they can't handle input files that are bigger than a computer's memory and can't handle infinite streams like socket connections. To overcome this, you can use unbuffered versions of the character and token streams, which keep just a small sliding window into the streams: UnbufferedCharStream and UnbufferedTokenStream.

As a demonstration, here's a modification of the comma-separated-value grammar from Section 6.1, *Parsing Comma-Separated Values*, on page 86 that sums the floating-point values in a two-column file:

api/CSV.g4
```
/** Rows are two real numbers:
    0.9962269825793676, 0.9224608616182103
    0.91673278673353,  -0.6374985722530822
    0.9841464019977713, 0.03539546030010776
    ...
 */
grammar CSV;

@members {
double x, y; // keep column sums in these fields
}

file: row+ {System.out.printf("%f, %f\n", x, y);} ;

row : a=field ',' b=field '\r'? '\n'
      {
      x += Double.valueOf($a.start.getText());
      y += Double.valueOf($b.start.getText());
      }
    ;

field
    : TEXT
    ;

TEXT : ~[,\n\r]+ ;
```

If all you care about are the sums of the columns, you need to keep only one or two tokens in memory at once. To prevent complete buffering, there are three things to do. First, use the unbuffered streams instead of the usual ANTLFileStream and CommonTokenStream. Second, pass the lexer a token factory that copies characters from the input stream into the text of the tokens. Otherwise, the getText() method for tokens would try to access the input character stream, which probably would no longer be available. (See the diagram in Section 2.4, *Building Language Applications Using Parse Trees*, on page 16 that shows the relationship between tokens and the character stream.) Finally, ask the parser not to create parse trees. The following test rig has the key lines highlighted:

api/TestCSV.java
```
import org.antlr.v4.runtime.CharStream;
import org.antlr.v4.runtime.CommonToken;
import org.antlr.v4.runtime.CommonTokenFactory;
```

```
import org.antlr.v4.runtime.Token;
import org.antlr.v4.runtime.TokenStream;
import org.antlr.v4.runtime.UnbufferedCharStream;
import org.antlr.v4.runtime.UnbufferedTokenStream;

import java.io.FileInputStream;
import java.io.InputStream;
public class TestCSV {
    public static void main(String[] args) throws Exception {
        String inputFile = null;
        if ( args.length>0 ) inputFile = args[0];
        InputStream is = System.in;
        if ( inputFile!=null ) {
            is = new FileInputStream(inputFile);
        }
        CharStream input = new UnbufferedCharStream(is);
        CSVLexer lex = new CSVLexer(input);
        // copy text out of sliding buffer and store in tokens
        lex.setTokenFactory(new CommonTokenFactory(true));
        TokenStream tokens = new UnbufferedTokenStream<CommonToken>(lex);
        CSVParser parser = new CSVParser(tokens);
        parser.setBuildParseTree(false);
        parser.file();
    }
}
```

Here's a sample build and test sequence using a 1,000-line sample file:

```
$ antlr4 CSV.g4
$ javac TestCSV.java CSV*.java
$ wc sample.csv
    1000    2000   39933 sample.csv # 1000 lines, 2000 words, 39933 char
$ java TestCSV sample.csv
1000.542053, 1005.587845
```

To verify that the recognizer is not buffering up everything, I ran a 310M CSV input file with 7.8M value pairs into the test rig while restricting the Java VM to just 10M RAM.

```
$ wc big.csv
 7800000 15600000 310959090 big.csv # 7800000 lines, ...
$ time java -Xmx10M TestCSV big.csv
11695395.953785, 7747174.349207

real    0m43.415s # wall clock duration to compute the sums
user    0m51.186s
sys     0m6.195s
```

These unbuffered streams are useful when efficiency is the top concern. (You can even combine them with the technique from the previous section.) Their disadvantage is that you are forced to buffer things up manually. For example, you can't use $text in an action embedded within a rule because it goes to the input stream and asks for the text (and the text isn't being buffered).

13.9 Altering ANTLR's Code Generation

ANTLR uses two things to generate code: a StringTemplate[4] group file (containing templates) and a Target subclass called *Language*Target where *Language* is the grammar language option. The StringTemplate group file is org/antlr/v4/tool/templates/codegen/*Language*.stg. If you would like to tweak the code generation templates for, say, Java, all you have to do is copy and modify org/antlr/v4/tool/templates/codegen/Java.stg. Then, put it in the CLASSPATH *before* ANTLR's jar. ANTLR uses a resource loader to get those templates so it'll see your modified version first.

The templates just generate code specific to a grammar. Most of the common functionality has been factored out into the runtime library. So, Lexer, Parser and so on are all part of the runtime library, not generated by ANTLR.

To add a new target for language *L*, you might need to create class *L*Target. If so, place it in package org.antlr.v4.codegen and put it before ANTLR's jar in the CLASSPATH. You need this class only if your target needs to alter some of the default functionality in Target. If no *L*Target class is found, ANTLR uses the Target base class. (This is what it does for the Java language target.)

4. http://www.stringtemplate.org

CHAPTER 14

Removing Direct Left Recursion

In Section 5.4, *Dealing with Precedence, Left Recursion, and Associativity*, on page 71, we saw that the natural way to specify arithmetic expressions grammatically is ambiguous. For example, the following expr can interpret 1+2*3 as (1+2)*3 or 1+(2*3). By giving precedence to the alternatives specified first, however, ANTLR neatly sidesteps the ambiguity.

left-recursion-removal/Expr.g4

```
stat: expr ';' ;

expr:   expr '*' expr       // precedence 4
    |   expr '+' expr       // precedence 3
    |   INT                 // primary (precedence 2)
    |   ID                  // primary (precedence 1)
    ;
```

Rule expr is still left-recursive, though, which traditional top-down grammars (for example, ANTLR v3) cannot handle. In this chapter, we're going to explore how ANTLR deals with left recursion and how it handles operator precedence. In a nutshell, ANTLR replaces left recursion with a (...)* that compares the precedence of the previous and next operators.

It's important to get familiar with the rule transformation because the generated code reflects the transformed rule, not the original. More importantly, when a grammar doesn't give the expected grouping or associativity for operators, we need to know why. Most users can stop reading after the next section that shows the valid recursive alternative patterns; advanced users interested in the implementation details can continue to the second section.

Let's start by looking at the transformations that ANTLR performs and then walk through an example to see the *precedence climbing* in action.[1]

---

1. Theodore Norvell coined the term (http://www.engr.mun.ca/~theo/Misc/exp_parsing.htm), but the original work was done by Keith Clarke (http://antlr.org/papers/Clarke-expr-parsing-1986.pdf).

14.1 Direct Left-Recursive Alternative Patterns

ANTLR examines any left-recursive rule looking for one of four subexpression operator patterns.

binary Any alternative of the form `expr` *op* `expr` or `expr` (*op1* | *op2* | ... | *opN*) `expr`. *op* can be a single-token or multitoken operator. For example, a Java grammar might treat angle brackets individually instead of treating operators <=> and >= as single tokens. Here's an alternative that handles comparison operators at the same precedence level:

```
expr: ...
    | expr ('<' '=' | '>' '=' | '>' | '<') expr
    ...
    ;
```

op can also be a rule reference. For example, we can factor out those tokens into another rule.

```
expr: ...
    | expr compareOps expr
    ...
    ;
compareOps : ('<' '=' | '>' '=' | '>' | '<') ;
```

ternary Any alternative of the form `expr` *op1* `expr` *op2* `expr`. *op1* and *op2* must be single-token references. This pattern handles the ?: operator in C-derived languages:

```
expr: ...
    | expr '?' expr ':' expr
    ...
    ;
```

unary prefix Any alternative of the form *elements* `expr`. ANTLR recognizes any sequence of elements followed by a tail-recursive rule reference as a unary prefix operation, as long as the alternative does not fit the binary or ternary pattern. Here are two alternatives with prefix operators:

```
expr: ...
    | '(' type ')' expr
    ...
    | ('+'|'-'|'++'|'--') expr
    ...
    ;
```

unary suffix Any alternative of the form `expr` *elements*. As with the prefix pattern, ANTLR recognizes alternatives with a direct left-recursive rule reference followed by any sequence of elements, as long as it doesn't fit the binary or ternary pattern. Here are two alternatives with suffix operators:

```
expr: ...
    | expr '.' Identifier
   ...
    | expr '.' 'super' '(' exprList? ')'
   ...
    ;
```

Any other alternative pattern is considered a *primary expression* element like an identifier or an integer but includes things like '(' expr ')' because it doesn't fit an operator pattern. This makes sense because the whole point of parentheses is to treat the enclosed expression as a single atomic element. These "other" alternatives can actually appear in any order. ANTLR collects and deals with them properly. The order of all other alternatives matters. Here are a few sample primary expression alternatives:

```
expr: ...
    |   literal
    |   Identifier
    |   type '.' 'class'
   ...
    ;
```

Unless otherwise specified, ANTLR assumes that all operators are left associative. In other words, 1+2+3 groups like this: (1+2)+3. Some operators, however, are right associative, such as assignment and exponentiation, as we saw in Section 5.4, *Dealing with Precedence, Left Recursion, and Associativity*, on page 71. To specify right associativity, use the assoc token option.

```
expr: expr '^'<assoc=right> expr
   ...
    | expr '='<assoc=right> expr
   ...
    ;
```

In the next section, we'll take a look at how ANTLR translates these patterns.

14.2 Left-Recursive Rule Transformations

If you turn on the -Xlog ANTLR command-line option, you can find the transformed left-recursive rules in the log file. Here's what happens to rules stat and expr from Expr.g4 shown earlier:

```
// use "antlr4 -Xlog Expr.g4" to see transformed rules
stat:   expr[0] ';' ;  // match an expr whose operators have any precedence

expr[int _p]           // _p is expected minimum precedence level
```

```
    :   ( INT          // match primaries (non-operators)
        | ID
        )
        // match operators as long as their precedence is at or higher than
        // expected minimum
        ( {4 >= $_p}? '*' expr[5]  // * has precedence 4
        | {3 >= $_p}? '+' expr[4]  // + has precedence 3
        )*
    ;
```

Whoa! That's quite a transformation. Don't worry about how ANTLR conjures up all of those parameters to expr. We're mainly interested in learning a bit about how those predicates test operator precedence to direct the parse and get the right groupings.

The key is deciding whether to match the next operator in the current invocation of expr or to let the calling invocation of expr match the next operator. The (...)* loop matches operator and right operand pairs. For input 1+2*3, the loop would match +2 and *3. The purpose of the predicates in the loop alternatives is to decide whether the parser should match the operator/operand pair immediately or fall out of the current invocation of expr. For example, predicate {3 >= $_p}? deactivates the addition alternative if the addition operator's precedence, 3, is below the expected minimum precedence, _p, for the current subexpression.

This Ain't Operator Precedence Parsing

Don't confuse this mechanism with *operator precedence parsing*, despite what you read on Wikipedia.[a] Operator precedence parsing can't handle things like the minus sign that has two different precedences, one for unary negation and one for binary subtraction operators. It also can't handle alternatives that have two adjacent rule references like expr ops expr. See *Compilers: Principles, Techniques, and Tools [ALSU06]* to get the real definition.

a. http://en.wikipedia.org/wiki/Operator-precedence_parser

Parameter _p's value is always derived from the precedence of the previous operator. _p starts at 0, since nonrecursive calls to expr pass 0, like stat does: expr[0]. To see _p in action, let's look at some parse trees derived from the transformed rule (showing the value of parameter _p in square brackets). Note that these parse trees are not what ANTLR would build for us from the original left-recursive rule. These are the parse trees for the transformed rule, not the original. Here are some sample inputs and associated parse trees:

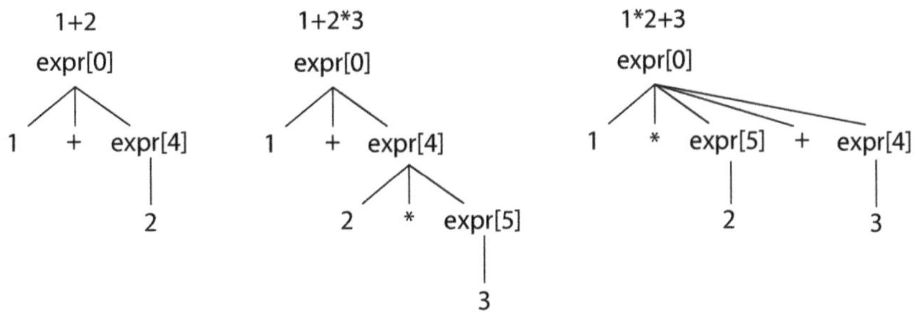

In the first tree, the initial call to expr has _p of 0, and expr immediately matches the 1 to the (INT|ID) subrule. Now expr has to decide whether it will match the + or skip the loop entirely and return. The predicate evaluates as {3>=0}? and so we enter the loop to match + and then call expr recursively with an argument of 4. That invocation matches 2 and immediately returns because there is no more input. expr[0] then returns to the original call to expr in stat.

The second tree illustrates how expr[0] matches 1, and again {3>=0}? allows us to match the + operator followed by the second operand, expr[4]. The recursive call to expr[4] matches the 2 and then evaluates {4 >= 4}?, which lets the parser proceed to match the * operator followed by the last operand, 3, via a call to expr[5].

The third parse tree is the most interesting. The initial invocation, expr[0], matches 1 and then decides to match the * operation because {4>=0}? is true. That loop then recursively calls expr[5], which immediately matches 2. Now, inside the call to expr[5], the parser should not match the + because otherwise the 2+3 would evaluate before the multiply. (In the parse tree, we would see expr[5] with 2+3 as children instead of just the 2.) Predicate {3 >= 5}? deactivates that alternative and so expr[5] returns without matching the +. After returning, expr[0] matches +3 since {3>=0}? is true.

I hope this gives you a good feel for the precedence climbing mechanism. If you'd like to learn more, Norvell's description[2] goes into a lot of detail.

2. http://www.engr.mun.ca/~theo/Misc/exp_parsing.htm

CHAPTER 15

Grammar Reference

Most of this book is a guide to using ANTLR. This chapter is a reference and summarizes grammar syntax and the key semantics of ANTLR grammars. It is not meant as an isolated and complete description of how to use ANTLR. The source code for all examples in this book is a good resource and is available at the website.[1]

15.1 Grammar Lexicon

The lexicon of ANTLR is familiar to most programmers because it follows the syntax of C and its derivatives with some extensions for grammatical descriptions.

Comments

There are single-line, multiline, and Javadoc-style comments.

```
/** This grammar is an example illustrating the three kinds
 *  of comments.
 */
grammar T;

/* a multi-line
   comment
 */

/** This rule matches a declarator for my language */
decl : ID ; // match a variable name
```

The Javadoc comments are sent to the parser and are not ignored. These are allowed only at the start of the grammar and any rule.

1. http://pragprog.com/book/tpantlr2/the-definitive-antlr-4-reference

Identifiers

Token names always start with a capital letter and so do lexer rules as defined by Java's Character.isUpperCase() method. Parser rule names always start with a lowercase letter (those that fail Character.isUpperCase()). The initial character can be followed by uppercase and lowercase letters, digits, and underscores. Here are some sample names:

```
ID, LPAREN, RIGHT_CURLY // token names/rules
expr, simpleDeclarator, d2, header_file // rule names
```

Like Java, ANTLR accepts Unicode characters in ANTLR names.

```
grammar 外;
a:'外';
```

To support Unicode parser and lexer rule names, ANTLR uses the following rule:

```
ID  :   a=NameStartChar NameChar*
        {
        if ( Character.isUpperCase(getText().charAt(0)) ) setType(TOKEN_REF);
        else setType(RULE_REF);
        }
    ;
```

NameChar identifies the valid identifier characters.

```
fragment
NameChar
    :   NameStartChar
    |   '0'..'9'
    |   '_'
    |   '\u00B7'
    |   '\u0300'..'\u036F'
    |   '\u203F'..'\u2040'
    ;
```

NameStartChar is the list of characters that can start an identifier (rule, token, or label name).

```
fragment
NameStartChar
    :   'A'..'Z' | 'a'..'z'
    |   '\u00C0'..'\u00D6'
    |   '\u00D8'..'\u00F6'
    |   '\u00F8'..'\u02FF'
    |   '\u0370'..'\u037D'
    |   '\u037F'..'\u1FFF'
    |   '\u200C'..'\u200D'
```

```
    |   '\u2070'..'\u218F'
    |   '\u2C00'..'\u2FEF'
    |   '\u3001'..'\uD7FF'
    |   '\uF900'..'\uFDCF'
    |   '\uFDF0'..'\uFFFD'
    ;
```

These more or less correspond to isJavaIdentifierPart() and isJavaIdentifierStart() in Java's Character class. Make sure to use the -encoding option on the ANTLR tool if your grammar file is not in UTF-8 format so that ANTLR reads characters properly.

Literals

ANTLR does not distinguish between character and string literals like most languages do. All literal strings that are one or more characters in length are enclosed in single quotes such as ';', 'if', '>=', and '\'' (refers to the one-character string containing the single quote character). Literals never contain regular expressions.

Literals can contain Unicode escape sequences of the form \uXXXX, where XXXX is the hexadecimal Unicode character value. For example, '\u00E8' is the French letter *e* with a grave accent: 'è'. ANTLR also understands the usual special escape sequences: '\n' (newline), '\r' (carriage return), '\t' (tab), '\b' (backspace), and '\f' (form feed). You can use Unicode characters directly within literals or use the Unicode escape sequences. See code/reference/Foreign.g4.

```
grammar Foreign;
a:'外';
```

The recognizers that ANTLR generates assume a character vocabulary containing all Unicode characters. The input file encoding assumed by the runtime library depends on the target language. For the Java target, the runtime library assumes files are in UTF-8. Using the constructors, you can specify a different encoding. See, for example, ANTLR's ANTLRFileStream.

Actions

Actions are code blocks written in the target language. You can use actions in a number of places within a grammar, but the syntax is always the same: arbitrary text surrounded by curly braces. You don't need to escape a closing curly character if it's in a string or comment: {"}"} or {/*}*/;}. If the curlies are balanced, you also don't need to escape }: {{...}}. Otherwise, escape extra curlies with a backslash: {\{} or {\}}. The action text should conform to the target language as specified with the language option.

Embedded code can appear in @header and @members named actions, parser and lexer rules, exception catching specifications, attribute sections for parser rules (return values, arguments, and locals), and some rule element options (currently predicates).

The only interpretation ANTLR does inside actions relates to grammar attributes; see *Token Attributes*, on page 273, as well as Chapter 10, *Attributes and Actions*, on page 177. Actions embedded within lexer rules are emitted without any interpretation or translation into generated lexers.

Keywords

Here's a list of the reserved words in ANTLR grammars: import, fragment, lexer, parser, grammar, returns, locals, throws, catch, finally, mode, options, tokens. Also, although it is not a keyword, do not use the word rule as a rule or alternative label name since it results in RuleContext as a context object; RuleContext clashes with the built-in class. Further, do not use any keyword of the target language as a token, label, or rule name. For example, rule if would result in a generated function called if().

15.2 Grammar Structure

A grammar is essentially a grammar declaration followed by a list of rules but has the following general form:

```
/** Optional Javadoc-style comment */
grammar Name; ①
options {...}
import ... ;
tokens {...}
@actionName {...}

«rule1» // parser and lexer rules, possibly intermingled
...
«ruleN»
```

The filename containing grammar *X* must be called *X*.g4. You can specify options, imports, token specifications, and actions in any order. There can be at most one each of options, imports, and token specifications. All of those elements are optional except for the header ① and at least one rule. Rules take the following basic form:

```
ruleName : «alternative1» | ... | «alternativeN» ;
```

Parser rule names must start with a lowercase letter, and lexer rules must start with a capital letter.

Grammars defined without a prefix on the grammar header are *combined* grammars that can contain both lexical and parser rules. To make a parser grammar that allows only parser rules, use the following header:

```
parser grammar Name;
...
```

And, naturally, a pure lexer grammar looks like this:

```
lexer grammar Name;
...
```

Only lexer grammars can contain mode specifications.

Section 15.5, *Lexer Rules*, on page 279 and Section 15.3, *Parser Rules*, on page 263 contain details on rule syntax. Section 15.8, *Options*, on page 294 describes grammar options, and Section 15.4, *Actions and Attributes*, on page 273 has information on grammar-level actions. We'll look at grammar imports, token specifications, and named actions next.

Grammar imports

Grammar imports let you break up a grammar into logical and reusable chunks, as we saw in *Importing Grammars*, on page 38. ANTLR treats imported grammars very much like object-oriented programming languages treat superclasses. A grammar inherits all of the rules, tokens specifications, and named actions from the imported grammar. Rules in the "main grammar" override rules from imported grammars to implement inheritance.

Think of import as more like a smart include statement (which does not include rules that are already defined). The result of all imports is a single combined grammar; the ANTLR code generator sees a complete grammar and has no idea there were imported grammars.

To process a main grammar, the ANTLR tool loads all of the imported grammars into subordinate grammar objects. It then merges the rules, token types, and named actions from the imported grammars into the main grammar. In the following diagram, the grammar on the right illustrates the effect of grammar MyELang importing grammar ELang:

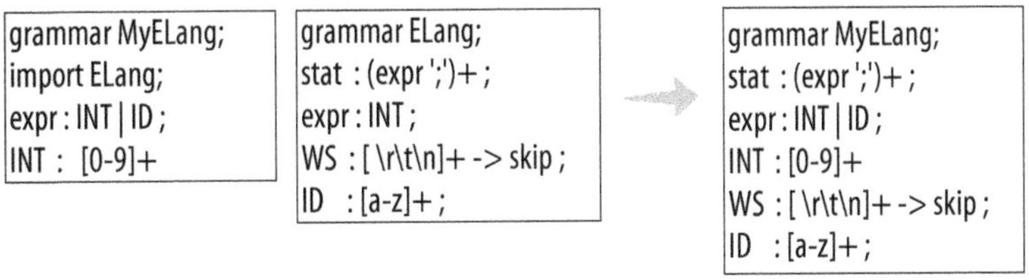
grammar MyELang;
import ELang;
expr : INT | ID ;
INT : [0-9]+
grammar ELang;
stat : (expr ';')+ ;
expr : INT ;
WS : [\r\t\n]+ -> skip ;
ID : [a-z]+ ;
grammar MyELang;
stat : (expr ';')+ ;
expr : INT | ID ;
INT : [0-9]+
WS : [\r\t\n]+ -> skip ;
ID : [a-z]+ ;

MyELang inherits rules stat, WS, and ID, but it overrides rule expr and adds INT. Here's a sample build and test run that shows MyELang can recognize integer expressions whereas the original ELang can't. The third, erroneous input statement triggers an error message that also demonstrates the parser was looking for MyELang's expr, not ELang's.

```
⇒ $ antlr4 MyELang.g4
⇒ $ javac MyELang*.java
⇒ $ grun MyELang stat
⇒ 34;
⇒ a;
⇒ ;
⇒ EOF
❮ line 3:0 extraneous input ';' expecting {<EOF>, INT, ID}
```

If there were any tokens specifications, the main grammar would merge the token sets. Any named actions such as @members would be merged. In general, you should avoid named actions and actions within rules in imported grammars since that limits their reuse. ANTLR also ignores any options in imported grammars.

Imported grammars can also import other grammars. ANTLR pursues all imported grammars in a depth-first fashion. If two or more imported grammars define rule r, ANTLR chooses the first version of r it finds. In the following diagram, ANTLR examines grammars in the following order: Nested, G1, G3, G2:

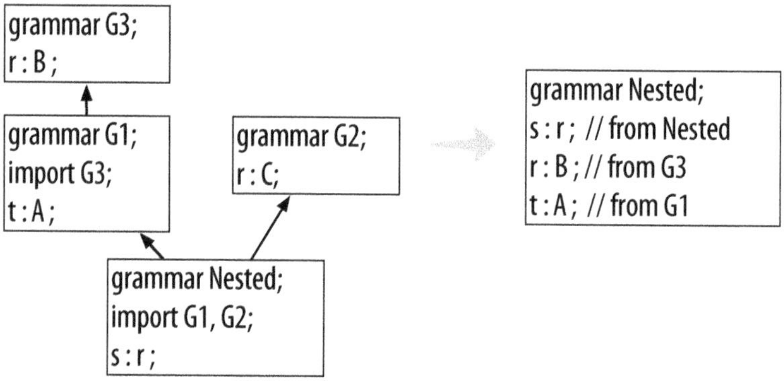

Nested includes the r rule from G3 because it sees that version before the r in G2.

Not every kind of grammar can import every other kind of grammar.

- Lexer grammars can import lexer grammars.
- Parser grammars can import parser grammars.
- Combined grammars can import lexer or parser grammars.

- Combined grammars can import combined grammars (except, for the time being, ones using lexical modes).

ANTLR adds imported rules to the end of the rule list in a main lexer grammar. That means lexer rules in the main grammar get precedence over imported rules. For example, if a main grammar defines rule `IF : 'if' ;` and an imported grammar defines rule `ID : [a-z]+ ;` (which also recognizes `if`), the imported `ID` won't hide the main grammar's `IF` token definition.

tokens Section

The purpose of the `tokens` section is to define token types needed by a grammar for which there is no associated lexical rule. The basic syntax is as follows:

```
tokens { «Token1», ..., «TokenN» }
```

Most of the time, the `tokens` section is used to define token types needed by actions in the grammar (as we did in Section 10.3, *Recognizing Languages Whose Keywords Aren't Fixed*, on page 187).

```
// explicitly define keyword token types to avoid implicit definition warnings
tokens { BEGIN, END, IF, THEN, WHILE }
@lexer::members {   // keywords map used in lexer to assign token types
Map<String,Integer> keywords = new HashMap<String,Integer>() {{
    put("begin", KeywordsParser.BEGIN);
    put("end",   KeywordsParser.END);
    ...
}};
}
```

The `tokens` section really just defines a set of tokens to add to the overall set.

```
$ cat Tok.g4
grammar Tok;
tokens { A, B, C }
a : X ;
$ antlr4 Tok.g4
warning(125): Tok.g4:3:4: implicit definition of token X in parser
$ cat Tok.tokens
A=1
B=2
C=3
X=4
```

Actions at the Grammar Level

Using Actions Outside of Grammar Rules, on page 178, illustrates the use of named actions at the top level of the grammar file. Currently there are only two defined actions (for the Java target): `header` and `members`. The former injects code into the generated recognizer class file, before the recognizer class definition, and the latter injects code into the recognizer class definition, as fields and methods.

For combined grammars, ANTLR injects the actions into both the parser and the lexer. To restrict an action to the generated parser or lexer, use @parser::*name* or @lexer::*name*.

Here's an example where the grammar specifies a package for the generated code:

reference/foo/Count.g4

```
grammar Count;

@header {
package foo;
}

@members {
int count = 0;
}

list
@after {System.out.println(count+" ints");}
    : INT {count++;} (',' INT {count++;} )*
    ;

INT : [0-9]+ ;
WS : [ \r\t\n]+ -> skip ;
```

The grammar itself should be in directory foo so that ANTLR generates code in that same foo directory (at least when not using the -o ANTLR tool option).

```
$ cd foo
$ antlr4 Count.g4   # generates code in the current directory (foo)
$ ls
Count.g4                CountLexer.java         CountParser.java
Count.tokens            CountLexer.tokens
CountBaseListener.java  CountListener.java
$ javac *.java
$ cd ..
$ grun foo.Count list
9, 10, 11
EOF
3 ints
```

The Java compiler expects classes in package foo to be in directory foo.

Now that we've seen the overall structure of a grammar, let's dig into the parser and lexer rules.

15.3 Parser Rules

Parsers consist of a set of parser rules in either a parser or a combined grammar. A Java application launches a parser by invoking the rule function, generated by ANTLR, associated with the desired start rule. The most basic rule is just a rule name followed by a single alternative terminated with a semicolon.

```
/** Javadoc comment can precede rule */
retstat : 'return' expr ';' ;
```

Rules can also have alternatives separated by the | operator.

```
stat:   retstat
    |   'break' ';'
    |   'continue' ';'
    ;
```

Alternatives are either a list of rule elements or empty. For example, here's a rule with an empty alternative that makes the entire rule optional:

```
superClass
    :   'extends' ID
    |                   // empty means other alternative(s) are optional
    ;
```

Alternative Labels

As we saw in Section 7.4, *Labeling Rule Alternatives for Precise Event Methods*, on page 119, we can get more precise parse-tree listener events by labeling the outermost alternatives of a rule using the # operator. All alternatives within a rule must be labeled, or none of them should be. Here are two rules with labeled alternatives:

reference/AltLabels.g4

```
grammar AltLabels;
stat: 'return' e ';' # Return
    | 'break'    ';' # Break
    ;
e   : e '*' e        # Mult
    | e '+' e        # Add
    | INT            # Int
    ;
```

Alternative labels do not have to be at the end of the line, and there does not have to be a space after the # symbol.

ANTLR generates a rule context class definition for each label. For example, here is the listener that ANTLR generates:

```
public interface AltLabelsListener extends ParseTreeListener {
    void enterMult(AltLabelsParser.MultContext ctx);
    void exitMult(AltLabelsParser.MultContext ctx);
    void enterBreak(AltLabelsParser.BreakContext ctx);
    void exitBreak(AltLabelsParser.BreakContext ctx);
    void enterReturn(AltLabelsParser.ReturnContext ctx);
    void exitReturn(AltLabelsParser.ReturnContext ctx);
    void enterAdd(AltLabelsParser.AddContext ctx);
    void exitAdd(AltLabelsParser.AddContext ctx);
    void enterInt(AltLabelsParser.IntContext ctx);
    void exitInt(AltLabelsParser.IntContext ctx);
}
```

There are enter and exit methods associated with each labeled alternative. The parameters to those methods are specific to alternatives.

You can reuse the same label on multiple alternatives to indicate that the parse-tree walker should trigger the same event for those alternatives. For example, here's a variation on rule e that reuses label BinaryOp:

```
e   : e '*' e        # BinaryOp
    | e '+' e        # BinaryOp
    | INT            # Int
    ;
```

ANTLR would generate the following listener methods for e:

```
void enterBinaryOp(AltLabelsParser.BinaryOpContext ctx);
void exitBinaryOp(AltLabelsParser.BinaryOpContext ctx);
void enterInt(AltLabelsParser.IntContext ctx);
void exitInt(AltLabelsParser.IntContext ctx);
```

ANTLR gives errors if an alternative name conflicts with a rule name. Here's another rewrite of rule e where two alternative labels conflict with rule names:

reference/Conflict.g4

```
e   : e '*' e        # e
    | e '+' e        # Stat
    | INT            # Int
    ;
```

The context objects generated from rule names and labels get capitalized, so label Stat conflicts with rule stat.

```
$ antlr4 Conflict.g4
error(124): Conflict.g4:6:23: rule alt label e conflicts with rule e
error(124): Conflict.g4:7:23: rule alt label Stat conflicts with rule stat
warning(125): Conflict.g4:2:13: implicit definition of token INT in parser
```

Rule Context Objects

ANTLR generates methods to access the rule context objects (parse-tree nodes) associated with each rule reference. For rules with a single rule reference, ANTLR generates a method with no arguments. Consider the following rule:

```
inc : e '++' ;
```

ANTLR generates this context class:

```
public static class IncContext extends ParserRuleContext {
    public EContext e() { ... } // return context object associated with e
    ...
}
```

ANTLR also provides support to access context objects when there is more than a single reference to a rule.

```
field : e '.' e ;
```

ANTLR generates a method with an index to access the *i*th element as well as a method to get context for all references to that rule.

```
public static class FieldContext extends ParserRuleContext {
    public EContext e(int i) { ... }    // get ith e context
    public List<EContext> e() { ... }   // return ALL e contexts
    ...
}
```

If we had another rule, s, that references field, an embedded action could access the list of e rule matches performed by field.

```
s : field
    {
    List<EContext> x = $field.ctx.e();
     ...
    }
  ;
```

A listener or visitor could do the same thing. Given a pointer to a FieldContext object, f, f.e() would return List<EContext>.

Rule Element Labels

You can label rule elements using the = operator to add fields to the rule context objects.

```
stat: 'return' value=e ';' # Return
    | 'break'          ';' # Break
    ;
```

Here value is the label for the return value of rule e, which is defined elsewhere.

Labels become fields in the appropriate parse-tree node class. In this case, label value becomes a field in ReturnContext because of the Return alternative label.

```
public static class ReturnContext extends StatContext {
    public EContext value;
    ...
}
```

It's often handy to track a number of tokens, which you can do with the += "list label" operator. For example, the following rule creates a list of the Token objects matched for a simple array construct:

```
array : '{' el+=INT (',' el+=INT)* '}' ;
```

ANTLR generates a List field in the appropriate rule context class.

```
public static class ArrayContext extends ParserRuleContext {
    public List<Token> el = new ArrayList<Token>();
    ...
}
```

These list labels also work for rule references.

```
elist : exprs+=e (',' exprs+=e)* ;
```

ANTLR generates a field holding the list of context objects.

```
public static class ElistContext extends ParserRuleContext {
    public List<EContext> exprs = new ArrayList<EContext>();
    ...
}
```

Rule Elements

Rule elements specify what the parser should do at a given moment just like statements in a programming language. The elements can be a rule, a token, or a string literal like expression, ID, and 'return'. Here's a complete list of the rule elements (we'll look at actions and predicates in more detail later):

Syntax	Description
T	Match token *T* at the current input position. Tokens always begin with a capital letter.
'*literal*'	Match the string literal at the current input position. A string literal is simply a token with a fixed string.
r	Match rule *r* at the current input position, which amounts to invoking the rule just like a function call. Parser rule names always begin with a lowercase letter.

Syntax	Description
r[«*args*»]	Match rule *r* at the current input position, passing in a list of arguments just like a function call. The arguments inside the square brackets are in the syntax of the target language and are usually a comma-separated list of expressions.
{«*action*»}	Execute an action immediately after the preceding alternative element and immediately before the following alternative element. The action conforms to the syntax of the target language. ANTLR copies the action code to the generated class verbatim, except for substituting attribute and token references such as `$x` and `$x.y`.
{«*p*»}?	Evaluate semantic predicate «*p*». Do not continue parsing past a predicate if «*p*» evaluates to false at runtime. Predicates encountered during prediction, when ANTLR distinguishes between alternatives, enable or disable the alternative(s) surrounding the predicate(s).
.	Match any single token except for the end-of-file token. The "dot" operator is called the *wildcard*.

When you want to match everything but a particular token or set of tokens, use the ~ "not" operator. This operator is rarely used in the parser but is available. `~INT` matches any token except the `INT` token. `~','` matches any token except the comma. `~(INT|ID)` matches any token except an `INT` or an `ID`.

Token, string literal, and semantic predicate rule elements can take options. See *Rule Element Options*, on page 295.

Subrules

A rule can contain alternative blocks called *subrules* (as allowed in Extended BNF Notation [EBNF]). A subrule is like a rule that lacks a name and is enclosed in parentheses. Subrules can have one or more alternatives inside the parentheses. Subrules cannot define attributes with `locals` and `returns` like rules can. There are four kinds of subrules (x, y, and z represent grammar fragments).

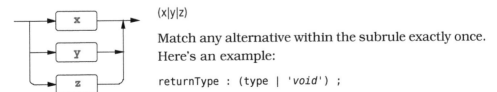

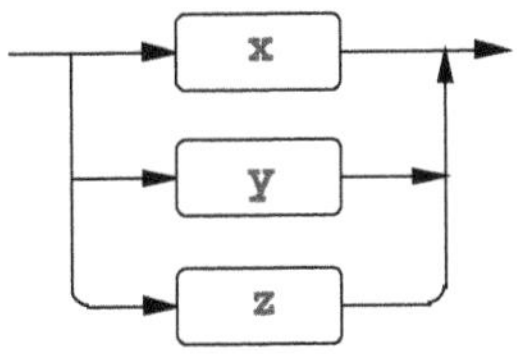

(x|y|z)

Match any alternative within the subrule exactly once. Here's an example:

```
returnType : (type | 'void') ;
```

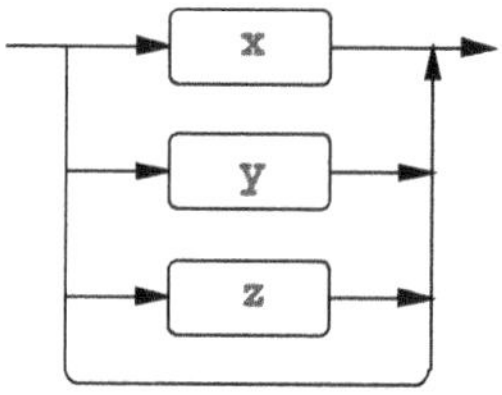

(x|y|z)?

Match nothing or any alternative within the subrule. Here's an example:

```
classDeclaration
    :   'class' ID (typeParameters)? ('extends' type)?
        ('implements' typeList)?
        classBody
    ;
```

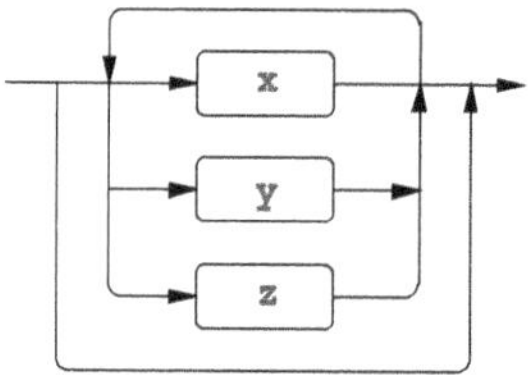

(x|y|z)*

Match an alternative within the subrule zero or more times. Here's an example:

```
annotationName : ID ('.' ID)* ;
```

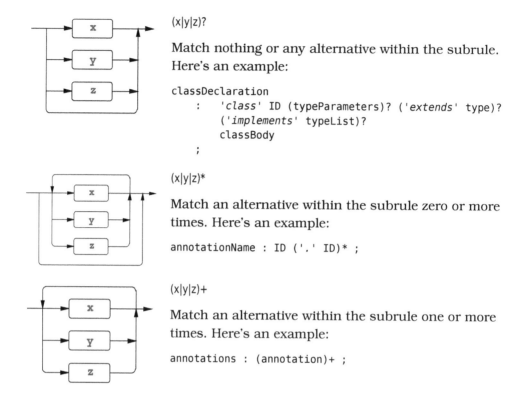

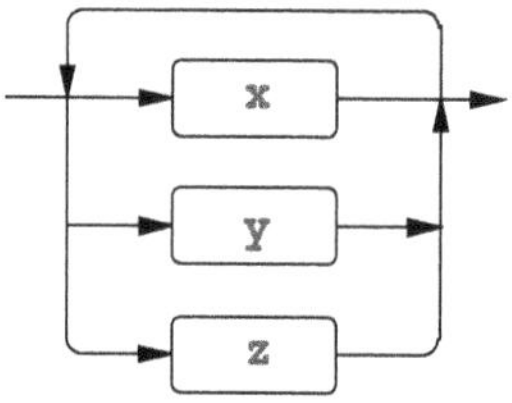

(x|y|z)+

Match an alternative within the subrule one or more times. Here's an example:

```
annotations : (annotation)+ ;
```

You can suffix the ?, *, and + subrule operators with the nongreedy operator, which is also a question mark: ??, *?, and +?. See Section 15.6, *Wildcard Operator and Nongreedy Subrules*, on page 285.

As a shorthand, you can omit the parentheses for subrules composed of a single alternative with a single-rule element reference. For example, annotation+ is the same as (annotation)+, and ID+ is the same as (ID)+. Labels also work with the shorthand. ids+=INT+ make a list of INT token objects.

Catching Exceptions

When a syntax error occurs within a rule, ANTLR catches the exception, reports the error, attempts to recover (possibly by consuming more tokens), and then returns from the rule. Every rule is wrapped in a try/catch/finally statement.

```
void r() throws RecognitionException {
    try {
        «rule-body»
    }
    catch (RecognitionException re) {
        _errHandler.reportError(this, re);
```

```
        _errHandler.recover(this, re);
    }
    finally {
        exitRule();
    }
}
```

In Section 9.5, *Altering ANTLR's Error Handling Strategy*, on page 173, we saw how to use a strategy object to alter ANTLR's error handling. Replacing the strategy changes the strategy for all rules, however. To alter the exception handling for a single rule, specify an exception after the rule definition.

```
r   :   ...
    ;
    catch[RecognitionException e] { throw e; }
```

That example demonstrates how to avoid default error reporting and recovery. r rethrows the exception, which is useful when it makes more sense for a higher-level rule to report the error. Specifying any exception clause prevents ANTLR from generating a clause to handle RecognitionException.

You can specify other exceptions as well.

```
r   :   ...
    ;
    catch[FailedPredicateException fpe] { ... }
    catch[RecognitionException e] { ... }
```

The code snippets inside curly braces and the exception "argument" actions must be written in the target language, Java, in this case.

When you need to execute an action even if an exception occurs, put it into the finally clause.

```
r   :   ...
    ;
    // catch blocks go first
    finally { System.out.println("exit rule r"); }
```

The finally clause executes right before the rule triggers exitRule() before returning. If you want to execute an action after the rule finishes matching the alternatives but before it does its cleanup work, use an after action.

Here's a complete list of exceptions:

Exception name	Description
RecognitionException	The superclass of all exceptions thrown by an ANTLR-generated recognizer. It's a subclass of RuntimeException to avoid the hassles of checked exceptions. This

Exception name	Description
	exception records where the recognizer (lexer or parser) was in the input, where it was in the ATN (internal graph data structure representing the grammar), the rule invocation stack, and what kind of problem occurred.
NoViableAltException	Indicates that the parser could not decide which of two or more paths to take by looking at the remaining input. This exception tracks the starting token of the offending input and also knows where the parser was in the various paths when the error occurred.
LexerNoViableAltException	The equivalent of NoViableAltException but for lexers only.
InputMismatchException	The current input Token does not match what the parser expected.
FailedPredicateException	A semantic predicate that evaluates to false during prediction renders the surrounding alternative nonviable. Prediction occurs when a rule is predicting which alternative to take. If all viable paths disappear, the parser will throw NoViableAltException. This exception gets thrown by the parser when a semantic predicate evaluates to false outside of prediction, during the normal parsing process of matching tokens and calling rules.

Rule Attribute Definitions

There are a number of action-related syntax elements associated with rules to be aware of. Rules can have arguments, return values, and local variables just like functions in a programming language. (Rules can have actions embedded among the rule elements, as we'll see in Section 15.4, *Actions and Attributes*, on page 273.) ANTLR collects all of the variables you define and stores them in the rule context object. These variables are usually called *attributes*. Here's the general syntax showing all possible attribute definition locations:

```
rulename[«args»] returns [«retvals»] locals [«localvars»] : ... ;
```

The attributes defined within those [...] can be used like any other variable. Here is a sample rule that copies parameters to return values:

```
// Return the argument plus the integer value of the INT token
add[int x] returns [int result] : '+=' INT {$result = $x + $INT.int;} ;
```

As with the grammar level, you can specify rule-level named actions. For rules, the valid names are init and after. As the names imply, parsers execute init actions immediately before trying to match the associated rule and execute after actions immediately after matching the rule. ANTLR after actions do not execute as part of the finally code block of the generated rule function. Use the ANTLR finally action to place code in the generated rule function finally code block.

The actions come after any argument, return value, or local attribute definition actions. The row rule preamble from Section 10.2, *Accessing Token and Rule Attributes*, on page 184 illustrates the syntax nicely.

actions/CSV.g4
```
/** Derived from rule "row : field (',' field)* '\r'? '\n' ;" */
row[String[] columns] returns [Map<String,String> values]
locals [int col=0]
@init {
    $values = new HashMap<String,String>();
}
@after {
    if ($values!=null && $values.size()>0) {
        System.out.println("values = "+$values);
    }
}
```

Rule row takes argument columns, returns values, and defines local variable col. The "actions" in square brackets are copied directly into the generated code.

```
public class CSVParser extends Parser {
    ...
    public static class RowContext extends ParserRuleContext {
        public String[] columns;
        public Map<String,String> values;
        public int col=0;
        ...
    }
    ...
}
```

The generated rule functions also specify the rule arguments as function arguments, but they are quickly copied into the local RowContext object.

```
public class CSVParser extends Parser {
    ...
    public final RowContext row(String[] columns) throws RecognitionException {
        RowContext _localctx = new RowContext(_ctx, 4, columns);
        enterRule(_localctx, RULE_row);
        ...
    }
    ...
}
```

ANTLR tracks nested [...] within the action so that String[] columns is parsed properly. It also tracks angle brackets so that commas within generic type parameters do not signify the start of another attribute. Map<String,String> values is one attribute definition.

There can be multiple attributes in each action, even for return values. Use a comma to separate attributes within the same action.

```
a[Map<String,String> x, int y] : ... ;
```

ANTLR interprets that action to define two arguments, x and y.

```
public final AContext a(Map<String,String> x, int y)
    throws RecognitionException
{
    AContext _localctx = new AContext(_ctx, 0, x, y);
    enterRule(_localctx, RULE_a);
    ...
}
```

Start Rules and EOF

A *start rule* is the rule engaged first by the parser; it's the rule function called by the language application. For example, a language application that parses Java code might call parser.compilationUnit() on a JavaParser object called parser. Any rule in the grammar can act as a start rule.

Start rules don't necessarily consume all of the input. They consume only as much input as needed to match an alternative of the rule. For example, consider the following rule that matches one, two, or three tokens, depending on the input:

```
s : ID
  | ID '+'
  | ID '+' INT
  ;
```

Upon a+3, rule s matches the third alternative. Upon a+b, it matches the second alternative and ignores the final b token. Upon a b, it matches the first alternative, ignoring the b token. The parser does not consume the complete input in the latter two cases because rule s doesn't explicitly say that the end of file must occur after matching an alternative of the rule.

This default functionality is very useful for building things such as IDEs. Imagine the IDE wanting to parse a method somewhere in the middle of a big Java file. Calling rule methodDeclaration should try to match just a method and ignore whatever comes next.

On the other hand, rules that describe entire input files should reference special predefined-token EOF. If they don't, you might scratch your head for a while wondering why the start rule doesn't report errors for any input no matter what you give it. Here's a rule that's part of a grammar for reading configuration files:

```
config : element*; // can "match" even with invalid input.
```

Invalid input would cause config to return immediately without matching any input and without reporting an error. Here's the proper specification:

```
file : element* EOF; // don't stop early. must match all input
```

15.4 Actions and Attributes

In Chapter 10, *Attributes and Actions*, on page 177, we learned how to embed actions within grammars and looked at the most common token and rule attributes. This section summarizes the important syntax and semantics from that chapter and provides a complete list of all available attributes.

Actions are blocks of text written in the target language and enclosed in curly braces. The recognizer triggers them according to their locations within the grammar. For example, the following rule emits found a decl after the parser has seen a valid declaration:

```
decl: type ID ';' {System.out.println("found a decl");} ;
type: 'int' | 'float' ;
```

Most often, actions access the attributes of tokens and rule references.

```
decl: type ID ';'
      {System.out.println("var "+$ID.text+":"+$type.text+";");}
    | t=ID id=ID ';'
      {System.out.println("var "+$id.text+":"+$t.text+";");}
    ;
```

Token Attributes

All tokens have a collection of predefined, read-only attributes. The attributes include useful token properties such as the token type and text matched for a token. Actions can access these attributes via $*label*.*attribute* where *label* labels a particular instance of a token reference (a and b in the following example are used in the action code as $a and $b). Often, a particular token is referenced only once in the rule, in which case the token name itself can be used unambiguously in the action code (token INT can be used as $INT in the action). The following example illustrates token attribute expression syntax:

```
r   :   INT {int x = $INT.line;}
        ( ID {if ($INT.line == $ID.line) ...;} )?
        a=FLOAT b=FLOAT {if ($a.line == $b.line) ...;}
    ;
```

The action within the (...)? subrule can see the INT token matched before it in the outer level.

Because there are two references to the FLOAT token, a reference to $FLOAT in an action is not unique; you must use labels to specify which token reference you're interested in.

Token references within different alternatives are unique because only one of them can be matched for any invocation of the rule. For example, in the following rule, actions in both alternatives can reference $ID directly without using a label.

```
r   :   ... ID {System.out.println($ID.text);}
    |   ... ID {System.out.println($ID.text);}
    ;
```

To access the tokens matched for literals, you must use a label.

```
stat:   r='return' expr ';' {System.out.println("line="+$r.line);} ;
```

Most of the time you access the attributes of the token, but sometimes it is useful to access the Token object itself because it aggregates all the attributes. Further, you can use it to test whether an optional subrule matched a token.

```
stat: 'if' expr 'then' stat (el='else' stat)?
      {if ( $el!=null ) System.out.println("found an else");}
    | ...
    ;
```

$T and $l evaluate to Token objects for token name *T* and token label *l*. $ll evaluates to List<Token> for list label *ll*. $T.attr evaluates to the type and value specified in the following table for attribute *attr*:

Attribute	Type	Description
text	String	The text matched for the token; translates to a call to getText(). Example: $ID.text.
type	int	The token type (nonzero positive integer) of the token such as INT; translates to a call to getType(). Example: $ID.type.
line	int	The line number on which the token occurs, counting from 1; translates to a call to getLine(). Example: $ID.line.

Attribute	Type	Description
pos	int	The character position within the line at which the token's first character occurs counting from zero; translates to a call to getCharPositionInLine(). Example: $ID.pos.
index	int	The overall index of this token in the token stream, counting from zero; translates to a call to getTokenIndex(). Example: $ID.index.
channel	int	The token's channel number. The parser tunes to only one channel, effectively ignoring off-channel tokens. The default channel is 0 (Token.DEFAULT_CHANNEL), and the default hidden channel is Token.HIDDEN_CHANNEL. Translates to a call to getChannel(). Example: $ID.channel.
int	int	The integer value of the text held by this token; it assumes that the text is a valid numeric string. Handy for building calculators and so on. Translates to Integer.valueOf(text-of-token). Example: $INT.int.

Parser Rule Attributes

ANTLR predefines a number of read-only attributes associated with parser rule references that are available to actions. Actions can access rule attributes only for references that precede the action. The syntax is $*r*.*attr* for rule name *r* or a label assigned to a rule reference. For example, $expr.text returns the complete text matched by a preceding invocation of rule expr.

```
returnStat : 'return' expr {System.out.println("matched "+$expr.text);} ;
```

Using a rule label looks like this:

```
returnStat : 'return' e=expr {System.out.println("matched "+$e.text);} ;
```

You can also use $ followed by the name of the attribute to access the value associated with the currently executing rule. For example, $start is the starting token of the current rule.

```
returnStat : 'return' expr {System.out.println("first token "+$start.getText());} ;
```

$*r* and $*rl* evaluate to ParserRuleContext objects of type *R*Context for rule name *r* and rule label *rl*. $*rll* evaluates to List<*R*Context> for rule list label *rll*. $*r*.*attr* evaluates to the type and value specified in the following table for attribute *attr*:

Attribute	Type	Description
text	String	The text matched for a rule or the text matched from the start of the rule up until the point of the $text expression evaluation. Note that this includes the text for all tokens including those on hidden channels, which is what you want because usually that has all the whitespace and comments. When referring to the current rule, this attribute is available in any action including any exception actions.
start	Token	The first token to be potentially matched by the rule that is on the main token channel; in other words, this attribute is never a hidden token. For rules that end up matching no tokens, this attribute points at the first token that could have been matched by this rule. When referring to the current rule, this attribute is available to any action within the rule.
stop	Token	The last nonhidden channel token to be matched by the rule. When referring to the current rule, this attribute is available only to the after and finally actions.
ctx	ParserRuleContext	The rule context object associated with a rule invocation. All of the other attributes are available through this attribute. For example, $ctx.start accesses the start field within the current rules context object. It's the same as $start.

Dynamically Scoped Attributes

You can pass information to and from rules using parameters and return values, just like functions in a general-purpose programming language. Programming languages don't allow functions to access the local variables or parameters of invoking functions, however.

For example, the following reference to local variable x from a nested method call is illegal in Java:

```
void f() {
    int x = 0;
    g();
}
```

```
void g() {
    h();
}
void h() {
    int y = x; // INVALID reference to f's local variable x
}
```

Variable x is available only within the scope of f(), which is the text lexically delimited by curly brackets. For this reason, Java is said to use *lexical scoping.* Lexical scoping is the norm for most programming languages.[2] Languages that allow methods further down in the call chain to access local variables defined earlier are said to use *dynamic scoping.* The term *dynamic* refers to the fact that a compiler cannot statically determine the set of visible variables. This is because the set of variables visible to a method changes depending on who calls that method.

It turns out that, in the grammar realm, distant rules sometimes need to communicate with each other, mostly to provide context information to rules matched below in the rule invocation chain. (Naturally, this assumes you are using actions directly in the grammar instead of the parse-tree listener event mechanism.) ANTLR allows dynamic scoping in that actions can access attributes from invoking rules using syntax $r::x where r is a rule name and x is an attribute within that rule. It is up to the programmer to ensure that r is in fact an invoking rule of the current rule. A runtime exception occurs if r is not in the current call chain when you access $r::x.

To illustrate the use of dynamic scoping, consider the real problem of defining variables and ensuring that variables in expressions are defined. The following grammar defines the symbols attribute where it belongs in the block rule but adds variable names to it in rule decl. Rule stat then consults the list to see whether variables have been defined.

reference/DynScope.g4

```
grammar DynScope;

prog:   block
    ;

block
/* List of symbols defined within this block */
locals [
    List<String> symbols = new ArrayList<String>()
]
```

2. See http://en.wikipedia.org/wiki/Scope_(programming)#Static_scoping.

```
    :   '{' decl* stat+ '}'
        // print out all symbols found in block
        // $block::symbols evaluates to a List as defined in scope
        {System.out.println("symbols="+$symbols);}
    ;

/** Match a declaration and add identifier name to list of symbols */
decl:   'int' ID {$block::symbols.add($ID.text);} ';'
    ;

/** Match an assignment then test list of symbols to verify
 *  that it contains the variable on the left side of the assignment.
 *  Method contains() is List.contains() because $block::symbols
 *  is a List.
 */
stat:   ID '=' INT ';'
        {
        if ( !$block::symbols.contains($ID.text) ) {
            System.err.println("undefined variable: "+$ID.text);
        }
        }
    |   block
    ;

ID  :   [a-z]+ ;
INT :   [0-9]+ ;
WS  :   [ \t\r\n]+ -> skip ;
```

Here's a simple build and test sequence:

```
$ antlr4 DynScope.g4
$ javac DynScope*.java
$ grun DynScope prog
{
  int i;
  i = 0;
  j = 3;
}
EOF
undefined variable: j
symbols=[i]
```

There's an important difference between a simple field declaration in an @members action and dynamic scoping. symbols is a local variable, so there is a copy for each invocation of rule block. That's exactly what we want for nested blocks so that we can reuse the same input variable name in an inner block. For example, the following nested code block redefines i in the inner scope. This new definition must hide the definition in the outer scope.

reference/nested-input
```
{
  int i;
  int j;
  i = 0;
  {
    int i;
    int x;
    x = 5;
  }
  x = 3;
}
```

Here's the output generated for that input by DynScope:

```
$ grun DynScope prog nested-input
symbols=[i, x]
undefined variable: x
symbols=[i, j]
```

Referencing $block::symbols accesses the symbols field of the most recently invoked block's rule context object. If you need access to a symbols instance from a rule invocation further up the call chain, you can walk backward starting at the current context, $ctx. Use getParent() to walk up the chain.

15.5 Lexer Rules

A lexer grammar is composed of lexer rules, optionally broken into multiple modes, as we saw in *Issuing Context-Sensitive Tokens with Lexical Modes*, on page 223. Lexical modes allow us to split a single lexer grammar into multiple sublexers. The lexer can return only those tokens matched by rules from the current mode.

Lexer rules specify token definitions and more or less follow the syntax of parser rules except that lexer rules cannot have arguments, return values, or local variables. Lexer rule names must begin with an uppercase letter, which distinguishes them from parser rule names.

```
/** Optional document comment */
TokenName : «alternative1» | ... | «alternativeN» ;
```

You can also define rules that are not tokens but rather aid in the recognition of tokens. These fragment rules do not result in tokens visible to the parser.

```
fragment HelperTokenRule : «alternative1» | ... | «alternativeN» ;
```

For example, DIGIT is a pretty common fragment rule.

```
INT : DIGIT+ ;          // references the DIGIT helper rule
fragment DIGIT : [0-9] ; // not a token by itself
```

Lexical Modes

Modes allow you to group lexical rules by context, such as inside and outside of XML tags. It's like having multiple sublexers, with one for context. The lexer can return only those tokens matched by entering a rule in the current mode. Lexers start out in the so-called default mode. All rules are considered to be within the default mode unless you specify a mode command. Modes are not allowed within combined grammars, just lexer grammars. (See grammar XMLLexer from *Tokenizing XML*, on page 228.)

```
«rules in default mode»
...
mode MODE1;
«rules in MODE1»
...
mode MODEN;
«rules in MODEN»
...
```

Lexer Rule Elements

Lexer rules allow two constructs that are unavailable to parser rules: the .. range operator and the character set notation enclosed in square brackets, [*characters*]. Don't confuse character sets with arguments to parser rules. [*characters*] only means character set in a lexer. Here's a summary of all lexer rule elements:

Syntax	**Description**
'*literal*'	Match that character or sequence of characters. Here's an example: 'while' or '='.
[*char set*]	Match one of the characters specified in the character set. Interpret *x-y* as a set of characters between range *x* and *y*, inclusively. The following escaped characters are interpreted as single special characters: \n, \r, \b, \t, and \f. To get], \, or -, you must escape them with \. You can also use Unicode character specifications: \uXXXX. Here are a few examples:

```
WS : [ \n\u000D] -> skip ;    // same as [ \n\r]
ID : [a-zA-Z] [a-zA-Z0-9]* ; // match usual identifier spec
DASHBRACK : [\-\]]+ ;        // match - or ] one or more times
```

Syntax	**Description**
'*x*'..'*y*'	Match any single character between range *x* and *y*, inclusively. Here's an example: 'a'..'z'. 'a'..'z' is identical to [a-z].
T	Invoke lexer rule *T*; recursion is allowed in general but not left recursion. *T* can be a regular token or fragment rule.

Syntax	Description
	(continued)

```
ID          :   LETTER (LETTER|'0'..'9')* ;
fragment
LETTER      :   [a-zA-Z\u0080-\u00FF_] ;
```

. The dot is a single-character wildcard that matches any single character. Here's an example:

```
ESC : '\\' . ; // match any escaped \x character
```

{«action»} Lexer actions must appear at the end of the outermost alternative. If a lexer rule has more than one alternative, enclose them in parentheses and put the action afterward.

```
END : ('endif'|'end') {System.out.println("found an end");} ;
```

The action conforms to the syntax of the target language. ANTLR copies the action's contents into the generated code verbatim; there is no translation of expressions such as $x.y like there is in parser actions.

{«p»}? Evaluate semantic predicate «*p*». If «*p*» evaluates to false at runtime, the surrounding rule becomes "invisible" (nonviable). Expression «*p*» conforms to the target language syntax. While semantic predicates can appear anywhere within a lexer rule, it is most efficient to have them at the end of the rule. The one caveat is that semantic predicates must precede lexer actions. See *Predicates in Lexer Rules*, on page 292.

~x Match any single character not in the set described by *x*. Set *x* can be a single character literal, a range, or a subrule set like ~('x'|'y'|'z') or ~[xyz]. Here is a rule that uses ~ to match any character other than characters using ~[\r\n]*:

```
COMMENT :   '#' ~[\r\n]* '\r'? '\n' -> skip ;
```

Just as with parser rules, lexer rules allow subrules in parentheses and EBNF operators: ?, *, +. The COMMENT rule illustrates the * and ? operators. A common use of + is [0-9]+ to match integers. Lexer subrules can also use the nongreedy ? suffix on those EBNF operators.

Recursive Lexer Rules

ANTLR lexer rules can be recursive, unlike most lexical grammar tools. This comes in handy when you want to match nested tokens like nested action blocks: {...{...}...}.

reference/Recur.g4
```
lexer grammar Recur;

ACTION : '{' ( ACTION | ~[{}] )* '}' ;

WS     : [ \r\t\n]+ -> skip ;
```

Redundant String Literals

Be careful that you don't specify the same string literal on the right side of multiple lexer rules. Such literals are ambiguous and could match multiple token types. ANTLR makes this literal unavailable to the parser. The same is true for rules across modes. For example, the following lexer grammar defines two tokens with the same character sequence:

reference/L.g4
```
lexer grammar L;
AND : '&' ;
mode STR;
MASK : '&' ;
```

A parser grammar cannot reference literal '&', but it can reference the name of the tokens.

reference/P.g4
```
parser grammar P;
options { tokenVocab=L; }
a : '&' // results in a tool error: no such token
    AND // no problem
    MASK // no problem
  ;
```

Here's a build and test sequence:

```
$ antlr4 L.g4   # yields L.tokens file needed by tokenVocab option in P.g4
$ antlr4 P.g4
error(126): P.g4:3:4: cannot create implicit token for string literal '&'
                      in non-combined grammar
```

Lexer Rule Actions

An ANTLR lexer creates a Token object after matching a lexical rule. Each request for a token starts in Lexer.nextToken(), which calls emit() once it has identified a token. emit() collects information from the current state of the lexer to build the token. It accesses fields _type, _text, _channel, _tokenStartCharIndex, _tokenStartLine, and _tokenStartCharPositionInLine. You can set the state of these with the various setter methods such as setType(). For example, the following rule turns enum into an identifier if enumIsKeyword is false:

```
ENUM : 'enum' {if (!enumIsKeyword) setType(Identifier);} ;
```

ANTLR does no special *$x* attribute translations in lexer actions (unlike v3).

There can be at most a single action for a lexical rule, regardless of how many alternatives there are in that rule.

Lexer Commands

To avoid tying a grammar to a particular target language, ANTLR supports *lexer commands*. Unlike arbitrary embedded actions, these commands follow specific syntax and are limited to a few common commands. Lexer commands appear at the end of the outermost alternative of a lexer rule definition. Like arbitrary actions, there can be only one per token rule. A lexer command consists of the -> operator followed by one or more command names that can optionally take parameters.

TokenName : *«alternative»* -> *command-name*

TokenName : *«alternative»* -> *command-name*(*«identifier or integer»*)

An alternative can have more than one command separated by commas. Here are the valid command names:

skip Do not return a token to the parser for this rule. This is typically used for whitespace:

```
WS : [ \r\t\n]+ -> skip ;
```

more Match this rule but continue looking for a token. The token rule that matches next will include the text matched for this rule. This is typically used with modes. Here's an example that matches string literals with a mode:

reference/Strings.g4

```
lexer grammar Strings;
LQUOTE : '"' -> more, mode(STR) ;
WS     : [ \r\t\n]+ -> skip ;

mode STR;

STRING : '"' -> mode(DEFAULT_MODE) ; // token we want parser to see
TEXT   : .   -> more ;               // collect more text for string
```

Here's a sample run:

```
⇒ $ antlr4 Strings.g4
⇒ $ javac Strings.java
⇒ $ grun Strings tokens -tokens
⇒ "hi"
⇒ "mom"
⇒ EOF
```

```
❮ [@0,0:3='"hi"',<2>,1:0]
  [@1,5:9='"mom"',<2>,2:0]
  [@2,11:10='<EOF>',<-1>,3:0]
```

type(*T*) Set the token type for the current token. Here's an example that forces two different tokens to use the same token type:

reference/SetType.g4
```
lexer grammar SetType;

tokens { STRING }

DOUBLE : '"' .*? '"'   -> type(STRING) ;
SINGLE : '\'' .*? '\'' -> type(STRING) ;
WS     : [ \r\t\n]+ -> skip ;
```

Here's a sample run. You can see that both tokens come back as token type 1.

```
⇒ $ antlr4 SetType.g4
⇒ $ javac SetType.java
⇒ $ grun SetType tokens -tokens
⇒ "double"
⇒ 'single'
⇒ EOF
❮ [@0,0:7='"double"',<1>,1:0]
  [@1,9:16=''single'',<1>,2:0]
  [@2,18:17='<EOF>',<-1>,3:0]
```

channel(*C*) Set the channel for the current token. The default is Token.DEFAULT_CHANNEL. You can define constants and then use it or an integer literal above Token.DEFAULT_CHANNEL in value (0). There's a generic hidden channel called Token.HIDDEN_CHANNEL with value 1.

```
@lexer::members { public static final int WHITESPACE = 1; }
...
WS  :   [ \t\n\r]+ -> channel(WHITESPACE) ;
```

mode(*M*) After matching this token, switch the lexer to mode *M*. The next time the lexer tries to match a token, it will look only at rules in mode *M*. *M* can be a mode name from the same grammar or an integer literal. See grammar Strings earlier.

pushMode(*M*) This is the same as mode except that it pushes the current mode onto a stack as well as setting the mode *M*. It should be used in conjunction with popMode.

popMode Pop a mode from the top of the mode stack and set the current mode of the lexer to that. This is used in conjunction with pushMode.

15.6 Wildcard Operator and Nongreedy Subrules

EBNF subrules like (...)?, (...)*, and (...)+ are *greedy*—they consume as much input as possible, but sometimes that's not what's needed. Constructs like .* consume until the end of the input in the lexer and sometimes in the parser. We want that loop to be *nongreedy*, so we need to use different syntax: .*? borrowed from regular expression notation. We can make any subrule that has a ?, *, or + suffix nongreedy by adding another ? suffix. Such nongreedy subrules are allowed in both the parser and the lexer, but they are used much more frequently in the lexer.

Nongreedy Lexer Subrules

Here's the very common C-style comment lexer rule that consumes any characters until it sees the trailing '*/':

```
COMMENT : '/*' .*? '*/' -> skip ; // .*? matches anything until the first */
```

Here's another example that matches strings that allow \" as an escaped quote character:

reference/Nongreedy.g4

```
grammar Nongreedy;
s : STRING+ ;
STRING : '"' ( '\\"' | . )*? '"' ; // match "foo", "\"", "x\"\"y", ...
WS     : [ \r\t\n]+ -> skip ;
```

```
⇒ $ antlr4 Nongreedy.g4
⇒ $ javac Nongreedy*.java
⇒ $ grun Nongreedy s -tokens
⇒ "quote:\""
⇒ EOF
❮ [@0,0:9='"quote:\""',<1>,1:0]
  [@1,11:10='<EOF>',<-1>,2:0]
```

Nongreedy subrules should be used sparingly because they complicate the recognition problem and sometimes make it tricky to decipher how the lexer will match text. Here is how the lexer chooses token rules:

- The primary goal is to match the lexer rule that recognizes the most input characters.

```
INT   : [0-9]+ ;
DOT   : '.' ;         // match period
FLOAT : [0-9]+ '.' ;  // match FLOAT upon '34.' not INT then DOT
```

- If more than one lexer rule matches the same input sequence, the priority goes to the rule occurring first in the grammar file.

```
DOC : '/**' .*? '*/' ; // both rules match /** foo */,  resolve to DOC
CMT : '/*' .*? '*/' ;
```

- Nongreedy subrules match the fewest characters that still allow the surrounding lexical rule to match.

```
/** Match anything except \n inside of double angle brackets */
STRING : '<<' ~'\n'*? '>>' ; // Input '<<foo>>>>' matches STRING then END
END    : '>>' ;
```

- After crossing through a nongreedy subrule *within* a lexical rule, all decision making from then on is "first match wins."

  For example, alternative `'ab'` in the rule right-side `.*? ('a'|'ab')` is dead code and can never be matched. If the input is `ab`, the first alternative, `'a'`, matches the first character and therefore succeeds. `('a'|'ab')` by itself on the right side of a rule properly matches the second alternative for input `ab`. This quirk arises from a nongreedy design decision that's too complicated to go into here.

To illustrate the different ways to use loops within lexer rules, consider the following grammar, which has three different action-like tokens (using different delimiters so that they all fit within one example grammar):

reference/Actions.g4

```
ACTION1 : '{' ( STRING | . )*? '}' ;    // Allows {"foo}
ACTION2 : '[' ( STRING | ~'"' )*? ']' ; // Doesn't allow ["foo]; nongreedy *?
ACTION3 : '<' ( STRING | ~[">] )* '>' ; // Doesn't allow <"foo>; greedy *
STRING : '"' ( '\\"' | . )*? '"' ;
```

Rule `ACTION1` allows unterminated strings, such as `{"foo}`, because input `"foo` matches to the wildcard part of the loop. It doesn't have to go into rule `STRING` to match a quote. To fix that, rule `ACTION2` uses `~'"'` to match any character but the quote. Expression `~'"'` is still ambiguous with the `']'` that ends the rule, but the fact that the subrule is nongreedy means that the lexer will exit the loop upon a right square bracket. To avoid a nongreedy subrule, make the alternatives explicit. Expression `~[">]` matches anything but the quote and right angle bracket. Here's a sample run:

```
$ antlr4 Actions.g4
$ javac Actions*.java
$ grun Actions tokens -tokens
{"foo}
EOF
[@0,0:5='{"foo}',<1>,1:0]
[@1,7:6='<EOF>',<-1>,2:0]
$ grun Actions tokens -tokens
["foo]
```

```
⇒ EOF
❮ line 1:0 token recognition error at: '["foo]\n'
  [@0,7:6='<EOF>',<-1>,2:0]
⇒ $ grun Actions tokens -tokens
⇒ <"foo>
⇒ EOF
❮ line 1:0 token recognition error at: '<"foo>\n'
  [@0,7:6='<EOF>',<-1>,2:0]
```

Nongreedy Parser Subrules

Nongreedy subrules and wildcards are also useful within parsers to do "fuzzy parsing" where the goal is to extract information from an input file without having to specify the full grammar. In contrast to nongreedy lexer decision making, parsers always make globally correct decisions. A parser never makes a decision that will ultimately cause valid input to fail later during the parse. Here is the central idea: *nongreedy parser subrules match the shortest sequence of tokens that preserves a successful parse for a valid input sentence.*

For example, here are the key rules that demonstrate how to pull integer constants out of an arbitrary Java file:

reference/FuzzyJava.g4

```
grammar FuzzyJava;
/** Match anything in between constant rule matches */
file : .*? (constant .*?)+ ;

/** Faster alternate version (Gets an ANTLR tool warning about
 *  a subrule like .* in parser that you can ignore.)
 */
altfile : (constant | .)* ; // match a constant or any token, 0-or-more times

/** Match things like "public static final SIZE" followed by anything */
constant
     : 'public' 'static' 'final' 'int' Identifier
       {System.out.println("constant: "+$Identifier.text);}
     ;
Identifier : [a-zA-Z_$] [a-zA-Z_$0-9]* ; // simplified
```

The grammar contains a greatly simplified set of lexer rules from a real Java lexer; the whole file about 60 lines. The recognizer still needs to handle string and character constants as well as comments so it doesn't get out of sync, trying to match a constant inside of the string, for example. The only unusual lexer rule performs the "match any character not matched by another lexer rule" functionality.

reference/FuzzyJava.g4

```
OTHER : . -> skip ;
```

This catchall lexer rule and the .*? subrule in the parser are the critical ingredients for fuzzy parsing.

Here's a sample file that we can run into the fuzzy parser:

reference/C.java
```
import java.util.*;
public class C {
    public static final int A = 1;
    public static final int B = 1;
    public void foo() { }
    public static final int C = 1;
}
```

And here's the build and test sequence:

```
$ antlr4 FuzzyJava.g4
$ javac FuzzyJava*.java
$ grun FuzzyJava file C.java
constant: A
constant: B
constant: C
```

Notice that it totally ignores everything except for the public static final int declarations. This all happens with only two parser rules.

15.7 Semantic Predicates

Semantic predicates, {...}?, are Boolean expressions written in the target language that indicate the validity of continuing the parse along the path "guarded" by the predicate. Predicates can appear anywhere within a parser rule just like actions can, but only those appearing on the left edge of alternatives can affect prediction (choosing between alternatives). We discussed predicates in detail in Chapter 11, *Altering the Parse with Semantic Predicates*, on page 191. This section provides all of the fine print regarding the use of semantic predicates in parser and lexer rules. Let's start by digging deeper into how the parser incorporates predicates into parsing decisions.

Making Predicated Parsing Decisions

ANTLR's general decision-making strategy is to find all *viable alternatives* and then ignore the alternatives guarded with predicates that currently evaluate to false. (A viable alternative is one that matches the current input.) If more than one viable alternative remains, the parser chooses the alternative specified first in the decision.

Consider a variant of C++ where array references also use parentheses instead of square brackets. If we predicate only one of the alternatives, we still have an ambiguous decision in expr.

```
expr:                ID '(' expr ')' // array reference (ANTLR picks this one)
    |   {istype()}? ID '(' expr ')' // ctor-style typecast
    |               ID '(' expr ')' // function call
    ;
```

In this case, all three alternatives are viable for input x(i). When x is not a type name, the predicate evaluates to false, leaving only the first and third alternatives as possible matches for expr. ANTLR automatically chooses the first alternative matching the array reference to resolve the ambiguity. Leaving ANTLR with more than one viable alternative because of too few predicates is probably not a good idea. It's best to cover n viable alternatives with at least n-1 predicates. In other words, don't build rules like expr with too few predicates.

Sometimes, the parser finds *multiple* visible predicates associated with a single choice. No worries. ANTLR just combines the predicates with appropriate logical operators to conjure up a single meta-predicate on-the-fly.

For example, the decision in rule stat joins the predicates from both alternatives of expr with the || operator to guard the second stat alternative.

```
stat:   decl | expr ;
decl:   ID ID ;
expr:   {istype()}? ID '(' expr ')'  // ctor-style typecast
    |   {isfunc()}? ID '(' expr ')'  // function call
    ;
```

The parser will predict an expr from stat only when istype()||isfunc() evaluates to true. This makes sense because the parser should choose to match an expression only if the upcoming ID is a type name or function name. It wouldn't make sense to test just one of the predicates in this case. Note that when the parser gets to expr itself, the parsing decision tests the predicates individually, one for each alternative.

If multiple predicates occur in a sequence, the parser joins them with the && operator. For example, consider changing stat to include a predicate before the call to expr.

```
stat:   decl | {java5}? expr ;
```

In this case, the parser would predict the second alternative only if java5&&(istype()||isfunc()) evaluated to true.

Turning to the code inside the predicates themselves now, keep in mind the following guidelines:

Use meaningful predicates.
ANTLR assumes that your predicates actually resolve the ambiguity. For example, ANTLR has no idea that the following predicates don't meaningfully resolve the ambiguity between the two alternatives:

```
expr:   {isTuesday()}?  ID '(' expr ')'  // ctor-style typecast
    |   {isHotOutside}? ID '(' expr ')'  // function call
    ;
```

Predicates must be free from side effects. ANTLR assumes that it can evaluate your predicates out of order or even multiple times, so don't use predicates like `{$i++ < 10}?`. It's almost certain that such predicates won't behave like you want.

Even when the parser isn't making decisions, predicates can deactivate alternatives, causing rules to fail. This happens when a rule has only a single alternative. There is no choice to make, but ANTLR evaluates the predicate as part of the normal parsing process, just like it does for actions. That means the following rule always fails to match:

```
prog:   {false}? 'return' INT ; // throws FailedPredicateException
```

ANTLR converts `{false}?` in the grammar to a conditional in the generated parser.

```
if ( !false ) throw new FailedPredicateException(...);
```

So far, all of the predicates we've seen have been visible and available to the prediction process, but that's not always the case.

Finding Visible Predicates

The parser will not evaluate predicates during prediction that occur after an action or token reference. Let's think about the relationship between actions and predicates first.

ANTLR has no idea what's inside the raw code of an action, so it must assume any predicate could depend on side effects of that action. Imagine an action that computed value `x` and a predicate that tested `x`. Evaluating that predicate before the action executed to create `x` would violate the implied order of operations within the grammar.

More importantly, the parser can't execute actions until it has decided which alternative to match. That's because actions have side effects and we can't undo things like print statements. For example, in the following rule, the parser can't execute the action in front of the `{java5}?` predicate before committing to that alternative:

```
@members {boolean allowgoto=false;}
stat: {System.out.println("goto"); allowgoto=true;} {java5}? 'goto' ID ';'
    | ...
    ;
```

If we can't execute the action during prediction, we shouldn't evaluate the {java5}? predicate because it depends on that action.

The prediction process also can't see through token references. Token references have the side effect of advancing the input one symbol. A predicate that tested the current input symbol would find itself out of sync if the parser shifted it over the token reference. For example, in the following grammar, the predicates expect getCurrentToken() to return an ID token:

```
stat: '{' decl '}'
    | '{' stat '}'
    ;
decl: {istype(getCurrentToken().getText())}? ID ID ';' ;
expr: {isvar(getCurrentToken().getText())}?  ID ;
```

The decision in stat can't test those predicates because, at the start of stat, the current token is a left curly. To preserve the semantics, ANTLR won't test the predicates in that decision.

Visible predicates are those that prediction encounters before encountering an action or token. The prediction process ignores nonvisible predicates, treating them as if they don't exist.

In rare cases, the parser won't be able to use a predicate, even if it's visible to a particular decision. That brings us to our next fine print topic.

Using Context-Dependent Predicates

A predicate that depends on a parameter or local variable of the surrounding rule is considered a *context-dependent predicate.* Clearly, we can evaluate such predicates only within the rules in which they're defined. For example, it makes no sense for the decision in the following prog to test the context-dependent predicate {$i<=5}?. That $i local variable is not even defined in prog.

```
prog:   vec5
    |   ...
    ;
vec5
locals [int i=1]
    :   ( {$i<=5}? INT {$i++;} )* // match 5 INTs
    ;
```

ANTLR ignores context-dependent predicates that it can't evaluate in the proper context. Normally the proper context is simply the rule defining the predicate, but sometimes the parser can't even evaluate a context-dependent predicate from within the same rule! Detecting these cases is done on-the-fly at runtime during adaptive *LL(*)* prediction.

For example, prediction for the optional branch of the else subrule in stat here "falls off" the end of stat and continues looking for symbols in the invoking prog rule:

```
prog:   stat+ ; // stat can follow stat
stat
locals [int i=0]
    :   {$i==0}? 'if' expr 'then' stat {$i=5;} ('else' stat)?
    |   'break' ';'
    ;
```

The prediction process is trying to figure out what can follow an if statement other than an else clause. Since the input can have multiple stats in a row, the prediction for the optional branch of the else subrule reenters stat. This time, of course, it gets a new copy of $i with a value of 0, not 5. ANTLR ignores context-dependent predicate {$i==0}? because it knows that the parser isn't in the original stat call. The predicate would test a different version of $i, so the parser can't evaluate it.

The fine print for predicates in the lexer more or less follows these same guidelines, except of course lexer rules can't have parameters and local variables. Let's look at all of the lexer-specific guidelines in the next section.

Predicates in Lexer Rules

In parser rules, predicates must appear on the left edge of alternatives to aid in alternative prediction. Lexers, on the other hand, prefer predicates on the right edge of lexer rules because they choose rules after seeing a token's entire text. Predicates in lexer rules can technically be anywhere within the rule. Some positions might be more or less efficient than others; ANTLR makes no guarantees about the optimal spot. A predicate in a lexer rule might be executed multiple times even during a single token match. You can embed multiple predicates per lexer rule, and they are evaluated as the lexer reaches them during matching.

Loosely speaking, the lexer's goal is to choose the rule that matches the most input characters. At each character, the lexer decides which rules are still viable. Eventually, only a single rule will be still viable. At that point, the lexer creates a token object according the rule's token type and matched text.

Sometimes the lexer is faced with more than a single viable matching rule. For example, input enum would match an ENUM rule and an ID rule. If the next character after enum is a space, neither rule can continue. The lexer resolves the ambiguity by choosing the viable rule specified first in the grammar. That's why we have to place keyword rules before an identifier rule like this:

```
ENUM : 'enum' ;
ID   : [a-z]+ ;
```

If, on the other hand, the next character after input enum is a letter, then only ID is viable.

Predicates come into play by pruning the set of viable lexer rules. When the lexer encounters a false predicate, it deactivates that rule just like parsers deactivate alternatives with false predicates.

Like parser predicates, lexer predicates can't depend on side effects from lexer actions. That's because actions can execute only after the lexer positively identifies the rule to match. Since predicates are part of the rule selection process, they can't rely on action side effects. Lexer actions must appear after predicates in lexer rules. As an example, here's another way to match enum as a keyword in the lexer:

reference/Enum3.g4

```
ENUM:    [a-z]+ {getText().equals("enum")}?
         {System.out.println("enum!");}
    ;
ID  :    [a-z]+ {System.out.println("ID "+getText());} ;
```

The print action in ENUM appears last and executes only if the current input matches [a-z]+ and the predicate is true. Let's build and test Enum3 to see whether it distinguishes between enum and an identifier.

```
⇒ $ antlr4 Enum3.g4
⇒ $ javac Enum3.java
⇒ $ grun Enum3 tokens
⇒ enum abc
⇒ EOF
❮ enum!
  ID abc
```

That works great, but it's really just for instructional purposes. It's easier to understand and more efficient to match enum keywords with a simple rule like this:

```
ENUM : 'enum' ;
```

15.8 Options

You can specify a number of options at the grammar and rule element levels. (There are currently no rule options.) These change how ANTLR generates code from your grammar. The general syntax is as follows:

```
options { name1=value1; ... nameN=valueN; } // ANTLR not target language syntax
```

where a value can be an identifier, a qualified identifier (for example, a.b.c), a string, a multiline string in curly braces {...}, and an integer.

Grammar Options

All grammars can use the following options. In combined grammars, all options except language pertain only to the generated parser. Options may be set either within the grammar file using the options syntax (described earlier) or when invoking ANTLR on the command line, using the -D option (see Section 15.9, *ANTLR Tool Command-Line Options*, on page 296.) The following examples demonstrate both mechanisms; note that -D overrides options within the grammar:

superClass Set the superclass of the generated parser or lexer. For combined grammars, it sets the superclass of the parser.

```
$ cat Hi.g4
grammar Hi;
a : 'hi' ;
$ antlr4 -DsuperClass=XX Hi.g4
$ grep 'public class' HiParser.java
public class HiParser extends XX {
$ grep 'public class' HiLexer.java
public class HiLexer extends Lexer {
```

language Generate code in the indicated language, if ANTLR is able to do so. Otherwise, you will see an error message like this:

```
$ antlr4 -Dlanguage=C MyGrammar.g4
error(31):  ANTLR cannot generate C code as of version 4.0
```

tokenVocab ANTLR assigns token type numbers to the tokens as it encounters them in a file. To use different token type values, such as with a separate lexer, use this option to have ANTLR pull in the .tokens file. ANTLR generates a .tokens file from each grammar.

```
$ cat SomeLexer.g4
lexer grammar SomeLexer;
ID : [a-z]+ ;
$ cat R.g4
parser grammar R;
```

```
options {tokenVocab=SomeLexer;}
tokens {A,B,C} // normally, these would be token types 1, 2, 3
a : ID ;
$ antlr4 SomeLexer.g4
$ cat SomeLexer.tokens
ID=1
$ antlr4 R.g4
$ cat R.tokens
A=2
B=3
C=4
ID=1
```

TokenLabelType ANTLR normally uses type Token when it generates variables referencing tokens. If you have passed a TokenFactory to your parser and lexer so that they create custom tokens, you should set this option to your specific type. This ensures that the context objects know your type for fields and method return values.

```
$ cat T2.g4
grammar T2;
options {TokenLabelType=MyToken;}
a : x=ID ;
$ antlr4 T2.g4
$ grep MyToken T2Parser.java
    public MyToken x;
```

Rule Options

There are currently no valid rule-level options, but the tool still supports the following syntax for future use:

```
rulename
options {...}
    :   ...
    ;
```

Rule Element Options

Token options have the form *T<name=value>*, as we saw in Section 5.4, *Dealing with Precedence, Left Recursion, and Associativity*, on page 71. The only token option is assoc, and it accepts values left and right. Figure 13, *A sample grammar*, on page 296 shows a sample grammar with a left-recursive expression rule that specifies a token option on the '^' exponent operator token.

Semantic predicates also accept an option, per *Catching Failed Semantic Predicates*, on page 168. The only valid option is the fail option, which takes either a string literal in double quotes or an action that evaluates to a string.

reference/ExprLR.g4

```
grammar ExprLR;

expr : expr '^'<assoc=right> expr
     | expr '*' expr  // match subexpressions joined with '*' operator
     | expr '+' expr  // match subexpressions joined with '+' operator
     | INT            // matches simple integer atom
     ;

INT : '0'..'9'+ ;
WS  : [ \n]+ -> skip ;
```

Figure 13—A sample grammar

The string literal or string result from the action should be the message to emit upon predicate failure.

errors/VecMsg.g4

```
ints[int max]
locals [int i=1]
    :   INT ( ',' {$i++;} {$i<=$max}?<fail={"exceeded max "+$max}> INT )*
    ;
```

The action can execute a function as well as compute a string when a predicate fails: {...}?<fail={doSomethingAndReturnAString()}>.

15.9 ANTLR Tool Command-Line Options

If you invoke the ANTLR tool without command-line arguments, you'll get a help message.

```
$ antlr4
ANTLR Parser Generator  Version 4.0
 -o ___              specify output directory where all output is generated
 -lib ___            specify location of grammars, tokens files
 -atn                generate rule augmented transition network diagrams
 -encoding ___       specify grammar file encoding; e.g., euc-jp
 -message-format ___ specify output style for messages in antlr, gnu, vs2005
 -listener           generate parse tree listener (default)
 -no-listener        don't generate parse tree listener
 -visitor            generate parse tree visitor
 -no-visitor         don't generate parse tree visitor (default)
 -package ___        specify a package/namespace for the generated code
 -depend             generate file dependencies
 -D<option>=value    set/override a grammar-level option
 -Werror             treat warnings as errors
 -XdbgST             launch StringTemplate visualizer on generated code
 -Xforce-atn         use the ATN simulator for all predictions
 -Xlog               dump lots of logging info to antlr-timestamp.log
```

Here are more details on the options:

-o *outdir*

ANTLR generates output files in the current directory by default. This option specifies the output directory where ANTLR should generate parsers, listeners, visitors, and .tokens files.

```
$ antlr4 -o /tmp T.g4
$ ls /tmp/T*
/tmp/T.tokens               /tmp/TListener.java
/tmp/TBaseListener.java     /tmp/TParser.java
```

-lib *libdir*

When looking for .tokens files and imported grammars, ANTLR normally looks in the current directory. This option specifies which directory to look in instead.

```
$ cat /tmp/B.g4
parser grammar B;
x : ID ;
$ cat A.g4
grammar A;
import B;
s : x ;
ID : [a-z]+ ;
$ antlr4 -lib /tmp A.g4
```

-atn

This generates DOT graph files that represent the internal augmented transition network (ATN) data structures that ANTLR uses to represent grammars. The files come out as *Grammar*.*rule*.dot. If the grammar is a combined grammar, the lexer rules are named *Grammar*Lexer.*rule*.dot.

```
$ cat A.g4
grammar A;
s : b ;
b : ID ;
ID : [a-z]+ ;
$ antlr4 -atn A.g4
$ ls *.dot
A.b.dot          A.s.dot          ALexer.ID.dot
```

-encoding *encodingname*

By default ANTLR loads grammar files using the UTF-8 encoding, which is a very common character file encoding that degenerates to ASCII for characters that fit in one byte. There are many character file encodings from around the world. If that grammar file is not the default encoding for your locale, you need this option so that ANTLR can properly interpret grammar files (such as the one below). This does not affect the input to the generated parsers, just the encoding of the grammars themselves.

```
# my locale is en_US on a Mac OS X box
# I saved this file with a UTF-8 encoding to handle grammar name 外 (\uCDE2)
# inside the grammar file
$ cat 外.g4
grammar 外;
a : 'foreign' ;
$ antlr4 -encoding UTF-8 外.g4
$ ls 外*.java
外BaseListener.java    外Listener.java
外Lexer.java           外Parser.java
$ javac -encoding UTF-8 外*.java
```

-message-format *format*

ANTLR generates warning and error messages using templates from directory tool/resources/org/antlr/v4/tool/templates/messages/formats. By default, ANTLR uses the antlr.stg (StringTemplate group) file. You can change this to gnu or vs2005 to have ANTLR generate messages appropriate for Emacs or Visual Studio. To make your own called *X*, create resource org/antlr/v4/tool/templates/messages/formats/*X* and place it in the CLASSPATH.

-listener

This option tells ANTLR to generate a parse-tree listener and is the default.

-no-listener

This option tells ANTLR not to generate a parse-tree listener.

-visitor

ANTLR does not generate parse-tree visitors by default. This option turns that feature on. ANTLR can generate both parse-tree listeners and visitors; this option and -listener aren't mutually exclusive.

-no-visitor

Tell ANTLR not to generate a parse-tree visitor; this is the default.

-package

Use this option to specify a package or namespace for ANTLR-generated files. Alternatively, you can add an @header {...} action, but that ties the grammar to a specific language. If you use this option and @header, make sure that the header action does not contain a package specification; otherwise, the generated code will have two of them.

-depend

Instead of generating a parser and/or lexer, generate a list of file dependencies, one per line. The output shows what each grammar depends on and what it generates. This is useful for build tools that need to know ANTLR grammar dependencies. Here's an example:

```
$ antlr4 -depend T.g
T.g: A.tokens
TParser.java : T.g
T.tokens : T.g
TLexer.java : T.g
TListener.java : T.g
TBaseListener.java : T.g
```

If you use -lib libdir with -depend and grammar option tokenVocab=A, then the dependencies include the library path as well: T.g: libdir/A.tokens. The output is also sensitive to the -o outdir option: outdir/TParser.java : T.g.

-D<option>=value

Use this option to override or set a grammar-level option in the specified grammar or grammars. This option is useful for generating parsers in different languages without altering the grammar. (I expect to have other targets in the near future.)

```
$ antlr4 -Dlanguage=Java T.g4  # default
$ antlr4 -Dlanguage=C T.g4
error(31):  ANTLR cannot generate C code as of version 4.0
```

-Werror

As part of a large build, ANTLR warning messages could go unnoticed. Turn on this option to have warnings treated as errors, causing the ANTLR tool to report failure back to the invoking command-line shell.

There are also some extended options that are useful mainly for debugging ANTLR itself.

-XdbgST

For those building a code generation target, this option brings up a window showing the generated code and the templates used to generate that code. It invokes the StringTemplate inspector window.

-Xforce-atn

ANTLR normally builds traditional "switch on token type" decisions where possible (one token of lookahead is sufficient to distinguish between all alternatives in a decision). To force even these simple decisions into the adaptive *LL(*)* mechanism, use this option.

-Xlog

This option creates a log file containing lots of information messages from ANTLR as it processes your grammar. If you would like to see how ANTLR translates your left-recursive rules, turn on this option and look in the resulting log file.

```
$ antlr4 -Xlog T.g4
wrote ./antlr-2012-09-06-17.56.19.log
```

APPENDIX 1

Bibliography

[ALSU06] Alfred V. Aho, Monica S. Lam, Ravi Sethi, and Jeffrey D. Ullman. *Compilers: Principles, Techniques, and Tools* . Addison-Wesley Longman, Reading, MA, Second, 2006.

[Gro90] Josef Grosch. Efficient and Comfortable Error Recovery in Recursive Descent Parsers. *Structured Programming.* 11[3]:129–140, 1990.

[Par09] Terence Parr. *Language Implementation Patterns.* The Pragmatic Bookshelf, Raleigh, NC and Dallas, TX, 2009.

[Top82] Rodney W. Topor. A note on error recovery in recursive descent parsers. *SIGPLAN Notices.* 17[2]:37–40, 1982.

[Wir78] Niklaus Wirth. *Algorithms + Data Structures = Programs.* Prentice Hall, Englewood Cliffs, NJ, 1978.

Index

I

J

K

L

M

N

O

P

Seven in Seven

From Web Frameworks to Concurrency Models, see what the rest of the world is doing with this introduction to seven different approaches.

Whether you need a new tool or just inspiration, *Seven Web Frameworks in Seven Weeks* explores modern options, giving you a taste of each with ideas that will help you create better apps. You'll see frameworks that leverage modern programming languages, employ unique architectures, live client-side instead of server-side, or embrace type systems. You'll see everything from familiar Ruby and JavaScript to the more exotic Erlang, Haskell, and Clojure.

Jack Moffitt, Fred Daoud
(302 pages) ISBN: 9781937785635. $38
http://pragprog.com/book/7web

Your software needs to leverage multiple cores, handle thousands of users and terabytes of data, and continue working in the face of both hardware and software failure. Concurrency and parallelism are the keys, and *Seven Concurrency Models in Seven Weeks* equips you for this new world. See how emerging technologies such as actors and functional programming address issues with traditional threads and locks development. Learn how to exploit the parallelism in your computer's GPU and leverage clusters of machines with Map-Reduce and Stream Processing. And do it all with the confidence that comes from using tools that help you write crystal clear, high-quality code.

Paul Butcher
(300 pages) ISBN: 9781937785659. $38
http://pragprog.com/book/pb7con

Put the "Fun" in Functional

Elixir puts the "fun" back into functional programming, on top of the robust, battle-tested, industrial-strength environment of Erlang.

You want to explore functional programming, but are put off by the academic feel (tell me about monads just one more time). You know you need concurrent applications, but also know these are almost impossible to get right. Meet Elixir, a functional, concurrent language built on the rock-solid Erlang VM. Elixir's pragmatic syntax and built-in support for metaprogramming will make you productive and keep you interested for the long haul. This book is *the* introduction to Elixir for experienced programmers.

Dave Thomas
(240 pages) ISBN: 9781937785581. $36
http://pragprog.com/book/elixir

A multi-user game, web site, cloud application, or networked database can have thousands of users all interacting at the same time. You need a powerful, industrial-strength tool to handle the really hard problems inherent in parallel, concurrent environments. You need Erlang. In this second edition of the best-selling *Programming Erlang*, you'll learn how to write parallel programs that scale effortlessly on multicore systems.

Joe Armstrong
(548 pages) ISBN: 9781937785536. $42
http://pragprog.com/book/jaerlang2

The Pragmatic Bookshelf

The Pragmatic Bookshelf features books written by developers for developers. The titles continue the well-known Pragmatic Programmer style and continue to garner awards and rave reviews. As development gets more and more difficult, the Pragmatic Programmers will be there with more titles and products to help you stay on top of your game.

Visit Us Online

This Book's Home Page

http://pragprog.com/book/tpantlr2
Source code from this book, errata, and other resources. Come give us feedback, too!

Register for Updates

http://pragprog.com/updates
Be notified when updates and new books become available.

Join the Community

http://pragprog.com/community
Read our weblogs, join our online discussions, participate in our mailing list, interact with our wiki, and benefit from the experience of other Pragmatic Programmers.

New and Noteworthy

http://pragprog.com/news
Check out the latest pragmatic developments, new titles and other offerings.

Save on the eBook

Save on the eBook versions of this title. Owning the paper version of this book entitles you to purchase the electronic versions at a terrific discount.

PDFs are great for carrying around on your laptop—they are hyperlinked, have color, and are fully searchable. Most titles are also available for the iPhone and iPod touch, Amazon Kindle, and other popular e-book readers.

Buy now at *http://pragprog.com/coupon*

Contact Us

Online Orders:	*http://pragprog.com/catalog*
Customer Service:	*support@pragprog.com*
International Rights:	*translations@pragprog.com*
Academic Use:	*academic@pragprog.com*
Write for Us:	*http://pragprog.com/write-for-us*
Or Call:	+1 800-699-7764

Milton Keynes UK
Ingram Content Group UK Ltd.
UKHW031011240924
448749UK00004B/10